The Tutoring Revolution

Applying Research for Best Practices, Policy Implications, and Student Achievement

Edward E. Gordon, Ronald R. Morgan,
Charles J. O'Malley, and Judith Ponticell

ROWMAN & LITTLEFIELD EDUCATION
Lanham • New York • Toronto • Plymouth, UK

Published in the United States of America
by Rowman & Littlefield Education
A Division of Rowman & Littlefield Publishers, Inc.
A wholly owned subsidiary of The Rowman & Littlefield Publishing Group, Inc.
4501 Forbes Boulevard, Suite 200, Lanham, Maryland 20706
www.rowmaneducation.com

Estover Road
Plymouth PL6 7PY
United Kingdom

British Library Cataloguing in Publication Information Available

Library of Congress Cataloging-in-Publication Data

Gordon, Edward E.
  The tutoring revolution : applying research for best practices, policy implications, and
  student achievement / Edward E. Gordon ... [et al.].
    p. cm.
  Includes bibliographical references and index.
  ISBN-13: 978-1-57886-532-1 (cloth : alk. paper)
  ISBN-10: 1-57886-532-8 (cloth : alk. paper)
  1. Tutors and tutoring—United States. 2. Education—United States. I. Title.
 LC41.G595 2006
 371.3'94—dc22   2006017760

⊗™ The paper used in this publication meets the minimum requirements of American
National Standard for Information Sciences—Permanence of Paper for Printed Library
Materials, ANSI/NISO Z39.48-1992.
Manufactured in the United States of America.

Dedicated to the use of best practices
and research by all who tutor

Contents

Foreword

Each year, millions of students in America meet with a tutor, either at their kitchen table, in the library, in a retail center, on the Web, or at school. We know that the number of children seeking support from a tutor is increasing each year. Some seek homework help while others want to do better in Advanced Placement classes. Most often the call for tutorial support arises with a poor grade in school, triggering the anxious parent to ask a friend or the classroom teacher for a referral to a tutor.

Whichever the reason, and each is valid, tutoring is maturing as an industry. In fact, consumers reach into their family's discretionary spending budget and spend between $4 and $6 billion each year (2006) on tutoring for their children. Spending is growing at about 18 percent a year, up from about an 8 percent growth between 2000 and 2002 (Eduventures Learning Market and Opportunities Report).

This growth in spending (or as I prefer to call it, investment) has recently been spurred by several factors, including increased competition for college and media coverage of local school performance under the federal No Child Left Behind Act. Local headlines decry schools that have been labeled as failing or, as the bureaucrats prefer, "in need of improvement."

Perhaps most significant to the increasing popularity of tutoring is the federal government's checkbook that now has over $2 billion set aside for tutoring of low-income/low-achieving students. Even if you do not participate in Supplemental Education Services (SES), as this federal tutoring program is called, rest assured that it will leave a big footprint in the history of tutoring. Practitioners, schools of education, parents, and policy wonks will now view the evolution of tutoring through the coloring of massive new federal spending in tutoring.

And this is where noted practitioner and researcher Edward Gordon and his colleagues, in *The Tutoring Revolution: Applying Research for Best Practices, Policy Implications, and Student Achievement* have stepped into the education research literature with their timely, thoughtful book. Consumers of privately financed education make up their minds about the value of the services they and their family receive from tutors. They may see a 100-point jump on a college admissions test, or a D in algebra may become a B. But when public tax dollars are injected into the equation, especially in times of increasing fiscal restraint, hard questions about accountability and return on investment are raised.

Thus this book comes at an important time in public education spending because it gives us a thorough grounding in the literature of research on tutoring, mapping out what we know and don't know about the differential effects of tutoring. It also gives policy makers a useful research-based framework for viewing and evaluating public investments in SES. We have in one volume a complete review of tutoring best practices spanning a variety of delivery models that are positively correlated to gains in student achievement. We know that:

- Tutoring increases specific skills in education content—math, reading, writing, and so on.
- All children can benefit from specialized support when sufficient time is available.
- Diagnostic assessment of the student's strengths and weaknesses, followed by individualized instructional materials, is one of the essential success factors of tutoring.
- Frequent mastery testing and feedback to the learner are essential to the goal of helping the student believe in himself or herself. "I can succeed!" replaces "I am a failure."
- Effective tutors must know their material and connect with their tutee in a respectful relationship. A teaching credential does not create an effective tutor just as it does not create an effective classroom teacher.
- Tutors and their employers must conduct themselves to the highest standards of program quality and business ethics and subject themselves to compliance that is enforced by government regulators and marketplace forces.

Critical to writing the next chapter in the government's evaluation of tutoring is the design of this research, including a fair estimate of how much academic growth should be expected for a relatively short-term intervention like SES. Researchers need to construct sophisticated models that isolate regular classroom instruction from the effects of tutoring, control for demographic characteristics of the students, compare different instructional models of the many tutoring options, and use standardized or other testing models that are fine enough to detect small changes in specific skills.

And somehow student, parent, and teacher feedback must be part of the study to ensure the qualitative evidence that the student feels more confident, participates more actively in class, or doesn't resist doing homework. As Gordon and colleagues show in this volume, these outcomes are just as exciting and valid as a two–standard deviation, or 2 sigma, increase in math skills on a standardized test.

Throughout this journey, tutors, education service providers, and publishers have the Education Industry Association (EIA) available to them providing a collective voice of public policy while promoting high standards in the industry. With over 600 members, EIA is the nation's leading umbrella organization for companies that serve parents, schools, universities, and communities with education services and products. As a long-term EIA member, Ed Gordon continues his service to the industry through the publication of this latest book.

All children can learn more, and I am hopeful that tutors will find the means to ensure that none will be left behind on the learning highway of tomorrow.

Steve Pines
Executive Director
Education Industry Association
Potomac, Maryland

Acknowledgments

The authors wish to acknowledge some of the hundreds of people who gave us information, ideas, constructive criticism, and long-term support while we were preparing this book. This is not our first book on tutoring. Prior to *The Tutoring Revolution*, Judy, Ron, and Ed collaborated on the use of tutoring for adults in the workplace—see *Closing the Literacy Gap in American Business* (1991), *FutureWork: The Revolution Reshaping American Business* (1994), and *Enhancing Learning in Training and Adult Education* (1998). Some research and ideas presented in these books have been applicable to our current work.

Many researchers have made contributions that are reflected in this new book: Eunice Askov, Distinguished Professor Emerita of Education, Codirector Emerita, Institute for the Study of Adult Literacy and the Goodling Institute for Research in Family Literacy, Pennsylvania State University; Daniel F. Bassill, President, Chief Executive Officer, Tutor/Mentor Connection, Chicago; James E. Baumhart, President, Chief Executive Officer, Better Business Bureau of Chicago and Northern Illinois; George Clowes, School Reform News; James Giovannini, Founder and Owner, Academic Tutoring Centers, Park Ridge, Illinois; Kenneth Hunter, President, Council of Better Business Bureaus, Arlington, Virginia; Yvonne Jones, Project Manager, 10,000 Tutors Program, Chicago Public Schools; John Kemp, Illinois Director, North Central Association of Colleges and Schools; Suzanne Knell, Executive Director, Illinois Library Resource Development Center, Champagne, Illinois; Noreen Lopez, National Coalition for Literacy, Washington, D.C.; Jerry Loyett, Illinois Director, North Central Association of Colleges and Schools; Robert Slavin, Johns Hopkins University, Baltimore, Maryland; Donovan Walling, Phi Delta Kappa International, Bloomington, Indiana; and Chris Yelich,

Administrative Director, Education Industry Association, Watertown, Wisconsin Office.

We also wish to acknowledge the important contributions of the many tutors/trainers and administrators of both Imperial Tutoring and Educational Services and Imperial Corporate Training and Development. For thirty-three years they provided both children and adults with tutoring services throughout the Chicagoland area.

Both Valerie J. Collier and Mary H. (Bonnie) Cloer have assisted us with their editing and computer skills. We express our deepest appreciation to both of them for their invaluable assistance.

Elaine Gordon, a professional writer and experienced university librarian, provided invaluable assistance in gathering information, dispersing materials to the author team, and editing for clarity. However, for any factual errors contained in this book, the authors take sole responsibility.

Edward E. Gordon
Chicago, Illinois/Palm Desert, California

Ronald R. Morgan
Chicago, Illinois/Huntington, West Virginia

Charles J. O'Malley
Boynton Beach, Florida

Judith Ponticell
Tampa, Florida

Introduction

The Benefits of Tutoring Research

For many years, the author team of *The Tutoring Revolution: Applying Research for Best Practices, Policy Implications, and Student Achievement* has studied tutoring from different perspectives: curriculum practices, the psychology of learning, research strategies, teacher/tutor education, and education policy. In part, we were motivated to prepare this book by the ever-increasing demand for tutoring across American society. Also, the No Child Left Behind (NCLB) Act contained a requirement for schools to begin offering failing students supplemental educational services, often some form of tutoring. As a result, we believed that the time had arrived for a serious discussion of what research can tell us concerning tutoring best practices and the future of tutoring research.

The authors agree with Wasik and Slavin (1993) that "a great deal of work is needed to understand why tutoring is effective." *The Tutoring Revolution* is the authors' attempt to begin offering a "more sophisticated understanding of the cognitive and motivational processes activated in tutoring that are not activated in the same degree in the regular classroom," as called for by Wasik and Slavin.

The Tutoring Revolution presents a broad, comprehensive, empirically derived perspective related to what we know and don't know about tutoring. We try to link the theories, research, and practice of tutoring together in a coherent, internally consistent manner to form the foundation for specific recommendations and strategies for tutoring.

The Tutoring Revolution focuses on the following:

1. Integration of theories, research findings, and practices
2. Comprehensive and objective review of extant literature related to tutoring

3. Comprehensive review and critical analysis of the knowledge structure related to tutoring documented by empirically based or more inclusive qualitatively disciplined methods of inquiry
4. The development of public education policy regarding the use of tutoring in the schools
5. A review of contemporary tutoring issues in America
6. The effort to develop ethical and regulatory tutoring standards
7. A discussion of future tutoring research issues and how to better integrate tutoring and classroom teaching as part of overall U.S. education reform

The Tutoring Revolution includes detailed descriptions of prominent models of learning and instruction. Since the authors have chosen to anchor this book within the context of the discipline of educational psychology, most of the work cited relates to learning in school. However, much of the research literature we use to support our views is based on laboratory findings and findings related to tutoring studies conducted in school-like settings. For the most part, we assume that there are few differences in the learning dynamics among adults, children, and adolescents. Of course, it is our burden to convince our readers that these laboratory-based and school-based research findings are relevant to them.

A number of common themes appear throughout *The Tutoring Revolution*. At center stage are a cognitive science perspective, an outcome-based education approach, a behaviorally anchored mastery learning model embellished with cognitive science components, and a collaborative instructional consultation model of service delivery. In addition, we emphasize evidence-based practices and encourage our readers to view tutoring education as research.

The authors recognize that there is a literate bias in education. An effort is made to build a strong case for the desirability of this literate bias. With the exception of biologically determined maturational stages of development, we assume that the learning characteristics among adults, children, and youths are similar. We give special attention to the cognitive aspects of tutoring (time on task, attention, and level of difficulty) and the social aspects of tutoring associated with L. S. Vygotsky—social learning, mentoring, and constructionist perspectives that are viewed as being of importance to designers of tutoring environments. We emphasize modifying individual differences among learners over which we have some control.

In sum, throughout *The Tutoring Revolution* we attempt to build a case for the notion that we can use tutorial education settings as natural laboratories in which to articulate educational, psychological, and sociological theories of tutoring. We recommend that our readers take a test-tutor-test hypothesis-testing-and-generating approach to solving education-related problems.

Many tutoring instructional systems have been tested in highly controlled laboratory, field experimental, and applied settings. What seems to be needed at this time is a greater focus on and appreciation for attempts to relate recent findings in cognitive science, social learning theory, mentoring, and constructionist teaching practices to tutoring. It is our view that greater sensitivity to the possibility of relating cognitive variables and social variables to our existing models of tutoring instruction will enhance our instructional options and help account for and minimize individual differences among learners.

Four themes are presented throughout *The Tutoring Revolution*—a cognitive science perspective, an outcome-based education approach, a behaviorally anchored mastery learning model embellished with cognitive science components, and a collaborative instructional consultation model of service delivery. Certain components of the chapters are designed to overlap. These knowledge structures are listed below. Readers may find it helpful to refer to these points as they progress through the book. This arrangement is intended to provide a smooth transition from one chapter to the next and encourage the reader to relate new information to what is already known.

ORGANIZING KNOWLEDGE STRUCTURES OF THE TUTORING REVOLUTION

- A behaviorally anchored mastery tutoring model embellished with cognitive science components
- An outcome-based education tutorial approach
- A collaborative instructional consultation model of tutoring service delivery
- Theoretical comparisons among behavioral–associationistic, gestalt, cognitive developmental, and information-processing views of thinking, problem solving, and creativity
- Viewing a cognitive template view of information processing with filtering as an automatic process and pigeonholing as a cognitive classification process
- Viewing development as development of attention
- Viewing differences between children and adults, expert and novice learners, and typical and atypical learners as differences in attention, cognitive-style expectancies, and memory organization
- Assuming that biologically determined individual differences consist of differences in attention, temperament, and maturational stages of development
- Assuming there is a literate bias in schooling

- Identifying six cognitive constructs of lasting value—intelligence, personality, the mind, information-processing conceptualizations of learning and instruction-memory organization, motivation, and cognitive-style expectancies
- Understanding of knowledge as consisting of content knowledge, content-procedural knowledge, and procedural knowledge (general problem solving strategies), with emphasis on automatizing content-procedural and procedural knowledge to free up working memory space for content
- Emphasizing the zone of proximal development—L. S. Vygotsky's social framework model-cognitive apprenticeship and reciprocal teaching models
- Promising areas of research consisting of expert–novice comparisons/behavioral-cognitive task analyses/computer simulations of thinking and problem solving; early interventions; prose learning/schema activators; tutoring/mastery learning/personalized systems of instruction; intelligence and personality; and behavior management

In chapter 1, "Tutoring and Reinventing Title I," we review how Title I has evolved since 1965. The passage of the NCLB brought major policy changes and introduced the federal funding of supplemental services (most often tutoring). We will explore the broader implications for school districts, teachers, and policy makers across America.

Chapter 2, "The Tutoring Revolution," provides the broader social and historical context on how the demand for tutoring in the United States began and developed to our own time. Then we review the many different types of tutoring services available in most urban areas. We also discuss the federal, state, and local community roles in the development of tutoring consumer standards.

In chapter 3, "Learning, Research, Assessment: Where Do We Stand?" we describe the conceptual frameworks, organized knowledge structures, politics and policies, and methodological issues used to frame the content of the book. In regard to this conceptual framework, we spotlight several areas of scholarship: learning theories and their influence on instruction; cognitive, social, and cultural constructivist views of learning theory and teaching; the creation of functional learning environments; a critical pedagogy of place; the reconceptualized curriculum movement—the divide between curriculum theories and practices; the achievement–self-esteem debate, cognitive load theory, and instructional design; Sternberg's balance theory of wisdom; and the psychology of school subjects. In additional to the conceptual frameworks, current politics and policies strongly influenced the knowledge structures used to frame this book. Recent changes related to school reforms, accountability systems, high-stakes testing, implications of the requirements associated with the NCLB, and school choice initiatives have been described and critically evaluated by educational researchers. Finally, methodological issues, or disciplined methods of inquiry, represent another set of organizational structures that were used as frameworks in the design of the book. The methodological issues specifically addressed in the chapter include the following: scientific research in education and the case for evidence-based reasoning in educational research, alternative forms of data representation, design experiments, and the teacher research movement.

In the first half of chapter 4, "Tutoring and the Advancement of Learning," we introduce a cognitive science perspective to the study of tutoring. We begin with a discussion of three models of instruction (tutoring, mastery learning, and personalized systems of instruction). Emphasis is given to the commonalities across the three models (e.g., their emphasis on continuous assessment, remediation, encouragement, and support) rather than the differences. We make a special effort to relate contemporary developments reported in the cognitive science literature to John B. Carroll's (1963) original behaviorally based model of tutoring and mastery learning. Particular attention is given to possible instructional correctives and the special problems related to the application of these models to atypical and nontraditional learners.

Cognitive scientists claim that the major differences in learning characteristics between novice and expert human learners are found primarily in the cognitive mediation differences of attention, cognitive-style expectancies, and memory organization. Individual differences among learners are broken down further into biological differences (attention, maturation stages, and temperament) and psychological differences (knowledge, language memory organization, mood, attitudes, personality, cognitive-style expectancies, and motivation). Although the biologically determined differences cannot be modified, we assume that we can modify many of the environmentally determined psychological individual differences. Most of the individual difference characteristics of interest to a cognitive scientist are believed to be learnable.

In the second half of chapter 4, we describe the 2 sigma effect and the search for methods of instruction to yield a 2 sigma effect. Barriers to reaching the 2 sigma level of performance are also described. Special attention is given to recommendations related to the improvement of teaching higher mental processes and the better use of multimedia learning and instructional technologies. The final sections of the chapter contain detailed reviews of what we know and don't know about a social learning perspective, mentorship, the development of expertise, and constructivist teaching practices.

In the final section of chapter 4, the Individualized Instruction Program—the authors' research program—is briefly described. Our purpose in presenting this brief description early in the book is to set the stage for encouraging our readers to view tutoring as research. We state throughout this book that there is no best method of instruction that can be applied to all persons in all settings. Most content-laden knowledge has a shelf life of five years or so. In contrast to content-laden knowledge structures, research methodology seems to have considerable staying power. Therefore, we believe that it is appropriate to put research methodology at the center of the stage, to use the knowledge yielded from an empirically based research program to anchor our work and to guide our tutoring practices. That said, it is our view that all tutors should view their work as research. We recommend that readers view tutoring settings as natural laboratories in which to explore and articulate educational, psychological, and sociological theories.

Chapter 5, "Tutoring Research," includes a review of the research syntheses that have been published related to tutoring. We make systematic efforts to draw connections between tutoring research findings and the NCLB and focus on a critical examination of evidence-based tutoring practices and recent developments in national educational policies that are likely to have some impact on tutoring.

What do we know about tutoring? Is tutoring effective? Does tutoring always work? Does tutoring work for all students? Is tutoring the best intervention? Is tutoring more effective for younger or older students? Do tutors need training? How much tutoring is beneficial? Why does tutoring work? In chapter 5, we describe and interpret what other reviewers have reported in their research syntheses related to tutoring.

Chapter 6, "Has Tutoring Worked?" presents a review of best practices. Often the quality of tutoring depends on how the tutoring was provided and who provided it. We discuss twelve promising best practice areas supported by tutoring research and summarize ten key components supporting high-quality tutoring.

In chapter 7, "The Ethics of Tutoring," we offer three different but complementary perspectives on tutoring ethical standards and trade practices from the Better Business Bureau, the Education Industry Association (the largest professional tutoring association), and model rules and regulations of tutoring standards for state education agencies prepared by the authors.

Chapter 8, "The Future of Tutoring," addresses the important cultural questions related to the effective use of professional tutors that need to be addressed throughout American society in general and the schooling community in particular. The authors again stress promising future research areas of inquiry. We think that additional research will enable tutoring to become effectively integrated with the teaching process as an essential component of contemporary education reform.

In *The Tutoring Revolution*, the authors have developed an important resource for school district administrators, teachers, tutors, education policy leaders, and researchers. This book is a beginning to the process of education inquiry—research on tutoring as a vital education practice to help more children and adults better reach their personal learning potential.

The Tutoring Revolution is designed to help teachers begin creating and refining their own ideas on the tutoring process. For a true tutoring revolution to benefit American education, your professional participation will be essential to compiling additional research on why tutoring can be effective.

Tutoring and Reinventing Title I

This chapter is designed to address key public policy implications of Public Law 107-110, the No Child Left Behind Act (NCLB). I will not address the merits or the successes—or lack thereof—of supplemental services. My colleagues will address those issues in subsequent chapters.

In order to more effectively accomplish that goal, we will provide the reader with:

Definitions of public policy and supplemental services
A brief history of NCLB
Pertinent excerpts from the NCLB and the U.S. Department of Education's regulations and guidance
A snapshot of the U.S. Department of Education's regulatory process
A discussion of select provisions of NCLB
Identification and discussion of public policy concerns
Observations

DEFINITIONS OF PUBLIC POLICY AND SUPPLEMENTAL SERVICES

Let us first provide a mini snapshot of what public policy is, and then address the role of public policy in decision making. The following quote from the June 27, 2002, *Washington Post* provides an excellent example of what public policy is:

The Pledge of Allegiance, recited by millions of American children at the start of each school day, is unconstitutional because it describes the United States as "one Nation, under God," a federal appeals court ruled yesterday. A three-judge panel of the U.S. Court of Appeals for the 9th Circuit ruled 2 to 1 that the reference to God, which was added to the pledge by Congress in 1954, amounts to an official endorsement of mono-theism. Thus, the San Francisco-based court said, both the 1954 law and a California school district's policy requiring teachers to lead children in the pledge violate the First Amendment prohibition against the establishment of a state religion.

If the ruling is allowed to stand, schoolchildren could no longer recite the pledge, at least in the nine western states covered by the court. (Lane, 2002, p. A1)

The issue of the Pledge of Allegiance becomes important, controversial, and an object of public attention. The general public debated the wisdom—or lack thereof—of the federal appeals court's decision. People spoke out on behalf of the decision—or against the decision. The next steps exemplified public policy.

State legislatures introduced bills eliminating the phrase "one nation under God" in order to comply with the court's decision. State legislatures passed laws or resolutions encouraging students to continue pledging allegiance as they had been doing. Democrats and Republicans in Congress sought to use the appeal court's decision as a rationale for pursuing their respective party ideology. The issues became:

1. Will this decision eventually be a factor in bringing down the wall of separation between church and state?
2. Will the decision become a factor in raising that wall?

These and similar questions vividly illustrate the role of public policy. Let's take a look at some of the terminology we'll be discussing in this chapter.

> *Public policy:* In any society, governmental entities enact laws, make policies, and allocate resources. This is true at all levels. Public policy can be generally defined as a system of laws, regulatory measures, courses of action, and funding priorities concerning a given topic promulgated by a governmental entity or its representatives. Individuals and groups often attempt to shape public policy through education, advocacy, or mobilization of interest groups (Kilpatrick, 2000).
> *Policy: Black's Law Dictionary* (1999) defines policy as "1. The general principles by which a government is guided in its management of public affairs." *The Cambridge Dictionary of American English* (2004) defines policy as "(n): a set of ideas or a plan for action followed by a business, a government, a political party, or a group of people." For the purposes

of discussion, we are defining public policy as the rationale for supporting or opposing specific initiatives based on political, ideological, reli-
gious, or pragmatic basis, usually long-term in impact.

Supplemental services: The U.S. Department of Education website defines
supplemental services as "extra help provided to students in reading, language arts and math. This extra help can be provided before or after
school, on weekends" (www.ecs.org/html/Document.asp?chouseid=3725,
2006).

A BRIEF HISTORY OF NCLB

Forty years ago, with the very strong support of President Lyndon Baines Johnson, Congress passed the Elementary and Secondary Education Act (ESEA) of
1965—part of President Johnson's "Great Society"—which significantly increased the visibility of the Federal government in American education. (Dr. Edward D'Alessio, interview, October 14, 1979)

ESEA contained several titles—statutory provisions that addressed areas of
special concern, including compensatory education, library materials, innovative education, special education, and bilingual education. However, for the
purposes of this discourse, the authors will focus on the largest, most heavily
funded title—Title I. This title channeled additional federal dollars to schools
with high concentrations of economically and educationally disadvantaged
children attending both public and private schools. Remedial reading and remedial mathematics programs were designed to bring the eligible students to
grade level, with dollars targeted to those students with greatest educational
need.

As is the case with most congressionally mandated programs, ESEA was
scheduled for reauthorization every five years. Congress evaluates the effectiveness of the laws it passes, strengthens perceived problem areas through
amendments, and reevaluates the appropriations.

NCLB was the result of the ESEA reauthorization process. In 1999 Congress began its review of ESEA; however, election year politics and other
events delayed action on ESEA. During the 2000 presidential campaign, education was a major issue. Candidate George W. Bush proposed significant
changes to the existing law, including increased parental choice and strength-
ened accountability measures. His proposal was based on the Florida school
choice program initiated by his brother, Florida Governor Jeb Bush, and the
strong school accountability program Governor George W. Bush initiated in
Texas (Dr. Sandy Kress, interview, January 25, 2001).

Shortly after his inauguration in January 2001, President George W. Bush sent his NCLB proposal to Congress. Receiving strong leadership from House Education and Workforce Committee Chair John Boehner (R-OH) and Senator Judd Greg (R-NH), and bipartisan support from Senator Ted Kennedy (D-MASS) and Congressman George Miller (D-CA), NCLB was signed into law January 8, 2002.

GUIDANCE AND REGULATIONS

Since the enactment of NCLB, the U.S. Department of Education has provided state education agencies (SEAs) and local education agencies (LEAs) with guidance (formal and informal) designed to assist them with the implementation of NCLB's provisions. On August 26, 2004, the department disseminated informal guidance to each of the chief state school officers on NCLB's supplemental services provisions. The following excerpts illustrate the department's focus on key public policy concerns:

> Under the Title I statute, it is the responsibility of the SEA to develop and apply objective criteria for approval of potential providers based, among other things, on a demonstrated record of effectiveness, and to maintain an approved list of providers. The LEA then enters into agreements with approved providers selected by parents. Conditions relating to criteria for approval of a provider are the responsibility of the SEA and an LEA may not alter, or add to, those criteria. However, an LEA may impose reasonable administrative and operational requirements through its agreements with providers that are consistent with requirements imposed generally on the LEA's contractors and that do not limit educational options for parents.
>
> We understand that a number of LEAs have imposed, or are considering conditions related to issues of program design. They may, for example, be requiring that providers offer a certain number of hours of services in order to receive the statutory per-child amount for services that providers employ only State-certified teachers as tutors, or that they use one-to-one tutoring as their sole delivery mechanism. These types of requirements—which relate to whether a provider has an effective educational program—may not be imposed by LEAs, because they would undermine the State's authority to set criteria for approval of providers as having effective programs and to determine which providers meet those standards. In addition, these types of requirements may create a "one-size-fits-all" model for services that does not effectively take into consideration the varied needs of students, and undermine the parents' opportunity to select the most appropriate provider and services for their child. (Rod Paige, correspondence to chief state school officers, June 14, 2002)

On June 13, 2005, the U.S. Department of Education released its updated guidance on supplemental services, along with sample letters LEAs could use in working with providers and informing parents of the supplemental service option. This guidance was a response to implementation and policy questions addressed to the department.

SNAPSHOT OF THE U.S. DEPARTMENT OF EDUCATION'S REGULATORY PROCESS

A loose description of the department's regulatory process may be helpful at this point. Periodically the department reassesses the guidance or regulations it disseminates to entities participating in a particular federally funded program (e.g., state departments of education, local school districts, private education advocacy organizations, postsecondary institutions, community-based organizations, other policy-making and policy-implementing organizations, and the general public).

The department's decision may be predicated by a variety of circumstances, including:

1. SEAs or LEAs encountering difficulties in implementing or enforcing certain provisions
2. The targeted beneficiaries of the program not being provided the intended services
3. Areas of consistent disagreement between the implementing agencies and the U.S. Department of Education

The Department of Education will issue a public notice that it intends to prepare or update the law's regulations or guidance. This notice will invite interested organizations and agencies to submit comments regarding specific provisions and proposed language changes. Concurrently key offices with the department would begin their review process.

Since this chapter is designed to discuss public policy ramifications of NCLB's supplemental service provisions, let us take a look at some of the public policy concerns addressed by the guidance. This guidance updates and expands upon the Supplemental Educational Services Guidance that the Department released on August 22, 2003 (www.ed.gov/policy/elsec/guid/suppsvcsguid.doc). The following excerpts from the document's table of contents identify major public policy issues the U.S. Department of Education felt necessary to address:

Supplemental Education Services
Title I, Section 1116(e)

Table of Contents

D-7. What steps should an SEA take if it determines that an LEA is failing to implement supplemental educational services in a manner that is consistent with the statute, regulations, and guidance?

The very fact that these questions are listed indicates that there are major problems in these areas.

Public Law 107-110, NCLB

Excerpts of the statutory citation are referenced here to allow the reader to absorb the purpose, educational ramifications, and policy implications of this unique approach.

Public Law 107-110, the No Child Left Behind Act (NCLB)
Excerpts, Statutory Citation
Part A, Section 116

Sec. 1116. Academic Assessment and Local Educational Agency and School Improvement.

(5) FAILURE TO MAKE ADEQUATE YEARLY PROGRESS AFTER IDENTIFICATION [emphasis added]—In the case of any school served under this part that fails to make adequate yearly progress, as set out in the State's plan under section 1111(b)(2), by the end of the first full school year after identification under paragraph (1), the local educational agency serving such school—
　(A) shall continue to provide all students enrolled in the school with the option to transfer to another public school served by the local educational agency in accordance with subparagraphs (E) and (F);
　(B) shall make *SUPPLEMENTAL EDUCATIONAL SERVICES* [emphasis added] available consistent with subsection (e)(1); and
　(C) shall continue to provide technical assistance.

(6) NOTICE TO PARENTS-. . .
　(F) an explanation of the parents' option to transfer their child to another public school under paragraphs (1)(E), (5)(A), (7)(C)(i), (8)(A)(i), and subsection (c)(10)(C)(vii) (with transportation provided by the agency when required by paragraph (9)) or to obtain *SUPPLEMENTAL EDUCA-TIONAL SERVICES* [emphasis added] for the child, in accordance with subsection (e).

(7) CORRECTIVE ACTION- IN GENERAL-
AGENCY- In the case of any school served by a local educational agency under this part that fails to make adequate yearly progress, as defined by the State

under section 1111(b)(2), by the end of the second full school year after the identification under paragraph (1), the local educational agency shall—

(iii) continue to make *SUPPLEMENTAL EDUCATIONAL SERVICES* [emphasis added] available, in accordance with subsection (e), to children who remain in the school;

(8) RESTRUCTURING-

(A) FAILURE TO MAKE ADEQUATE YEARLY PROGRESS—If, after 1 full school year of corrective action under paragraph (7), a school subject to such corrective action continues to fail to make adequate yearly progress, then the local educational agency shall-

(ii) continue to make *SUPPLEMENTAL EDUCATIONAL SERVICES* [emphasis added] available, in accordance with subsection (e), to children who remain in the school; and

(10) FUNDS FOR TRANSPORTATION AND *SUPPLEMENTAL EDUCATIONAL SERVICES* [emphasis added] -

(A)IN GENERAL- Unless a lesser amount is needed to comply with paragraph (9) and to satisfy all requests for supplement educational services under subsection (e), a local educational agency shall spend an amount equal to 20 percent of its allocation under subpart 2, from which the agency shall spend-

(i) an amount equal to 5 percent of its allocation under subpart 2 to provide, or pay for, transportation under paragraph (9);

(ii) an amount equal to 5 percent of its allocation under subpart 2 to provide *SUPPLEMENTAL EDUCATIONAL SERVICES* [emphasis added] under subsection (e); and (iii) an amount equal to the remaining 10 percent of its allocation under subpart 2 for transportation under paragraph (9), *SUPPLEMENTAL EDUCATIONAL SERVICES* [emphasis added] under subsection (e), or both, as the agency determines.

DISCUSSION OF SELECT PROVISIONS: WHAT HAPPENED AFTER THE LAW WAS ENACTED

Shortly after the enactment of NCLB, the U.S. Department of Education and the Education Leaders Council (an organization composed of state school officers, school board members, and other education policy experts) cosponsored a one-day conference on the supplemental services provisions attended by representatives of local and state education agencies, national public policy organizations, supplemental educational service providers, congressional staff, and others. According to then–Undersecretary of Education Gene Hickok, because the U.S. Department of Education was in the process of drafting nonregulatory guidance, the dialogue from this conference was extremely valuable to the department chapter (Eugene Hickok, correspondence to Illinois State Board of Education, December 2, 2004). This conference will be addressed later in this chapter.

After President George W. Bush signed NCLB into law, the U.S. Department of Education, the administering agency for this law, developed a draft set of guidance that was made available for public comment (i.e., agencies, organizations, and individuals potentially impacted by NCLB were provided an opportunity to comment on the department's proposed regulations within a set period of time). This process was repeated several times, with the comments received by the department included in each iteration.

Concurrently, then–U.S. Secretary of Education Rod Paige, Deputy Secretary Hickok, and other key individuals within the Department of Education met with representatives of education organizations, state and local school district representatives, private school officials, potential supplemental education service providers, and others in a concerted effort to sell NCLB to those responsible for its implementation.

The comments were synthesized by the Department of Education, with those comments deemed appropriate by select offices within the department and the Office of Management and Budget going through an internal clearance process and ultimately approved for distribution to the general public.

Once the guidance was received by these organizations and agencies, many of them convened national, regional, or state conferences for their respective constituencies in order to discuss implementation of the NCLB provisions. In many instances, U.S. Department of Education representatives served as resources in these sessions.

IDENTIFICATION AND DISCUSSION OF PUBLIC POLICY CONCERNS

A cursory review of federal K–12 education statutes will reveal that historically federal dollars have been directed—with rare exception—to public schools, public school districts, and postsecondary education institutions. However, under NCLB, new players are added to the roster—for-profit tutorial programs, nonprofit community-based organizations, and faith-based organizations. This raised questions from (and in many instances hackles of) education organizations such as the National Education Association, American Federation of Teachers, Council of Chief State School Officers, and others.

Concerns were expressed regarding the quality of educational services provided by proprietary tutorial companies:

The companies did not have a demonstrably superior pedagogy, could not save on administrative costs, and incurred high marketing costs. The result might have been increased competition and expanded choices, but there was no evidence of significant gains in efficiency or improved achievement. (*American School Board Journal*, 2005, p. 31)

These organizations were joined by several constitutional experts in questioning the constitutionality of federal dollars being directed to faith-based organizations. Issues such as "entanglement between church and state," government money "assisting" church-related organizations, and "taking dollars away from public education."

Objections to Supplementary Education Services

It was objected that guidance was received too late by state and local officials, resulting in delayed and confusing implementation on state and local levels:

Throw into this mix the time given to complete the task—the law took effect July 1, and the tutoring was supposed to start in September—as well as the minimal guidance that school officials say they have received from the U.S. Education Department on how to proceed.

It is no wonder administrators say that school systems are struggling to comply. Here's an analogy of what it's been like . . . the research, evaluations and accountability officer Baltimore's school system. Let's say you are building a house, and all the materials are there. You have the lumber, the windows have arrived and the wiring, too. You know the materials are there to build a nice three-bedroom, 1 1/2-bath house, but what you haven't received are the blueprints. You don't know where anything is supposed to go. (Strauss, 2002, p. A16)

During the first year of implementation, there was considerable confusion regarding funding levels for supplemental education programs. For example, a conference entitled Serving All School Children and Increasing Options for Parents was held in Washington, D.C., on June 13–14, 2002, convened by the U.S. Department of Education and the Education Leaders Council. A conference attendee reported that her district estimated approximately $250 per student for supplemental services (the U.S. Department of Education projected around $950).

A second objection is the lack of quality research on supplemental education programs and providers. As Dr. Ed Gordon, my colleague and one of the coauthors of this work, has indicated on many occasions, little research is available on the success of tutorial programs—nor is there reputable research on the teaching methods utilized by tutorial centers.

A third objection is inability to identify quality supplemental education programs. During the early stages of NCLB's implementation, most state education agencies hadn't developed procedures to identify quality tutorial programs, nor did they have procedures in place to adequately assist parents of eligible children in the selection of tutorial programs.

The American Federation of Teachers (AFT) raised several concerns. The Department of Education had released a letter for states and locals on the implementation of the supplemental service provision of Title I of the ESEA. This provision of the law allows students who are in persistently failing schools to receive after-school tutoring or supplemental services.

The department's letter represented its current thinking on how supplemental service programs should be implemented. It should not be interpreted, nor does it carry the same weight, as regulations. The department will publish guidance and regulations later.

The AFT has several problems with the letter released by the Department of Education. Two of the most serious are that it prohibits states from requiring providers of supplemental service to hire certified teachers. In the AFT's February letter to the department on regulatory issues, the union recommended that only certified or licensed teachers or paraprofessionals (working under the supervision of a certified teacher) provide supplemental services.

In addition, the department does not require that supplemental service providers use scientifically based research in their "instructional strategies." Not requiring either the use of certified or licensed teachers or scientifically based research programs will diminish the quality of supplemental service programs, according to the AFT (Meroney, 2002).

At its annual conference in 2002, the Education Commission of the States (ECS)—a widely respected national public policy organizations—addressed several key questions regarding NCLB. Among them:

- How do current state goals complement (or conflict) with ESEA?
- What strategies can states pursue to bring their policies into alignment with NCLB?
- What are the most difficult issues faced by states in implementing the legislation, and how can they be addressed?
- What are the roles and responsibilities of policy makers, the business sector, local communities, and the philanthropic community?

The session, chaired by Dr. Chris Cross, former assistant secretary for educational research and improvement, U.S. Department of Education, ECS Distinguished Senior Fellow, was attended by chairs of state legislative committees, members of state boards of education, LEA representatives, representatives of philanthropic organizations, representatives of testing services, and national public policy groups.

Several state legislators and representatives of state departments of education asked ECS for assistance in implementing the tutorial and school improvement sections, especially in rural areas. There was considerable discussion regarding methods of informing parents regarding the choices available to them, including providing comprehensive information about providers (Charles J. O'Malley & Associates, memo to Douglas Becker, July 14, 2002).

Secretary Paige's letter also discussed supplemental services. It said, for instance, that states must ensure that all providers have a demonstrated record of effectiveness in improving achievement, though some officials at the conference suggested they needed more clarification on what that stipulation meant. At the same time, Secretary Paige said states may not require providers to hire only certified teachers (Rod Paige, correspondence to chief state school officers, June 14, 2002).

Jeff Simering, legislative director for the Washington-based Council of the Great City Schools, which represents large urban districts, said he was pleased with the department's preliminary guidance:

> We think that they followed the letter of the law and didn't embellish upon it, and that's what we were asking them to do, he said. I like to find areas where I can be critical of folks, but at this point, they've done a decent job. (Strauss, 2002)

Steven E. Drake, then vice president for communications, Sylvan Learning Systems, commented on Sylvan's perceptions of NCLB's supplemental education provisions:

> The more convenient and seamless you make it for the children and therefore their parents, the better your attendance levels and participation. It's not going to be popular, he said. First, it's a [poor] reflection on schools that aren't working. And second, in their minds, it's taking away funds from public schools. Our opinion is the money should go to help kids. (Strauss, 2002)

The following excerpt from *Education Week* describes the situations facing state education departments:

> At least five states have been operating under the impression—mistaken, according to the Department of Education—that none of their public schools must meet a key requirement in the new federal education law this school year.
>
> Interviews with state officials in about half the states have found a wide range of responses to the new requirements. Several of those states have already iden-

tified schools and drawn up lists of potential providers. But that's far from the case across the board.

In fact, officials reached in seven state education agencies have suggested that none of their schools must provide supplemental services this year.

In one case . . . a state official said that was because all schools had made sufficient academic improvement. That's considered an acceptable rationale by the federal government.

But in the other six, the reasons apparently have nothing to do with how the schools have performed. Officials in those states pointed to issues related to their state systems of testing or accountability and to the difficulty of adjusting those systems rapidly to the new federal law.

In interviews over the past two weeks, those officials said it was their understanding that their stance was acceptable to the federal government. Not so, says the Education Department, with one possible exception. The department, while still withholding judgment about Virginia, indicated last week that none of the other five states is free from requiring supplemental services in schools based on the reasons those states have cited. The agency is currently in discussions, or has scheduled talks, with officials in those states to clarify the federal requirements and ensure compliance (Robelen, 2002).

In an interview, Undersecretary of Education Eugene W. Hickok said the agency would not grant any special exceptions: "We have told no states, nor will we tell any state, that they can take a walk on . . . accountability this year. The law doesn't allow it; we wouldn't allow it" (Robelen, 2002).

At least two other states have already reversed course after hearing from the federal government that they cannot take a pass on supplemental services. It may not have helped matters that the Education Department issued draft guidelines and regulations on supplemental services only in August, although Secretary Paige sent states a letter in June briefly outlining the department's thinking on the subject.

Jack Jennings, the director of the Washington-based Center on Education Policy, suggested that difficulties and delays should not be surprising. "States face a heavy burden trying to meet a host of new federal demands, some delving into unfamiliar terrain," said Jennings, who was a longtime aide to the House Education Committee.

Other Public Policy Issues

In addition to the general and national policy questions addressed in this chapter, the application of NCLB's supplemental services provisions has encountered other obstacles. For example, in January 2003, Harlem parents filed the first class action suit under NCLB, alleging many New York schools failed to inform parents of their choices, including supplemental services, under NCLB, even when requested (Robelen 2002).

In another example, the Chicago Public Schools, Illinois State Department of Education, and the U.S. Department of Education recently worked out a compromise agreement resolving a situation wherein the Chicago Public Schools, although identified as "in need of improvement," designated itself as a supplemental services provider. The agreement in essence permits the Chicago Public Schools (CPS) to provide tutorial/supplemental services, using funds other than those provided under NCLB.

However, this decision does not mean that CPS must cease providing extended learning opportunities to its students. It means, rather, that the district cannot consider those programs as supplemental educational services under Title I, Part A, of ESEA, and it cannot consider expenses for those programs against the requirement that it spend an amount equal to 20 percent of its Title I, Part A, allocation on supplemental educational services and transportation for public school choice. Students who signed up for the CPS supplemental educational service program must now be offered the choice of enrolling in another provider's program (Eugene Hickok, interview, February 16, 2005).

CPS reported significant achievement by students in a control group. Chicago elementary school students who were lagging farthest behind reaped the biggest gains from a mandated $50 million tutoring program, according to a CPS study released Wednesday, August 11, 2005 (Dell'Angela 2005).

A similar situation arose in Prince George's County, Maryland. The school district sought to become a supplemental services provider although the district was identified as "in need of improvement." The following excerpt from Department of Education correspondence from Nina Rees (Deputy Under Secretary for Innovation and Improvement, U.S. Department of Education, October 4, 2004) to Prince George's County Superintendent Andre Hornsby addresses the LEA's request:

> As you are aware, Section 200.47(b)(iv)(B) of the Title I regulations (34 C.F.R. 200.47(b)(iv)(B)) states that a local educational agency (LEA) in need of improvement, corrective action, or restructuring may not be an SES provider.
>
> Although PGCPS was approved as a provider by the Maryland Department of Education in the spring of 2004, because PGCPS is currently in need of improvement, under federal regulations, it cannot provide SES to students until it is out of improvement status. Additionally, although PGCPS cannot be a provider itself, you may wish to consider encouraging schools within the district that have made AYP to apply to the State to become providers.

Secretary Paige's letter to the chief state school officers cited other concerns:

We understand that a number of LEAs have imposed, or are considering conditions related to issues of program design. They may, for example, be requiring that providers offer a certain number of hours of services in order to receive the statutory per-child amount for services, that providers employ only State-certified teachers as tutors, or that they use one-to-one tutoring as their sole delivery mechanism. These types of requirements—which relate to whether a provider has an effective educational program—may not be imposed by LEAs, because they would undermine the State's authority to set criteria for approval of providers as having effective programs and to determine which providers meet those standards. In addition, these types of requirements may create a "one-size-fits-all" model for services that does not effectively take into consideration the varied needs of students, and undermine the parents' opportunity to select the most appropriate provider and services for their child.

OBSERVATIONS

You have likely noted a change in perception among those responsible for the implementation of NCLB's supplemental education services provisions. Accordingly, the overall implementation of these tutoring programs remains in a great state of flux across the United States. There has been widespread opposition to many aspects of NCLB by the professional education community. This has been tempered by reports from national public policy organizations citing more parents increasingly interested in the supplemental service programs available to their sons and daughters. Can representatives of these diverse communities work out their differences, overcome their fears and concerns, and put aside their biases to contribute to the success of this program?

One of the goals of *The Tutoring Revolution* is to make a substantial contribution to policy makers as they search for tutoring best practices that implement the supplemental service provisions of NCLB. In the following chapters we will examine the research covering this area and other tutoring issues.

2

The Tutoring Revolution

Every year in June the Tutor/Mentor Connection, a Chicago-based nonprofit organization, hosts the annual year-end dinner for students and adult volunteers who have participated in this program. The tutor-mentors are young professional men and women who have, in some cases, tutored the same student during their elementary and high school years. As tutors they helped these students with their basic skills, daily homework, and the process of learning how to learn. By serving as mentors, they also acted as important coaches and adult role models for these students, many of whom live in the Cabrini-Green Homes, one of the most violent, drug- and gang-infested public housing projects in America. When the students entered adolescence, the tutor-mentors helped them cope with this destructive environment and, most importantly, stay in school.

This dinner marked a rite of passage for several students graduating from high school and the Tutor/Mentor Connection program. One high school senior was about to enter the University of Wisconsin, and another Carlton College. Other students were to attend Jackson State University, Syracuse University, and Elmhurst College. They joined fifteen previous high school graduates already in college. "These students beat tremendous odds to be here tonight. We hopefully have given each of them a firm launching pad for a successful and meaningful life," says Dan Bassill, the program's president. The dinner reconfirmed what many educators are now beginning to understand: that high-quality tutoring programs can made a significant contribution to an individual student's success in school (Gordon, Morgan, Ponticell, & O'Malley, 2004).

TUTORING AND SCHOOLING

Tutoring is as old as civilization itself. It has been around longer than the common school forms of education that we take for granted today. In the twenty-first century, schooling is synonymous with education. This was not always true. There is a sizable body of evidence that tutoring was a prominent form of education in its own right (Gordon & Gordon, 1990).

The history of tutoring methods can be traced to the European Renaissance and afterward. First, royalty and the upper classes employed tutors to teach their children. Prominent thinkers who also were tutors, such as Jean-Jacques Rousseau, John Locke, Maria Edgeworth, Johann Herbart, and Friedrich Froebel, wrote tutoring how-to books for parents and tutors. They championed such concepts as individualized education, teaching to a child's aptitudes and interests, and using positive motivation rather than corporal punishment.

Tutoring practices gradually spread to the families of the new professional and middle classes in Europe. By 1850 in England as many children (50,000) were being tutored at home as were attending school. Of course, at that time most children received no education at all.

Tutoring played a prominent role in the development of literacy in America. Parents, relatives, itinerant teachers, ministers, and others acted as the agents of literacy. They adapted their methods to the remote frontier environment during the westward expansion of the United States (Gordon, 2004b). The American one-room schoolhouse can trace its earliest roots to the schools begun in private homes. Only by the early twentieth century (1919) did tax-supported public schools with compulsory attendance for children from age seven to sixteen or eighteen become a legal requirement in all the states. These laws placed schooling rather than tutoring in the driver's seat for the education of American children (Gordon & Gordon, 2003).

As already noted, some of the most important educational philosophers of Western civilization developed educational curriculum theories based on their practical experience as tutors. Their tutorial philosophies later developed into many of today's modern educational principles. The progressive education movement embraced the concepts of individual differences and child-centered education as first proposed by the philosopher-tutors such as Erasmus, Thomas Elyot, Juan de Vives, Thomas More, John Locke, François Fénelon, Jean-Jacques Rousseau, Maria Edgeworth, and a host of others (Gordon & Gordon, 1990).

What were these tutorial concepts? The development of the individual student's thinking process became a fundamental educational goal. This recognition of individual differences guided the instruction of each student.

Education became a culturally broadening experience that recognized the student's own talents and prepared him or her for adulthood. Students learned far better through rewards than punishments. A tutor best motivated a student to study through expressing kindness, exciting natural curiosity, and recognizing personal interests and unique abilities. The most effective tutor established an ethical standard reinforced by personal example for the student. A student's education helped him or her acquire a sense of individual responsibility for the betterment of society through his or her personal contribution.

These curriculum concepts developed by the philosopher-tutors for their students from the fifteenth to nineteenth centuries were later adopted by the twentieth-century progressive education movement and adapted to the American public school. John Dewey, as well as other progressives, shifted the central focus of teaching back to the student "to facilitate and enrich the growth of the individual child" (Dewey, 1963). As part of this transition, during the late nineteenth to the early twentieth century, educators began to ignore tutoring as a distinctive form of instruction. The principal reason for their neglect was the social justification that schooling for the masses was superior to tutoring for a few individuals. Schools absorbed and began to use certain curriculum aspects of tutoring. Unfortunately Dewey and other progressives overlooked the fact that the original context of tutoring was one-to-one instruction, not large-group teaching. The progressives cast the teacher in an almost impossible role, attempting to carry out precise individualized classroom teaching originally formulated for a tutorial curriculum. The development of tutoring has continued to our own time. By the 1960s tutoring began to gain ground as a supplemental service for increasing student classroom achievement (Gordon & Gordon, 1990).

At the beginning of the twenty-first century, tutoring has again emerged as a prominent education phenomenon throughout American society. A 2000 *Newsweek* poll found that 42 percent of Americans believe there is a "great need" for children to receive private, outside tutoring (Kantrowitz, 2000). The marketing analysts at Bear Stearns now estimate that the parents of students in the top 5 percent and the bottom 16 percent of their classes are likely to seek tutoring (Nadel, 2000). This translates to almost 7 million elementary school students and many high school students as well. In 2002 estimates of annual tutoring expenditure show that tutoring has grown to a $5 billion to $8 billion professional service industry (Gordon, 2002a). Today the total private and public investment in tutoring is probably larger (between $8 and $12 billion).

Tutors today come in all shapes and sizes. Adult volunteers, homework hotlines, peer tutors, individual teachers, franchised learning centers, university clinics, Internet sites, and private professional agencies are among the different types of tutoring services (Franklin, 2003). They vary in quality and cost. Private tutoring practices are the most commonly available form of tutoring across the United States. Hundreds of thousands of teachers annually tutor millions of students for a fee in their own home, the child's residence, or local public schools and libraries. Most of these tutors are classroom teachers who also work after school, on weekends, or in the summer tutoring local children. But does all this tutoring activity help improve American education (Gordon, 2002a)? We may soon find out.

At a time of great controversy in American education, tutoring has been given new prominence by the No Child Left Behind (NCLB) Act of 2001, which has been structured to provide supplemental services to children in failing schools through the Twenty-First Century Community Learning Centers program. In the 2006 fiscal year up to $2 billion will be used for elementary and secondary school district tutoring programs, or for referrals to a wide variety of local community tutoring programs (U.S. Department of Education, 2006). To increase participation, federal officials started pilot programs (2005) allowing schools to offer tutoring in lieu of a transfer during the first year that students could switch to a higher-performing school (Lizama, 2005). The use of federal funds to provide tutoring will have an effect on virtually every school across America. But important questions remain unanswered. Do educators know enough about the tutoring process to locate and use high-quality supplemental education programs? Is the potential effectiveness of tutoring services being compromised by little attention to research findings and the lack of consensus on professional standards? To answer these and other questions, in later chapters we will be considering both the theoretical and empirical foundations of tutoring.

Contemporary practices and cultural attitudes regarding tutoring have an immediate influence on its daily role in education. They can be summarized under five headings:

1. The tutors
2. The popularity of tutoring
3. Consumer guidance
4. The regulation of tutoring
5. Tutoring research

THE TUTORS

There are more categories of tutoring options available today than are commonly recognized, as seen in Table 2.1. These options are for both children

Category	Annual Percentage of All Students Tutored
Professional tutors (individual teachers or groups of teachers)	30
Community/nonprofit tutors for children	20
Community/nonprofit tutors for adults	10
School-based volunteer tutors	10
College peer tutoring	10
Adult work force tutoring	6
Peer tutoring (elementary and secondary schools)	5
College/university clinical tutoring	3
Corporate-owned tutoring centers	3
Franchised tutoring centers	3

Table 2.1. 21st-Century Tutoring Options For Children and Adults
Source: E. Gordon, 2002a.

and adults. A national study by the authors identified ten major tutoring options that are commonly found in most urban areas of the United States.

Let us briefly review the four of the most prominent tutoring options for children.

Professional Tutors

About 30 percent of the children being tutored today are receiving help from professional tutors who are teachers tutoring outside of school hours or during the summer. Each year, many thousands of teachers tutor millions of students for a fee in the tutor's home, in the child's home, in a local library and, since NCLB, in classrooms across America. Many specialize in a subject or specific learning problem (i.e., reading, math, or a learning disability). Students with serious learning issues benefit from professional tutors because they can offer diagnostic/developmental instruction drawn from their professional experience and education.

They offer precisely individualized one-on-one instruction. Professional tutors coach students and parents on learning behaviors in the home and collaborate with the students' classroom teachers. Professional tutoring is usually short term (three to six months). Professional tutors are excellent at diagnosis, remediating skills, and helping students "learn how to learn" to foster increased classroom achievement and independent learning activities at home.

Often small groups of teachers organize a local tutoring practice. In 1990 these groups organized the Education Industry Association (EIA).

Community Volunteer Tutors and/or Mentors

Community volunteer tutors can provide important support for regular schooling. In many cases an adult volunteer also becomes a mentor willing to take a personal interest in a student's long-term development as a learner. The best community-based tutoring programs offer volunteers solid tutor training, ongoing retraining, and close supervision. Effective community volunteer tutors/mentors also can continue the ongoing, long-term educational development of a child who has already received instruction from a professional tutor.

Adult School Volunteer Tutors

Tutoring in a school by an adult volunteer tutor is usually offered after school hours one on one or in small groups. College students, parents, and other adults are the tutors. Homework assistance is often the focus. The better the adult tutor is trained in the school's tutoring program, the more remedial learning assistance he or she can give a student.

Student Peer or Cross-Age Tutoring

In thousands of elementary, secondary, and postsecondary schools across America, students tutor their peers or older students tutor children in a lower grade. A great amount of research has shown that both the tutor and the tutee can benefit from these programs. Student overlearning and improved self-esteem help in almost any subject area or grade level. Peer or cross-age tutoring programs are relatively easy for teachers to provide and are low in cost. They offer a great supplement to teacher instruction (Gordon, 2005a).

THE POPULARITY OF TUTORING

In the past forty years, growing numbers of parents have been seeking tutoring to help their children who are attending public or private elementary, secondary, and postsecondary schools. This educational phenomenon has been driven by several factors:

1. The increased identification of learning disabilities
2. Children failing in school
3. Parental desires for a child to attend a prestigious school or college
4. Test preparation to improve standardized test scores

Moreover, parental interest in tutoring may be fueled in part by national or international studies calling attention to the lackluster test scores, low literacy, and poor reading habits of U.S. students, such as the following:

1. The National Assessment of Educational Progress, the so-called nation's report card, which has been administered every two years since 1990, continues to show that overall student achievement in reading, math, and science is rising very slowly or remaining flat (U.S. Department of Education, Office of Educational Research 2001, 2002).
2. The Program for International Student Assessment found that only 2 percent of U.S. students scored at the highest levels in reading, math, and science, while 25 percent were at the lowest levels. In the 2003 comparison of twenty-nine Organization for Economic Co-operation and Development (OECD) members, the United States placed twenty-fourth in math, fifteenth in reading, and nineteenth in science (OECD, 2004).
3. The National Endowment for the Arts report, *Reading at Risk* (2004), showed that over the past twenty years, book reading among young adults aged eighteen to twenty-four has declined by 55 percent.
4. In *Losing Our Future,* the Civil Rights Project at Harvard University and the Urban Institute reported abysmal high school graduation rates of 50 percent or lower in America's urban public schools. This study found many inaccuracies in previous reports because of the assumption that many students who left school transferred rather than dropped out (Orfield, Losen, Wald, & Swanson, 2004).

A new impetus for parents to seek tutorial help for their children was the passage of NCLB requiring universal student achievement of state standards. NCLB seems to assume that improvement of student learning will be continuous and consistent and can be accomplished in a fixed amount of time regardless of a student's starting place or individual learning needs (Rose, 2004). With the dramatic increase in so-called high-stakes testing, many more parents, perhaps fearing that their child will be retained, are now seeking tutoring for their child.

In 2002, encouraged by the NCLB supplemental service program, more parents and educators began asking, "Where can we find the best-qualified tutors?" As we have seen a vast array of options already exist, including individual teachers, groups of educators, corporations, and franchises, all of them offering tutoring programs that vary in price and quality. Until the passage of NCLB, most of these educational activities were unregulated by state, federal, or private regulatory groups.

During the late 1960s, private learning disability tutoring programs first appeared in urban areas. Since then, for-profit tutoring corporations have made numerous promises to frustrated parents. Most have failed to live up to public expectations. School districts have become increasingly wary of referring a child to a private tutorial program. The classroom performance of students who took part in these programs seldom matched the glowing posttest scores issued by the tutoring agencies. As a result, school districts have tended not to make referrals to outside tutoring agencies. They could not predict program results and were concerned over potential liability issues.

Thus we have today's catch-22 situation. School administrators and parents lack the basic knowledge to ask in-depth questions regarding tutorial programs, and therefore a great tutoring information gap now exists. Educators and parents find themselves at the beginning of a steep learning curve as they seek to answer critical questions about the quality of tutors and tutoring services. They are pretty much at the same level of consumer knowledge regarding tutoring services as car buyers were in the early 1960s when Ralph Nader wrote *Unsafe at Any Speed*. Nader helped answer the basic consumer question, "Where do I find the best car?" Forty years later, a myriad of automotive consumer guides help educate people about every aspect of making sound car-buying decisions.

Tutors and tutoring programs are not machines, of course, and tutors are not all alike. As we will see later in our review of research, the best tutors are master teachers, coaches, and mentors who will inspire a child or an adult to learn. Unfortunately, most parents, adult learners, and educators know a lot more about finding a good doctor than about finding a good tutor. People understand that different doctors specialize and provide different levels of professional service. So do tutors. A "one-size-fits-all" model of tutoring will fail to help many students. A professional tutor is well suited to assess individual needs and then build a learning program tailored to address those needs (Gordon, 2003).

CONSUMER GUIDANCE

The NCLB website (nochildleftbehind.ed.gov) provides a variety of resources for educators and parents. It answers questions such as: What are supplemental services? How will I know if my child is eligible for supplemental services? What kinds of programs are offered? How to I choose a good program? The U.S. Department of Education (USDOE) has also established a Supplemental Educational Services Quality Center. Its website, www.tutors forkids.org, provides information on tutoring and NCLB.

These websites are a good start. But many parents are seeking tutors outside the NCLB supplemental service program. They need more information to make intelligent choices. School districts need a credible means of providing useful consumer information to parents on how to find and select the best tutor for their child. An examination of current school district information for parents on selecting a tutor often reveals questions written in "educationese" that have little relevance to the parent consumer.

An example of this tutoring information gap is the following letter from a frustrated Midwestern parent that was sent to *Education Week*:

> My son is considered to be a low-income student because I'm a single mom. But the schools he has attended are all high-achieving, so he does not qualify for any extra tutoring. He is in the 3rd grade now and has struggled every year since kindergarten. He still is reading at a 1st-grade level. He needs the extra help.
>
> As a concerned parent, I cannot sit back and hope that he will catch up. My son struggles, gets frustrated, calls himself a "dummy," and wants to give up. He's only 8 years old. The anger he displays when he's frustrated is scary.
>
> This summer, I had my son tested by XYZ Learning Centers. To bring him up to the level he needs to be and at which he will feel comfortable learning, I have had to take out a student loan for more than $10,000 to pay for tutoring. ("Why Offer," 2005, p. 41)

Surveying the range of available options before making a substantial financial commitment is always a prudent course of action. Did this parent investigate other tutoring alternatives before signing up for a $10,000 tutoring program? What are the testing and fee practices of other local tutors? Did she ask her school for guidance or consult other community information resources such as the local public library or the numerous local community groups that offer tutoring? Tutoring fees vary widely. Parents need to make inquiries about what the tutor will charge and what exactly the child will receive in terms of expert instruction. This needs to be explained in layman's terms that are understandable to all parents so they can make better informed decisions.

The questions in the following outline pertinent information that a teacher, parent, or adult student needs to collect in order to document the quality of a tutor or tutoring service. This information will require interviews over the phone or in person, the use of websites, and some study of written promotional materials. These questions fall into ten distinct categories:

1. Basic program information
2. References
3. Licensing/staff credentials
4. Program content and goals

5. Contracts and guarantees
6. Fees
7. Student progress reports
8. Procedures for handling questions and complaints
9. Providing a safe environment
10. Volunteer tutoring programs

Here are some specific questions that consumers might ask in screening each potential tutoring program:

1. What are the exact types of services offered by a tutor or tutoring service?
2. What is the age or grade-level range of the children or adults tutored?
3. Will the mode of treatment used in the program be adequately explained to me in layman's terms before my child begins the program?
4. Is there an intake or screening process to ensure that a student's learning needs can be met by the tutor or tutoring service?
5. What time frame is given for enrollment in the tutoring program?
6. What should my expectations be for success? Will this tutor or tutoring program give you any indication, after the initial screening, of its expectations for my child?
7. How long has this service or individual provided tutoring programs?
8. What are the specific professional credentials required for a tutor (degrees, certification, years of experience)?
9. Has the tutoring service received any professional approval, licensing, or accreditation?
10. What is the sum of all the fees charged by the tutor or tutoring program?
11. Will the tutor accept insurance reimbursement (major medical), state or federal aid in payment? (Gordon, 2002a)

Once parents have interviewed several potential tutors, the Consumer Tutoring Quality Rating Scale (see Appendix) can be useful in determining which tutor to employ.

The Importance of Consumer Information for Evaluating Tutoring

Unfortunately, we do not live in an ideal world. The tutoring profession is fraught with challenges. Teachers can resist the intrusion by an outside tutor in their classroom teaching. Parents can sometimes look for the quick fix, compelled by lack of time, interest, or funds (Franklin, 2003).

Parents need basic consumer information so that they can arm themselves with the information necessary for finding the best tutor for their children.

The need for tutoring is not an indictment of the local school. The tutor and teacher are not in competition with each other. Instead, tutoring and classroom teaching should work together in prompting a student's learning. Tutoring should complement the work of the school. Tutors can analyze a student's learning needs and then use this information to improve the student's learning experiences.

The decision to use a professional tutor may be one of the most important choices that parents make for their child's future. As a psycho-educational service, tutoring has the potential to provide significant support to a student's educational foundation of "learning how to learn." Weak or ineffective tutoring can further weaken this personal learning foundation or undermine a student's self-esteem and motivation to learn. For these reasons, the state has an important role to play in the regulation of these professional educational programs.

THE REGULATION OF TUTORING

Until the passage of NCLB, states had little or no experience in approving private tutoring programs (Robelen, 2002). Very few states provided consumer regulations or voluntary professional educational approval of private tutors or tutoring services' financial practices, advertising, guarantees, tutor qualifications, program administration, curricula, or written reports to parents or schools. Nor has the field of private tutoring policed itself. Few tutoring programs have sought voluntary accreditation through regional education agencies. In this unregulated tutoring environment the potential for consumer fraud in the tutoring industry is a real danger and has only increased with the new federal law (Gordon, 2003).

NCLB is an important watershed for tutoring in the United States. It has placed tutoring for the first time in an educational spotlight. However, the outcome will be determined by how well individual states and school districts establish meaningful standards that regulate tutoring.

From a broad perspective NCLB has let the tutor genie out of the bottle. The growing public demand for high-quality tutoring will make it difficult to rescind these supplemental services.

NCLB raises four major tutoring regulatory issues that need to be addressed at both the local and federal levels. These include:

1. State board of education recognition requirements for tutors
2. Federal clarification of the qualifications of a professional tutor versus a volunteer tutor

3. The need for state boards of education to address consumer complaints regarding private tutoring services
4. Federal NCLB recognition that tutoring services need to be research based

State Recognition of Tutors

State boards of education need to both simplify and improve the application process to qualify more local community tutors for NCLB. Many states adopted all parts of the Council of Chief State School Officers *State Educational Agency Toolkit on Supplemental Educational Services* (2002) for NCLB. This toolkit is much more appropriate as a model for certifying a school than approving a tutoring program. Upon careful study this complex document reminds the authors of the classic school-accreditation process. The toolkit is far too complex and fails to get the information that is pertinent to determine the quality of a professional tutoring service. A result of its widespread adoption by many states has been the relatively low numbers of "approved" supplemental service providers (i.e., tutors). This has triggered shortages of approved tutors in local communities across the United States, even though research shows that over 100,000 teachers provide tutoring on a private basis as solo practitioners (Gordon, 2002a).

At the other end of the regulatory spectrum, some states have adopted the opposite approval strategy. They have issued a two- or three-page tutoring program application. This limits the evaluation of pertinent background information and questions the credibility of the state's process in identifying qualified professional tutors.

Complex or simplistic tutor approval strategies are largely self-defeating. On one hand, by making this process so complex, many qualified local tutors have been discouraged from applying, and only larger corporate programs have received approval. (In an author interview, a state educational agency toolkit consultant affirmed this as a desirable outcome.) On the other hand, an application process that sets the bar very low in terms of experience and requirements leaves the door open to applicants of questionable competence.

A more impartial evaluation process needs to be designed around identifying the qualifications of professional tutors and the specific tutoring services they offer students. This will help each state develop meaningful regulations and encourage the availability of a larger number of individual tutors in local communities.

The authors have prepared a model of proposed rules and regulations in relation to nonpublic tutoring services. (See chapter 7.) A major percentage of the approved NCLB supplemental service providers will likely expand their activities into regular tutorial services, if they have not already done so. NCLB represents only the tip of an increasing national demand for professional tutoring. In order to aid both parents and schools, it is clearly in the public interest for each state board of education to develop meaningful voluntary regulation of all tutors and tutoring services. This will help persuade more tutors to also participate in the NCLB and offer schools and parents more highly qualified educational choices.

A survey conducted by the Center on Education Policy (2005) for the US-DOE found that during the 2004–2005 school year only 18 percent of eligible students in districts actually participated in supplemental service (tutoring) programs. A lack of local tutors was cited as a major obstacle.

Yet just as the demand for tutors is increasing, teacher shortages are also growing across America. The demographic shift has begun that will see many baby boomers retiring from the classroom. According to the Bureau of Labor Statistics by 2010, up to 2.6 million new teachers will be needed in the United States (Hecker, 2001). The supply of professional, expert tutors is going down particularly in the areas of reading disabilities, learning disabilities, and higher math and science. These areas have traditionally required the most tutors. The states need to do everything in their power to encourage more teachers to participate in the NCLB effort as tutors (Gordon, 2005b).

To that end the USDOE (2005) issued *Supplemental Educational Services Non-Regulatory Guidance* to encourage the participation of more teachers. If an individual teacher or a group of teachers organize a nonprofit or for-profit entity, they can seek state approval to provide tutoring services (Gerwertz 2005b).

By 2005 the need for tutors had become acute in many public school systems across America. In September 2005, the USDOE gave the Chicago Public Schools a one-year waiver to run its own tutoring program (Banchero, 2005). One month later (October 2005), New York City and Boston were given the same exemption (Gerwertz, 2005a). This means that teachers in the same school building where children are currently failing will be allowed to act as their tutors. Such a policy runs the clear risk of repeating the instructional practices that failed an individual student. A tutoring curriculum needs to be used that is significantly different than the teaching practices used on a daily basis. Teachers need to be trained in tutoring best practices that are more individualized than their regular classroom teaching methods. Finally, how do we raise student expectations and motivations? Will they expect the tutoring to help if the same teachers whom they associate with their daily learning failures are now their tutors as well (Banchero, 2005)?

Federal Clarification of Tutor Qualifications

NCLB has introduced the idea of the tutor as another education professional. However, as we have seen, there are many different types of tutors who vary in their personal educational background, training, and experience. The levels of tutorial services they provide are not all the same. Tutors range from the subject-certified, degreed teacher to the community volunteer. Without specific differentiation regarding their levels of tutoring expertise, NCLB supplemental services will remain a marginalized educational activity that is perceived by the educational establishment as largely nonprofessional in nature. Students also run the risk of never receiving the professional tutoring services they need to improve their classroom achievement.

The failure to properly identify the expertise level of tutors reflects the general public's and many educators' viewpoint that almost anybody can tutor, and all tutoring is the same. Thus the majority of parents and educators look for the lowest-price tutoring available in their community, in the same way they shop for the cheapest plane ticket.

The end result of this uninformed consumer culture is that in balancing the student's need for tutoring versus the perceived value of tutoring, quantity wins out over quality. In general, parents and schools see tutoring as a "one-size-fits-all" educational activity. If anyone can do it, why pay a higher price for an expert, professional tutor? The results will be the same. This unfortunate attitude is largely self-defeating.

In 2005, in response to this important issue America's largest professional tutoring association, the EIA issued Standards for Best Practice for Education Services Providers. These included Guidelines for Qualifications of the Tutor/Education Service Provider (EIA, 2005).

The EIA established guidelines to help its members classify individuals they employ as tutors in three categories: Master Tutor—at least a bachelor's degree and knowledge of the education service provider's model; Tutor—college student with at least sixty credit hours; and Education Assistant—a person trained as a tutor who has at least a high school diploma. (See chapter 7 for complete EIA standards.)

These standards are a move in the right direction. Schools need clarity regarding the tutor's background before making any referral or using a program within a school district. It is to be hoped that in the near future NCLB will adopt such a designation of tutor expertise categories for each individual program to clarify the potential quality that parents might expect from any individual tutoring program.

Addressing Consumer Complaints

Tutoring is a rapidly expanding professional service, which unfortunately carries a growing potential for consumer fraud. In particular, this includes such areas as guarantees, program endorsements, advertising claims, and consumer complaint resolution. Let us examine each in turn.

Guarantees

Some tutoring programs offer parents a guarantee. After a prescribed number of tutoring classes, the student's reading and math skills are guaranteed to improve by one grade level. If the guarantee is not met, the tutor will provide additional instruction at no extra charge until the test score goal is met.

However, if you read the fine print you may discover that the tutor has the right to select the pre- and posttests. By carefully selecting tests that are too easy or not age appropriate, letting the tutor "teach the test," repeatedly giving the same or very similar tests over and over again, or a combination of these strategies, the guarantee for the tutoring can appear to have been met.

For some tutors their "guarantee" of a grade level in reading improvement is fulfilled if the student reaches the prescribed testing levels in either comprehension or vocabulary, but not both. Math "guarantees" can also be met by reaching prescribed testing levels in either computation skills or math-concept application skills, but not both. However, very little professional research has been published that can verify any specific tutoring program's guarantee is attainable for most of the children who will use the program.

Tutoring is a complex psychological/educational service that must address the many different learning skill issues of each student. It is difficult (if not impossible) for any tutoring program to guarantee test score improvements for the wide variety of students referred to them.

Mrs. L's experience with her twelve-year-old daughter, Sue, is a far too typical example of a guaranteed testing result from tutoring. Sue's seventh-grade math teacher told Mrs. L that Sue was two years below grade level in math. Mrs. L enrolled Sue with a tutor who guaranteed results. The tutor's pretests showed Sue's math skills to be two and a half years below seventh grade level. After thirty hours of tutoring, a different standardized test indicated two full years of improvement in Sue's math skills. Mrs. L was ecstatic—until Sue failed math the next semester. Her teacher reported that she did not see any great improvement either in Sue's class work or test grades.

How did this happen? Who or what was wrong: the teacher or the tests? The truth is, neither. Mrs. L never thought to check whether the tests given by the tutor were appropriate for Sue's age. Test publishers market a variety of standardized tests, which may be too hard or too easy for a particular age-group. By giving a difficult pretest and an easier posttest, a tutoring center can show marvelous results and meet its "guarantee" (Gordon, 2002a)

Celebrity Endorsements

Using actors posing as parents or students and having a celebrity endorse a product or service are popular marketing methods for all sorts of things, including tutoring services. Professional athletes, actors, politicians, and even some educators lend their names to "proven educational programs." Sometimes the celebrity gives a testimonial to the effect that, if the "new proven educational method" had been available to help overcome his or her personal learning problem, how much easier life would have been. Actually, very few of the individuals who endorse such programs check on how effectively the program serves its clientele. Endorsements may sell cars, clothes, and cosmetics, but they are not a substitute for a parent or adult investigating the facts about a professional tutoring service.

Advertising Claims

Other appeals are used that play on parents' emotions. Guilt-ridden parents, feeling they may have failed their child, respond to glowing claims that the tutoring program will ensure "your child's future success." The ads talk vaguely about teaching the "basics," about "programs designed for the individual," or using the "latest advanced interactive learning computer technologies." They claim that after using their methods a student "performs remarkably better!" Exactly how all this is accomplished is left unsaid.

The ads of another tutor include an "Underachievement Profile," consisting of a series of questions for parents to answer about their child. This is followed by the statement, "Remember, most underachievers will deny they have a problem. It is you as parents who must make the decision to seek help." Parents who already feel guilty about their child's failure in school are invited to sign up for the center's motivational counseling program, even though they have little understanding of what a motivational counseling program can or cannot do to improve daily schoolwork.

Mrs. R contacted such a motivational counseling program for her teenage son, Roger, whom his teachers described as having considerable academic potential that he was not using. When Mrs. R took Roger to meet Ms. Prentice, a counselor at the motivational center, she was impressed with the friendliness and the insight Ms. Prentice seemed to have regarding Roger's behavior, even though she had just met him. After paying substantial fees for several weeks of individual and group counseling sessions at the center, Mrs. R had high hopes for improvement in Roger's schoolwork. It was not forthcoming.

The counseling at the motivation center was not coordinated with Roger's teachers at school. Ms. Prentice glossed over his need for additional intensive remedial work in reading and math skills from a qualified tutor and assured Mrs. R that these skills would improve automatically once Roger became "motivated" to do his schoolwork. Not only was Roger's weakness in basic skills ignored, but no plan was made to provide him with help in these skills by the center or through a referral, even if Roger had become willing to accept such help.

Regulation at the state level might require a tutoring service to identify its expertise and specialty areas and the process it follows to provide intervention. Parents must look beyond the hype of promotional literature that touts state-of-the-art e-learning or any other program that will solve any and all learning problems. There are no generic wonder programs that can help every student who arrives at the door of a tutoring service (Gordon, 2002a).

Consumer Complaint Resolution

When parents have a complaint regarding an approved tutoring service, whom should they contact? In an NCLB tutoring program, the local education agency (LEA) will probably receive most of these calls, and possibly the state education agency (SEA) will too. However, both the LEAs and SEAs have limited staff for investigating and resolving consumer tutoring complaints.

In 2001 the Council of Better Business Bureaus developed the first national consumer protection standards for the tutoring or supplemental businesses. A national committee of tutor-educators helped the council formulate these standards. Over 110 local Better Business Bureaus (BBBs) across the United States and Canada are now using these standards to resolve consumer complaints. What the authors propose is that a partnership involving a SEA, LEA, and BBB might be more effective in resolving many of these consumer issues.

"This is a natural for the BBB," according to James Baumhart, president of the Better Business Bureau of Chicago and Northern Illinois, "as it enabled us to develop a proactive set of standards before many complaints were received." Kenneth Hunter, president of the Council of Better Business Bureaus, believes that "in effect, we set standards for businesses to adhere to so they know the ground rules in advance." Each local BBB maintains a consumer complaint history on local businesses and reports whether a particular program meets its standards for general business practices and as a tutoring business. Consumers can contact a local BBB for information or file a complaint by using the national website, www.bbb.org, or by contacting the Council of Better Business Bureaus at 703-276-0100 (Gordon, 2003).

State boards of education need to be encouraged to collaborate with their local BBB in the mediation and settlement of consumer complaints regarding tutoring services. In 2001 the National Better Business Bureau Trade Practice Standards and Professional Guidelines for Educational Tutoring were published in *The Do's and Don'ts in Advertising Copy* (Council of Better Business Bureaus, Inc., 2000). These standards were written to provide a benchmark for this industry. The local BBBs in every state will use these standards to settle formal consumer complaints. Unsettled complaints could be turned over to the state boards of education for further necessary action.

Many state attorney generals already collaborate with their local BBBs to help settle complaints in other professional service areas. Each state board of education needs to consider a partnership with the BBB in the mediation and settlement of consumer tutoring complaints.

Tutoring Research

The public policy changes brought about by NCLB have been considerable. NCLB has combined the use of academic assessment with the broad use of supplemental tutoring services. As a result, NCLB has become the first step to institutionalize tutoring. Before NCLB, the educational establishment had largely dismissed the use of tutoring to improve student achievement. Commercial tutoring programs came and went. Little meaningful tutoring research was published or offered to classroom teachers as new methods to individualize student learning. For the first time, NCLB provides federal funds for the establishment of high-quality classroom curricula that need to be research based and specifically designed to increase student achievement. NCLB calls for "research-based" classroom learning programs taught by "highly qualified teachers." Why does NCLB not also require research-based tutoring programs taught by highly qualified professional tutors?

Some educators will object that we do not have any idea about what constitutes tutoring best practices, since little research has been published thus far in the field of tutoring. As a result, they say there is still no consensus about what constitutes success under NCLB.

"The last thing we need is a rush to judgment based on anecdotes and scarce data. If tutoring programs prove unsuccessful, then they should be changed. But it is too early to make that determination," said Jeffrey H. Cohen in testimony (2005) before the House Education and the Workforce Committee. Cohen is the president of Baltimore-based Catapult Learning, which is approved to provide NCLB tutoring in thirty-five states (Gerwertz, 2005c).

That lack of tutoring data may soon change. The Chicago Public Schools Office of Research, Evaluation, and Accountability (2005) issued a report on the second year of tutoring provided students as part of NCLB. The results offered a mixed picture. (We will undertake a detailed analysis of these results in chapter 7.) Overall student achievement in these Chicago programs seemed to have much to do with how the tutoring was provided and who provided it (Dell'Angela, 2005).

Tutoring programs that are based on research offer obvious advantages for learners of all ages. A review by the authors of contemporary research related to tutoring revealed more than 300 books and 7,000 articles that indicated the benefits of tutoring are clear. L. F. Annis (1983) reported that tutoring procedures appear to produce positive effects on both students and tutors. Summaries of research on tutoring (Cohen, Kulik, & Kulik, 1982; Gage & Berliner, 1992; Gordon, Morgan, & Ponticell 1991, 1994) have indicated that these positive effects have been consistently found in measures of achievement, affective measures of self-esteem, and intrinsic interest in the subject matter being taught. In addition, the results from numerous cross-age and peer-tutoring studies conducted with learners across the life span have yielded positive findings (P. Lippitt, 1969; P. Lippitt & Lippitt, 1970; R. Lippitt & M. Lippitt, 1968). In sum, it appears that tutoring offers a powerful technique for enhancing student learning across a wide sample of different types of students and content areas (Gordon, Morgan, Ponticell, & O'Malley, 2004).

Some of the research issues that the authors hope to address will help better define the basic who, what, why, when, where, and how of both tutors and tutoring:

- Who are the most effective tutors? What are the professional backgrounds of successful tutors?
- What constitutes tutoring best practices?
- Why does tutoring work?
- When does tutoring become effective? How much time on task is needed to achieve a learning improvement?
- Where does tutoring happen best? Under what conditions do we get better results?
- How do we develop tutoring practices derived from psychology of learning principles?

We believe that the current wave of education reform promoting research-based classroom teaching needs to encompass tutoring research. This will help improve both the attitudes and expectations of educators and parents by identifying the best practices of high-quality tutoring that enhances student classroom learning and supporting a tutoring revolution.

3

Learning, Research, Assessment:
Where Do We Stand?

INTRODUCTION

The No Child Left Behind (NCLB) Act of 2001 has created a whirlwind of controversy, as we are now being held accountable for the education of our children in ways never before seen. Schools may lose funding and possibly close if students do not make adequate progress. Districts all over the country are attempting to deal with details such as a choice provision that calls for underperforming schools to offer a better performing school to its children.

As school districts work to understand and implement the many facets of NCLB, those of us in the field of educational research find ourselves in a unique position. Educational researchers are concerned with theories and principles of human learning, teaching, and instruction within the context of theory-derived educational materials, programs, strategies, and techniques that can enhance lifelong educational activities and processes. As such, we can be instrumental in furthering the understanding of the many complex processes involved in education from the group to individual level. We have a rich history on which to draw for guidance in making difficult, multilayered, evidence-based educational decisions. We are also experienced in the study of student learning in terms of the processes and constructs involved and the manner in which they manifest themselves in diverse student bodies. With all of this experience and knowledge to draw on, how can we go about making a difference? How can we be certain that our voices are heard among the policy makers who may or may not have experience in dealing with education in a real-world sense? Before we can look forward to making additional, positive contributions, it is probably a good idea to reflect on where we have been to understand where we should go in proposing a tutoring revolution.

American Educational Psychology

Educational psychology has been recognized as a discipline within the larger field since psychology officially arrived in the United States with the founding of the American Psychological Association (APA) in 1892. Around the turn of the twentieth century, prominent figures in the field were making a case for developing connections between their beliefs about learning and teaching. Two early pioneers, John Dewey and Edward L. Thorndike, stood out. Both were known, among other things, for their work and contrasting beliefs regarding the psychology of learning.

For a good portion of the twentieth century, Thorndike's behaviorally based theories of learning were widely accepted by the mainstream (Bower & Hilgard, 1998). Thorndike advocated a connectionist view of learning with hallmark components such as the laws of exercise (practice) and effect (reinforcement). Thorndike's theories, like the majority that once filled the field and ultimately dictated the way in which our current educational system was created, were based on ideas that described behavior and learning in a behavioral, connectionist manner. While this viewpoint may have some utility, it did not include many of the aspects of learning that we have come to embrace today. In fact, Thorndike borrowed methods from the physical sciences, with an emphasis on measuring, isolating variables, and comparing quantitative outcomes. These behaviorally oriented developments produced an empirically based set of knowledge structures that were often represented in abstract forms that ignore contextual influences and isolate aspects of practice that cannot easily be reintegrated with interacting features of classrooms.

While Thorndike advocated for a learning theory that was visible and measurable, John Dewey pursued another direction. Dewey highlighted ideas such as the "psychologizing" of school subjects. Students were presented with material and asked to relate the material to themselves and their experiences to make meaning of what they had learned. This went beyond the stimulus–response notions of the connectionists, who argued that teachers present material and students learn it via repetition and reinforcement. Dewey's intention was to show students and everyone involved in the educational process that learning is a dynamic event that cannot simply be broken down into component parts to fit a stimulus–response paradigm. Rather, it is a deeply personal matter that involves creativity, imagination, and personal experience, all of which reside within the learner.

The point is that different theories about learning have been around since the field was formally established as an area of study. Which of the two viewpoints looks better today? Some continue to hold on to aspects of behavioristic views of learning theory and teaching. For example, within the realm of functional behavioral analysis, a small group of contemporary behaviorally oriented learning theorists and many special educators and school psychologists have embraced many of the ideals Thorndike put forth years ago.

Around 1960, a new era began with a shift from behaviorism toward cognitive psychology. Educational psychology was at the forefront of significant advances in the study of cognition and motivation, development and individual differences, language and thought, metagcognition, discourse structures, strategic instruction, and teacher decision making.

Cognitive psychology continued to emerge as the premier discipline within academic psychology and educational psychology during the past thirty-five years. These developments had a significant impact on education. For the past twenty-five years, constructivist viewpoints have prevailed in educational research. Constructivists hold the learning community and the impact of social and cultural influences as key pieces in student development and learning. These constructivist views are associated with the views of Dewey and Vygotsky.

The idea of the social and cultural influences impacting development and learning are key components in contemporary constructivist learning theory. They also reflect a change in methodological attitudes toward the construct of diversity. Where culture and ethnicity were once treated as control variables in research, we now look to learners' backgrounds and the social influences in which they developed as major factors in their development.

One goal of NCLB is to shrink the achievement gap between ethnic groups. Historically and currently, a gap continues to be present between Caucasian, African American, and other minority students. Educational researchers continue to struggle with the reasons for this gap and with the implementation of potential methodologies to close it. As noted above, ethnicity and culture have often been treated as control variables in research. To effectively understand and combat the achievement gap and other disparities between and within groups, we must move past the control variable quagmire. Ceci and Papierno (2005) described the rhetoric and reality of gap closing. Most research regarding minority students and academic success is focused on the examination of student failures. The factors that lead students to succeed are rarely mentioned, contributing further to the deficit model. There are many examples of minority students performing exceptionally well in the face of group-based inequalities. The focus today is to encourage future researchers to focus their efforts on the systematic study of these successes.

Fixing Our Schools

Efforts to correct problems in our schools have gone on for many years in America. We are always trying to come up with better ways to foster greater student achievement. As anyone who keeps up with the news of the day knows, NCLB has, among many, the goal that all students in the United States will be achieving at what is considered to be an appropriate level in core subject areas by the year 2013. There are many repercussions that schools may experience if they do not meet the specific standards set forth by NCLB, including the loss of funding through the outright closing of schools that are chronic failures.

Like many efforts to fix and/or reform our schools, the NCLB was created with a noble goal that was difficult to challenge. Who wouldn't want to see every student in America rise above substandard performance to a level of competence that would ultimately afford a better set of opportunities in life? The problem does not seem to be the goal of the act but the unforeseen consequences of its component parts. The media is filled with complaints that NCLB is an unfunded mandate that includes lofty goals without federal financial backing. Further, concerns are present in that the inclusion of special education student test scores on district assessments will lead to many, if not all, districts appearing on the federal watch list of underperforming schools. Many logistical problems also exist in terms of districts having to accommodate student choice provisions to attend better performing schools if their home school is not meeting standards.

With all of the concerns surrounding NCLB, what have schools done in the past to fix the problems that exist? Borman, Hewes, Overman, and Brown (2003) conducted a meta-analysis of comprehensive school reform efforts. They included school reform efforts that were implemented on a whole school level and funded by external sources. The authors reviewed the effect on student achievement of twenty-nine different comprehensive reform models. These reform efforts were designed to target chronically underperforming schools in high-poverty areas. In many instances, funding is provided via Title I, which began in 1965 as part of the Elementary and Secondary Education Act, which has since been renamed NCLB.

Many aspects of comprehensive school reform were described and critically evaluated by the authors within the context of this meta-analysis. One main finding was that the school reform efforts work if they are based, among other things, on evidence-based practices associated with randomized controlled trials and sound statistical documentation. Certainly the selection of a program to be implemented on a whole school basis must be solid in terms of proven capability to make positive changes if implemented correctly with the appropriate level of buy-in by teachers and administrators.

In keeping with large-scale reform efforts, focus must also be given to reform efforts directed at changes at the individual teacher level. This focus is considered to be vital if one assumes that schools will only be fixed through the efforts of individual teachers who may then gather collectively to effect positive changes. Building on the findings related to what we know and don't know about constructivist learning and teaching practices, Windschitl (2002) outlined many of the difficulties associated with the implementation of constructivist teaching practices. In short, educators who choose to adopt constructivism as a practice may find themselves fighting against what Shepard (2000) called the twentieth-century dominant paradigm. This paradigm included three primary components: a social efficiency curriculum focus, behaviorally based associationist learning theoretical views and applications, and objective measurements of student achievement. These early- to mid-twentieth-century views are different from today's emergent paradigm of a reformed vision of a socially and culturally inclusive curriculum, cognitive and constructivist learning theories, and classroom assessments.

Windschitl (2002) outlines several dilemmas regarding the utilization of a constructivist model of instruction. The dilemmas are organized into four clusters of issues—conceptual, pedagogical, cultural, and political. The four clusters of dilemmas are situated on a continuum ranging from a teacher's personal understanding of the details of constructivism (conceptual) to the broader community, including administrators, parents, and the community in general (political).

Many argue that evidence-based practices should be the only ones allowed in education. In their view we have come to a dangerous impasse in the education of our children with no more time to buy into the many trends that have come along with little or no scientific support. For the educational researchers on this side of the fence, it may be refreshing to see that the NCLB includes significant mention of the terms "scientific" and/or "evidence-based" related to research in education. It may come to pass that a large portion of the available funding for research will be limited to those who follow a scientific model in their study of education and learning. Is this a positive trend?

A Critical Examination of Evidence-Based Practices

For those in the field of psychology, the scientific method of study is introduced early on at the undergraduate level. In a brief review of the list of terms compiled as part of a study of psychological literacy, Boneau (1990) stated that there is a major focus on research methodological (evidence-based) topics that all psychologists are expected to know. We should all be well versed in statistics and evidence-based methodologies.

With this in mind, it can be argued that many psychologists enter the field with a set of biases toward the measurable and quantifiable when it comes to conducting studies and trusting the results of others. There is nothing wrong with this given our training background and the notion that we, as scientists and evidence-based practitioners, should be skeptical of studies and results that are not backed by strong empirical evidence as confirmation of a theory and/or intervention. One would hope that with something as serious as school reforms and the policies that govern them that only the research of the highest scientific quality be considered when decisions regarding funding and implementation are made.

While one would hope that continued reform efforts will be based on the bedrock of scientific proof via tightly controlled and replicated studies, the fact is that research in education is complex and seldom easy. Several researchers (Berliner, 2002; Erickson & Gutierrez, 2002; Pellegrino & Goldman, 2002) provide insightful commentaries related to the nature of educational research. Is it the place of a governmental body to dictate what scientific research is? Should we not admit that research in education is often so difficult that to attempt to equate it with research in the hard sciences such as chemistry or physics is futile?

In fact many alternative methods of inquiry have been developed that are equally as important as hard-line quantitative research in education. Qualitative research, when carried out according to strict guidelines in a trustworthy manner, can be just as useful as positivistic quantitative research. Gergen (2001) stated that the many developments that have taken place related to the way the views associated with postmodernists and neomodernists are controversial and difficult to understand. For many traditionally minded psychologists and educational researchers, these views remain controversial and difficult to assimilate into a narrow view of science and evidence-based practices. However, with a weathering of the controversies and disagreements, great things may become possible over the years to come.

What may be the most crucial component related to embracing collaborative, postmodern-based notions of research methodologies and evidence-based practices is the creation of research communities. The creation of research communities is described in a book edited by Shavelson and Towne (2002). The contributors describe the history of the issues and meanings associated with scientifically and/or evidence-based research practices in education. They note that it is crucial to engage in discussions of what constitutes science in education, lest we be restricted to whatever definition is handed down via the political arena. The educational research community is made up of those at the university level (faculty and students) as well as the membership of professional organizations such as the American Educational Research Association (AERA) who advocate for the use of sound research methodological practices in education. It may also be argued that practitioners in the field (teachers, administrators, and other certified personnel) have a great deal to add to the research methodological conversation, given that they (not the university-based educational researchers) are putting the school reform programs and instructional methods into place every day within the schools.

Feurer, Towne, and Shavelson (2002) argue that in addition to funding for research studies, the government should provide funding for the research infrastructure. These authors state that it is critically important to design research communities that foster communication and sharing of ideas and information among all persons (university researchers and students and field practitioners) associated with the educational research enterprise. Rather than focus our efforts solely on the mechanical aspects of our work, it is recommended that we include the continued building of a research community that is well connected with all of its members to ensure that the most effective educational reform practices are systematically developed and refined to ultimately bring about desired changes.

Conclusion

As a field, we have come to embrace many of the ideals held by Dewey as opposed to those held by Thorndike. This is not to discount Thorndike's numerous contributions; rather, it points to the growth away from associationist and connectionist views to those embraced currently in terms of what we have learned regarding the importance of cognitive, social, and cultural influences on learning. Pintrich (1994, 2000a, 2000b) describes not only the current favor of Dewey and his theories compared to behaviorally based views associated with Thorndike, but he also notes (via prediction) that educational researchers are likely to shift their focus from asking why students fail to asking why schools fail students. Given the current NCLB legislation, Pintrich could not have been more correct in his prediction. We appear to expect schools to fix themselves rather than look at the situation from the student's perspective. As stated earlier, there is nothing wrong with an attempt to mandate the improvement of student achievement. However, NCLB seems to restrict the autonomous and dynamic excitement associated with the overall educational process. The views of teachers and their students have become marginalized. The current educational reform effort focuses on test performance. Scoring well on standardized tests is now a matter of life or death for all students. The high-stakes testing, standards-based educational reform movement may well succeed in driving many highly qualified and inspirational teachers away from the field while cutting off a generation of students from the true joy of learning.

In sum, it is our view that we should be greatly concerned with the political backfiring of legislation aimed at dictating what constitutes evidence-based practices and true science in research. We are hopeful that as members of an evidence-based research and learning community, we can put aside our differences of opinion with regard to the better validity of one methodology over another to embrace an inclusive continuum of disciplined methods of inquiry (from the qualitative to the quantitative). By stating this, we are not advocating that policy changes be made based on the field notes created by a few researchers. However, there is no reason that sound, evidence-based decisions can't be based on the carefully documented set of field notes used to create a highly detailed set of case studies from a site-based teacher-researcher.

We can all make contributions to the community of researchers and learners. As scientists, we are naturally skeptics. Only through the active participation in a discussion can we come to understand the complex nature of research in education. Education is truly a field like no other. If we can all remember that we are in the field to help students grow holistically and if we keep the spirit of a learning and research community alive, we can influence the way that legislation and evidence-based practices are implemented.

WHAT WE NEED TO KNOW ABOUT
LEARNING THEORY AND INSTRUCTION

A Story from the Past

At the beginning of the twentieth century, John Dewey and his laboratory school colleagues were planting the seeds of a school-based, teacher-engaged system of building professional knowledge. But Dewey was succeeded by Charles Judd, who worked to bring a recognized science to education. Judd reached out to psychology for direction. Edward Thorndike had been developing a science of behavior that borrowed methods from the physical sciences, with an emphasis on measuring, isolating variables, and comparing quantitative outcomes. Thorndike's approach fit well with the increasingly popular notions of efficacy and division of labor for improving productivity. These behaviorally oriented developments produced an empirically based set of knowledge structures that were often represented in forms that are relatively abstract, ignore contextual influences, and isolate aspects of practice that cannot easily be reintegrated with interacting features of classrooms. In addition, this approach to school improvement stimulated the emergence of two professional communities (school practitioners and university researchers).

Lessons from the Past

Some have presumed that the costs of the past are due to pursuing an empirically based science of education. As J. Hiebert, Gallimore, and Stigler (2002) note in their article "A Knowledge Base for the Teaching Profession: What Would It Look Like and How Can We Get One?" it is a misinterpretation to assume that making education a science leads necessarily to the choices of the past. It is a mistake to interpret Thorndike's victory as one of scientific approaches over nonscientific approaches. Accepting the scientific versus nonscientific explanation leaves those who propose alternatives to the Judd and Thorndike legacy in the unappealing and unfounded position of advocating nonscientific approaches to study education.

A more appropriate reading is that Thorndike and his colleagues successfully promoted some scientific methods over others. Experimental comparative methods that rely on controlling and isolating variables became the methods of choice. But these are not the only scientific methods that yield dependable, trustworthy knowledge. Observations and replications across multiple trials can produce equally rigorous tests of quality and can, over time, produce dependable knowledge as well.

Clearly the growing numbers of case studies and ethnographies report information closer to the kind of knowledge that teachers hold (i.e., context sensitive, particular, readily descriptive knowledge). But we recognize that researchers' knowledge gathered through applying qualitative methods does not solve the larger problem. There often remains a difference in purpose between researchers and teachers, and there remains the task of building a reliable knowledge base that is tested across different contexts.

Definition of Educational Psychology

The science and profession of educational psychology is the branch of psychology that is concerned with the development, evaluation, and application of (1) theories and principles of human learning, teaching, and instruction and (2) theory-derived educational materials, programs, strategies, and techniques that can enhance lifelong educational activities and processes. Sophistication in cognitive psychology (particularly cognitive, social, and cultural constructivist views of learning and instruction) and familiarity with disciplined methods of inquiry (empirical and arts-based methods of educational research) are considered to be essential for analyzing and interpreting present and future research in educational psychology.

Educational psychology is expanding into nontraditional settings, such as tutoring, and is undergoing changes in focus. We believe that there are domains of scholarship and skills that are essential for the educational psychologist and that they are best represented in the academic subjects of emerging theoretical frameworks for research on classroom learning; empirical and arts-based post-modern views of educational research methodology and theory; cognitive, social, and cultural constructivist views of learning and instruction; diversity; and technology. A range of additional and sometimes related areas includes instructional design; school, community, and workplace-based consultations; cultural politics and educational research; school reforms; the educational psychology of special populations; teacher preparation and education (research on learning to teach and teacher efficacy, functional analyses of academic performance problems, principles of teaching for successful intelligence); corporate training and development (enhancing learning in training and adult education); mental health programming in schools and communities; the educational psychology of health and wellness; and the educational psychology of literacy.

Constructing a Knowledge Base for the Teaching Profession

Our focus has been and continues to be on the construction of an evidence-based knowledge base for the teaching profession. Concerns persist that educational research has too little influence on improving classroom teaching and learning (National Educational Research Policies and Priorities Board, 1999). To improve classroom teaching in a steady, lasting way, the teaching profession needs a knowledge base that grows and improves. In spite of the continuing effects of researchers, archived research knowledge has had little effect on the improvements of practice in the average classroom (Hiebert et al., 2002).

Robert Sternberg (2001), former Division 15 (Educational Psychology) president and former president of the APA, stated that "a teacher must know under what circumstances to teach one way, and under what circumstances to teach another. There is no one 'right' way of teaching material. How the teacher teaches depends on the students, the material, and the context of teaching."

Efforts to broaden the impact of research for teachers have taken a variety of forms, including government-produced summaries of "what works" in the classroom, interpretations of research for schools and districts wishing to improve, and prescriptions for effective teaching. Helpful as some of these efforts have been, educators recognize that translating research into forms useful for teachers is a continuing stubborn problem. Most approaches for bringing research to teachers assume that research knowledge is the best foundation on which to build a professional knowledge base because of its generalizable and trustworthy (scientific) character. An alternative view is that the knowledge teachers use is of a different kind than usually produced by educational researchers. Called craft knowledge by some, it is characterized more by its concreteness and contextual richness than its generalizability and context independence. From this point of view, bridging the gap between traditional research knowledge and teacher's practice is an inherently difficult, but not intractable, problem.

In our certification programs of study, we recognize the inherent difficulties of translating traditional research knowledge into forms teachers can use to improve their practices, and we recognize the value of teacher's craft knowledge. During the past two decades the teacher-as-researcher movement (G. Anderson & Herr, 1998) has oriented teachers to studying their own practices, thereby making them more public and testing their effectiveness. There has been an increased awareness of the richness of teacher's personal knowledge.

OUR CORE BODY OF KNOWLEDGE AND CONNECTIONS TO OTHER DISCIPLINES

Learning Theory and Teaching

Edward Lee Thorndike dominated educational psychology from the turn of the twentieth century until the end of World War II. At the outset, American psychology was pragmatic and functional. But partly as a result of Thorndike's influence, educational psychology moved away from the real world of students and teachers toward basic research on generalizable principles of learning and instruction. Investigations during the next period, roughly from 1930 to 1960, tended to depend on laboratory rather than field settings. Around 1960, a new era began with a shift from behaviorism toward cognitive psychology. Educational psychology was at the forefront of significant advances in the study of cognition and motivation, development and individual differences, language and thought, metacognition, discourse structures, strategic instruction, and teacher decision making. Dramatic changes in conceptual frameworks took place along with a renewed interest in the role of context, diversity, the psychology of school subjects, teaching and instruction, and combinations of quantitative and qualitative disciplined methods of inquiry. The prevailing view today is that methodologists need substantive knowledge, for it is recognized that the substantive questions are the most important aspects of inquiry.

Diversity

Educational psychologists seem to favor a methodological approach to culture-related educational problems that follow in the tradition of post hoc, aptitude–treatment interaction research. The way educational psychologists have dealt with ethnicity and culture mirrors how psychologists have addressed these issues in general, chiefly as areas outside their primary research concerns. Ethnicity and culture have been treated mainly as control variables in a literature where a focus on race, a pseudoscientific category, has overshadowed the study of culture and led to dubious assumptions for both theory and research. The theories that in the past helped with classroom management, instructional design, or measurement, or that advanced the cause of meaningful learning, have not been able to tackle effectively group-based inequalities.

Contemporary educational psychology is subject to two critiques related to diversity issues. First, it has been largely limited to playing a mediating role among the reigning paradigms in psychology and educational practices. These paradigms have tended to be acultural, ethnocentric, or both. Second, educational psychology has not capitalized on its strategic field position in advancing literature concerning ethnicity and culture. It is not focused on the study of teaching and learning as a joint process from a cultural and/or a developmental perspective. An argument can be made for educational psychology to align its mediational role and research priorities in a cultural direction.

Educational psychology emerged in the twentieth century in a period that was much less concerned about equity, and it evolved in ways not sensitive to group-based inequality or cultural phenomena in general. From the outset, educational psychology was more concerned with individual differences and the measurement of abilities than with facilitating culturally based student learning. Does educational psychology have anything to offer? The traditional answer has been mostly negative because group-based inequality is regarded mainly as a sociopolitical issue. From a critical pedagogical view, educational psychology may be viewed as part of the group-based inequality problem and may be unable to extricate itself sufficiently to be able to address it.

As long as teaching is regarded as separate from learning it may be argued that learning is not different for individuals regardless of origin but rather that teaching is experienced differently. On the other hand, if teaching and learning are regarded as a single unitary process, then it may be argued that the process is, in part, different for students from diverse cultures. An interdisciplinary cultural foundation in educational psychology remains a difficult challenge in a zeitgeist that is marked by research specialization. However, it is precisely through such a foundation that current educational psychology can address group-based inequalities.

Comparative Psychology of School Subjects

Educational psychology has had an on-again, off-again relationship with subject matter during the past century. The psychology of school subjects was center stage during the first two decades of the twentieth century, when it served to define the essential character of the discipline. The early prominence of school subjects for educational psychology faded by the mid-1920s. During the heyday of psychological theories of learning in the 1930s, 1940s, and 1950s, a vigorous search took place for the most simple and powerful mechanisms of learning. Today, the psychology of school subjects appears to be undergoing a renaissance, but in forms not foreseeable during its earlier incarnation. The assumption is that the conditions of teaching and learning are treated quite differently as a function of how knowledge and knowing are defined in the particular disciplines to be taught and learned.

OUR FUTURE

The Science of Learning Moves Mainstream

The term "science of learning" (or the "learning sciences," as some prefer) is back in vogue. We are now integrating what psychologists learned during the cognitive revolution (1970–1990) with many other areas of psychology, education science, computer science, linguistics, and other disciplines related to learning. Much of this work started in the early 1990s with the creation of the *Journal of Learning Science* and really took hold with the 1999 publication of a National Research Council report *How People Learn* (www.nap.edu/catalog/6160.html).

For years, top researchers such as Ann Brown, Joe Campione, David Berliner, Carol Dweck, Jim Greeno, Nora Newcomb, Marcia Linn, Jim Pellegrino, Susan Goldman, and many others have been attempting to move ideas born in the laboratory into classrooms. But their work has been slowed by the small size of traditional research grants, the complexity of the work, and the challenges of convincing schools to allow themselves to be used as laboratories.

The National Science Foundation (NSF) is now poised to launch a new program to support a cadre of science of learning centers—several a year at up to $5 million each year until there is a substantial cohort of centers around the country. With the centers, NSF hopes to enhance knowledge developments in a number of varied and often disconnected disciplines (developmental, social, cognitive science, linguistics, computer science) and core content domain-specific disciplines (e.g., biology, chemistry, and mathematics). Focus is given to increasing our understanding of how people learn and the best ways to teach them. The ultimate goal is to focus multidisciplinary research on learning in an effort to strengthen the foundation of evidence-based teaching now being pushed by the federal government.

Table 3.1.   Outline of Knowledge Structures Used to Frame the Book

Conceptual frameworks
Learning theory and teaching
Cognitive, social, and cultural constructivist views of learning theory and teaching
Creation of functional learning environments
A critical pedagogy of place
The reconceptualized curriculum movement: The divide between curriculum theories
    and practices
The achievement/self-esteem debate
Cognitive load theory used as a framework for instructional design
Sternberg's balance theory of wisdom
Computers as metacognitive tools for enhancing learning

Politics and policies
School reforms
Accountability systems and high stakes testing: Implications of the requirements of the
    No Child Left Behind Act of 2001
School choice initiatives

Methodological issues: Disciplined methods of inquiry
Scientific research in education: The case for evidence-based reasoning in educational
    research
Alternative forms of data representation
The teacher research movement

GENERAL ORGANIZING KNOWLEDGE STRUCTURES

There are several organizing structures in which this book is situated. Specifically, current research literature regarding conceptual frameworks, politics and policies, and methodological issues shaped the development of this book. An outline of the knowledge structures used to frame the book is presented in table 3.1. In what follows, a brief review of these areas of scholarship will be presented. A list of suggested readings related to each of these areas of scholarship is presented below.

Suggested Readings

I.   Conceptual frameworks
      A. Thinking, problem solving, and creativity
          Becker, C. (1994). *The subversive imagination: Artist, society, and social re-*
              sponsibility. New York: Routledge.
          Berliner, D.C., & Calfee, R.C. (1996). *Handbook of educational psychology.*
              New York: Macmillan.

Bransford, J.D., Brown, A.L., & Cocking, R.R. (Eds.) (1999). *How people learn: Brain, mind, experience, and school.* Washington, DC: National Academy Press.

Bruer, J.T. (1993). *Schools for thought: A science of learning in the classroom.* Cambridge, MA: The MIT Press.

Gardner, H. (1993). *Creating minds: An anatomy of creativity seen through the lives of Freud, Einstein, Picasso, Stravinsky, Eliot, Graham, and Gandhi.* New York: Basic Books.

Halpern, D.F. (2003). *Thinking critically about critical thinking.* Hillsdale, NJ: Lawrence Erlbaum.

Halpern, D.F. (2003). *Thought and knowledge: An introduction to critical thinking.* Hillsdale, NJ: Lawrence Erlbaum.

John-Steiner, V. (1997). *Notebooks of the mind: Explorations of thinking.* New York: Oxford University Press.

Lambert, N.M., & McCombs, B.L. (Eds.). (1998). *How students learn.* Washington, DC: American Psychological Association.

Mayer, R.E. (1999). *The promise of educational psychology: Learning in the content areas.* Upper Saddle River, NJ: Prentice Hall.

Phye, G.D. (1997). *Handbook of academic learning: Construction of knowledge.* New York: Academic Press.

Schank, R.C., & Cleary, C. (1995). *Engines for education.* Hillsdale, NJ: Lawrence Erlbaum.

B. Self-regulated learning

Martin, J. (2004). Self-regulated learning, social cognitive theory, and agency. *Educational Psychologist, 39*(2), 135–145.

Pintrich, P.R. (Ed.). (1995). Current issues in research on self-regulated learning: A discussion with commentaries. [Special issue]. *Educational Psychologist, 30*(4), 171–232.

Wolters, C.A. (2003). Regulation of motivation: Evaluating an underemphasized aspect of self-regulated learning. *Educational Psychologist, 38*(4), 189–206.

C. Transfer

DeCorte, E. (2003). Transfer as the productive use of acquired knowledge, skills, and motivations. *Current Directions in Psychological Science, 12*(4), 142–145.

D. The development of expertise

Alexander, P.A. (Ed.). (2003). Theme issue on expertise: Can we get there From here? [Special issue]. *Educational Researcher, 32*(8), 3–29.

Chi, M.T.N., Glaser, R., & Farr, M.J. (1988). *The nature of expertise.* Hillsdale, NJ: Erlbaum.

Hogan, T., Rabinowitz, M., & Craven, J.H. (2003). Representation in teaching: Inferences from research of expert and novice teachers. *Educational Psychologist, 38*(4), 235–248.

Sternberg, R.J. (1998). Abilities are forms of developing expertise. *Educational Researcher, 27*(3), 11–21.

E. Constructivist teaching practices

Caughlan, S. (2005). Considering pastoral power: A commentary on Aaron Schultz's rethinking domination and resistance: Challenging postmodernism. *Educational Researcher, 34*(2), 1, 14–16.

Mayer, R.E. (2004). Should there be a three-strikes rule against pure Discovery learning? The case for guided methods of instruction. *American Psychologist, 59*(1), 14–19.

Schultz, A. (2004). Rethinking domination and resistance: Challenging postmodernism. *Educational Researcher, 33*(1), 15–23.

Schultz, A. (2005). Theory illuminates (and conceals): A response to the critique by Samantha Caughlan. *Educational Researcher, 34*(2), 17–19.

Windschitl, M. (2002). Framing constructivism in practice as the negotiation of dilemmas: An analysis of the conceptual, pedagogical, cultural, and political challenges facing teachers. *Review of Educational Research, 72*(2), 131–176.

F. Creativity research

Plucker, J.A., Beghetto, R.A., & Dow, G.T. (2004). Why isn't creativity more important to educational psychologists? Potentials, pitfalls, and future directions in creativity research. *Educational Psychologist, 39*(2), 83–96.

Runco, M.A. (2004). Creativity. *Annual Review of Psychology, 55*, 657–687.

Sawyer, R.K. (2004). Creative teaching: Collaborative discussion as disciplined improvisation. *Educational Researcher, 33*(2), 12–20.

Sternberg, R.J. (2003). Creative thinking in the classroom. *Scandinavian Journal of Educational Research, 47*(3), 325–338.

Sternberg, R.J., Dess, N.K., et al. (2001). Creativity for the new millennium: A series of articles. *American Psychologist, 56*(4), 332–362.

Sternberg, R.J., & Lubart, T.I. (1996). Investing in creativity. *American Psychologist, 51*(7), 677–688.

Vallance, E. (1995). The public curriculum of orderly images. *Educational Researcher, 24*(2), 4–13.

G. Epistemic identity

Hofer, B.K. (Ed.). (2004). Personal epistemology: Paradigmatic approaches to understanding students' beliefs about knowledge and knowing. [Special issue]. *Educational Psychologist, 39*(1), 1–80.

H. The creation of functional learning environments

Barab, S.A., & Plucker, J.A. (2002). Smart people or smart contexts? Cognition, ability, and talent development in our age of situated approaches to knowing and learning. *Educational Psychologist, 37*(3), 165–182.

DeGrandpre, R.J. (2000). A science of meaning: Can behaviorism bring meaning to psychological science? *American Psychologist, 55*(7), 721–739.

Green, S.K., & Gredler, M.E. (2002). A review and analysis of constructivism for school-based practice. *School Psychology Review, 31*(1), 53–70.

Phye, G.D. (1997). *Handbook of academic learning: The construction of knowledge.* New York: Academic Press.

Shepard, L.A. (2000). The role of assessment in a learning culture. *Educational Researcher, 29*(7), 4–14.

I. A critical pedagogy of place

Borman, G.D., Hewes, G.M., Overman, L.T., Brown, S. (2003). Comprehensive school reform and achievement: A meta-analysis. *Review of Educational Research, 73*(2), 125–230.

Crosby, F.J., Iyer, A., Clayton, S., & Downing, R.A. (2003). Affirmative action: Psychological data and policy debates. *American Psychologist, 58*(2), 93–115.

Freire, P. (1995). *Pedagogy of the oppressed.* New York: Continuum. (Original work published 1970)

Giroux, H. (1988). *Teachers as intellectuals: Toward a critical pedagogy of learning.* South Hadley, MA: Bergin Garvey.

Gitlin, A. (2005). Inquiry, imagination, and the search for a deep politic. *Educational Researcher, 34*(3), 15–25.

Gruenewald, D.A. (2003). The best of both worlds: A critical pedagogy of place. *Educational Researcher, 32*(4), 3–12.

Haymes, S. (1995). *Race, culture, and the city: A pedagogy for black urban struggle.* Albany, NY: State University of New York Press.

Lee, C.D. (Ed.). (2003). Theme issue: Reconceptualized race and ethnicity in educational research. *Educational Researcher, 32*(5), 3–32.

McLaren, P. (2003). *Life in schools* (4th ed.). New York: Allyn & Bacon.

Portes, P.R. (1996). Ethnicity and culture in educational psychology. In D.C. Berliner & R.C. Calfee (Eds.), *Handbook of educational psychology* (pp. 331–357). New York: Macmillan.

J. The reconceptualized curriculum movement: The divide between curriculum theories and practices

Wraga, W.G. (1999). Extracting sun-beams out of cucumbers: The retreat from practice in reconceptualized curriculum studies. *Educational Researcher, 28*(1), 4–13.

K. The achievement–self-esteem debate

Baumeister, R.F., Campbell, J.D., Krueger, J.I., & Vohs, K.D. (2003). Does high self-esteem cause better performance, interpersonal success, happiness, or healthier lifestyles? *Psychological Science in the Public Interest, 4*(1), 1–44.

Spelke, E.S. (2005). Sex differences in intrinsic aptitude for mathematics and science? A critical review. *American Psychologist, 60*(9), 950–958.

L. Cognitive load theory and instructional design

Paas, F., Renkl, A., & Sweller, J. (Eds.) (2003). Special issue: Cognitive load theory and instructional design. *Educational Psychologist, 38*(1), 1–72.

M. Sternberg's balance theory: Wisdom

Sternberg, R.J. (2001). Why schools should teach for wisdom: The balance theory of wisdom in educational settings. *Educational Psychologist, 36*(4), 227–245.

N. The psychology of school subjects

Berliner, D.C., & Calfee, R.C. (Eds.). (1996). *Handbook of educational psychology*. New York: Macmillan.

Bruer, J.T. (1993). *Schools for thought: A science of learning in the classroom*. Cambridge, MA: MIT Press.

Phye, G.D. (1997). *Handbook of academic learning: Construction of knowledge*. New York: Academic Press.

O. School-based preventions

Ceci, S.J., & Papierno, P.B. (2005). The rhetoric and reality of gap closing: When the "have-nots" gain but the "haves" gain even more. *American Psychologist, 60*(2), 149–160.

Durlak, J.A. (1997). *Successful prevention programs for children and adolescents*. New York: Plenum Press.

Durlak, J.A., & Wells, A.M. (1997). Primary prevention mental health programs for children and adolescents: A meta-analysis review. *American Journal of Community Psychology, 25*, 115–152.

Greenberg, M.J., Weissberg, R.P., O'Brien, M.U., Zins, J.E., Fredericks, L., Resnick, H., et al. (2003). Enhancing school-based prevention and youth development through coordinated social, emotional, and academic learning. *American Psychologist, 58*(6/7), 466–474.

Kim, J.S., & Sunderman, G.L. (2005). Measuring academic proficiency under the No Child Left Behind Act: Implications for educational equity. *Educational Researcher, 34*(3), 3–13.

Wang, M.C., Haertel, G.D., & Walberg, H.J. (1997). Learning influences. In H.J. Walberg, & G.D. Haertel (Eds.), *Psychology and educational practice* (pp. 199–211). Berkeley, CA: McCatchen.

Weissberg, R.P., & Kumpfer, K.L. (Eds.). (2003). Prevention that works for children and youth. [Special issue]. *American Psychologist, 58*(6/7), 425–490.

Zins, J.E., Weissberg, R.P., Wang, M.C., & Walberg, H.J. (Eds.). (in press). *Building school success through social and emotional learning*. New York: Teachers College Press.

P. Mind–body relationships

Anderson, N.B., & Nicherson, K.J. (Eds.). (2005). Special issue: Genes, race, and psychology in the genome era. *American Psychologist, 60*(1), 5–128.

Damasio, A.R. (1999). *The feeling of what's happening: Body and emotion in the making of consciousness*. New York: Harcourt.

Eberhart, J.L. (2005). Imaging race. *American Psychologist, 60*(2), 181–190.

Hill, P.C., & Pargament, K.I. (2003). Advances in the conceptualization and measurement of religion and spirituality: Implications for physical and mental health research. *American Psychologist, 58*(1), 64–74.

Kier, F.J., & Davenport, D.S. (2004). Unaddressed problems in the study of spirituality and health. *American Psychologist, 59*(1), 53–54.

McCormick, D.J. (2004). Galton on spirituality, religion, and health. *American Psychologist, 59*(1), 52–52a.

Miller, W.R., & Thoresen, C.E. (2003). Spirituality, religion and health: An emerging research field. *American Psychologist, 58*(1), 24–35.

Powell, L.H., Shahabi, L., & Thoresen, C.E. (2003). Religion and spirituality: Linkages to physical health. *American Psychologist, 58*(1), 36–52.

Ray, O. (2004). How the mind hurts and heals the body. *American Psychologist, 29*(1), 29–40.

Q. Multimedia learning

Azevedo, R. (2005). Special issue: Computers as metacognitive tools for enhancing learning. *Educational Psychologist, 40*(4), 193–271.

Mayer, R.E. (1997). Multimedia learning: Are we asking the right questions? *Educational Psychologist, 32*(1), 1–20.

Mayer, R.E. (2001). *Multimedia learning.* New York: Cambridge University Press.

Mayer, R.E., Moreno, R., Boise, M., & Vagge, S. (1999). Maximizing constructivist learning from multimedia communications by minimizing cognitive load. *Journal of Educational Psychology, 91*(4), 638–643.

R. World conflict

Eidelson, R.J., & Eidelson, J.I. (2003). Dangerous ideas: Five beliefs that propel groups toward conflict. *American Psychologist, 58*, 182–192.

Kaiser, C.R., Vick, S.B., & Major, B. (2004). A prospective investigation of the relationship between just-world beliefs and the desire for revenge after September 11. *Psychological Science, 15*(7), 503–506.

Moghaddam, F.M. (2005). The staircase to terrorism: A psychological exploration. *American Psychologist, 60*(2), 161–169.

S. Popular psychology versus psychological science in the public interest

Anderson, C.A., Berkowitz, L., Donnerstein, E., Huesmann, L.R. Johnson, J.D., Lintz, D., et al. (2003). The influence of media violence on youth. *Psychological Science in the Public Interest, 4*(3), 81–110.

Baumeister, R.F., Campbell, J.D., Krueger, J.I., & Vohs, K.D. (2003). Does high self-esteem cause better performance, interpersonal success, happiness, or healthier life-styles? *Psychological Science in the Public Interest, 4*(1), 1–44.

Hollon, S.D., Thase, M.E., & Markowitz, J.C. (2002). Treatment and prevention of depression. *Psychological Science in the Public Interest, 3*(2), 39–77.

McNally, R.J., Bryant, R.A., & Ehlers, A. (2003). Does early psychological intervention promote recovery from post traumatic stress? *Psychological Science in the Public Interest, 4*(2), 45–79.

II. Politics and policies

A. School reforms

Borman, G.D., Hewes, G.M., Overman, L.T., & Brown, S. (2003). Comprehensive school reform and achievement: A meta-analysis. *Review of Educational Research, 73*(2), 125–230.

Burbules, N.C. (2004). Ways of thinking about educational quality. *Educational Researcher, 33*(6), 4–10.

Cochran-Smith, M. (2005). The new teacher education: For better or worse? *Educational Researcher, 34*(7), 3–17.

Leonardo, S. (2004). Critical social theory and transformative knowledge. *Educational Researcher, 33*(6), 11–18.

B. Accountability systems: Implications of requirements of the NCLB

Linn, R.L., Baker, E.L., & Betebenner, D.W. (2002). Accountability systems: Implications of requirements of the No Child Left Behind Act of 2001. *Educational Researcher, 31*(6), 3–16.

C. Teacher education reforms

Borman, K.M., Kromrey, J.D., Hines, C.V., & Hogarty, K.Y. (2002). Special issue on standards-based reforms and accountability. *Review of Educational Research, 72*(3), 343–546.

Cochran-Smith, M., & Fries, M.K. (2001). Sticks, stones, and ideology: The discourse of reform in teacher education. *Educational Researcher, 30*(8), 3–15.

Cochran-Smith, M., & Zeichner, K.M. (Eds.). (2005). *Studying teacher education: The report of the AERA panel on research and teacher education.* Washington, DC: American Educational Research Association.

Darling-Hammond, L., & Youngs, P. (2002). Defining "highly qualified teachers": What does "scientifically-based research" actually tell us? *Educational Researcher, 31*(9), 13–25.

Furlong, J. (2002). Ideology and reform in teacher education in England: Some reflections on Cochran-Smith and Fries. *Educational Researcher, 31*(6), 23–25.

Mattingly, D.J., Prislin, R., McKenzie, T.L., Rodriquez, J.L., & Kayzar, B. (2002). Evaluating evaluations: The case of parent involvement programs. *Review of Educational Research, 72*(4), 549–576.

D. School choice

Fowler, F.C. (2003). School choice: Silver bullet, social threat, or sound policy? *Educational Researcher, 32*(2), 33–39.

E. Educational policy under cultural pluralism

Fuller, B. (2003). Educational policy under cultural pluralism. *Educational Researcher, 32*(9), 15–24.

III. Methodological issues: Disciplined methods of inquiry

A. Scientific research in education: The case for evidence-based reasoning in educational research

Berliner, D.C. (2002). The hardest science of all. *Educational Researcher, 31*(8), 18–20.

Erickson, F., & Gutierrez, K. (2002). Culture, rigor, and science in educational research. *Educational Researcher, 31*(8), 21–24.

Feuer, M.J., Towne, L., & Shavelson, R.J. (2002a). Reply to commentators on "Scientific Culture and Educational Research." *Educational Researcher, 31*(8), 28–29.

Feuer, M.J., Towne, L., & Shavelson, R.J. (2002b). Scientific culture and educational research. *Educational Researcher*, *31*(8), 4–14.

Gergen, K.J. (2001). Psychological science in a postmodern context. *American Psychologist*, *56*(10), 803–813.

Hosteller, K. (2005). What is "good" education research? *Educational Researcher*, *34*(6), 16–21.

Johnson, R.B., & Onwegbuzie, A.J. (2004). Mixed methods research: A research paradigm whose time has come. *Educational Researcher*, *33*(7), 14–26.

Pellegrino, J.W., & Goldman, S.R. (2002). Be careful what you wish for—you may get it: Educational research in the spotlight. *Educational Researcher*, *31*(8), 15–17.

Slavin, R.E. (2002). Evidence-based educational policies: Transforming educational practice and research. *Educational Researcher*, *31*(7), 15–21.

Smardon, R. (2005). Where the action is: The microsociological turn in education research. *Educational Researcher*, *34*(1), 20–25.

St. Pierre, E.A. (2002). "Science" rejects postmodernism. *Educational Researcher*, *31*(8), 25–27.

Whitehurst, G.J. (Ed.). (2003). *Identifying and implementing educational practices supported by rigorous evidence: A user friendly guide*. Washington, DC: U.S. Department of Education.

B. Qualitative research issues

Cacroppo, J.T., Semin, G.R., & Beritsom, G.G. (2004). Realism, instrumentalism, and scientific symbiosis: Psychological theory as a search for truth and the discovery of solutions. *American Psychologist*, *59*(4), 214–223.

DeCuir, J.T., & Dixson, A.D. (2004). "So when it comes out, they aren't that surprised that it is there": Using critical race theory as a tool of analysis of race and racism in education. *Educational Researcher*, *33*(5), 26–31.

Murphy, P.K. (Ed.). (2003). Rediscovering the philosophical roots of educational psychology. [Special issue]. *Educational Psychologist*, *38*(3), 129–186.

Rosiek, J. (2003). A qualitative research methodology psychology can call its own: Dewey's call for qualitative experimentalism. *Educational Psychologist*, *38*(3), 165–176.

C. Alternative forms of data representation

Eisner, E.W. (1997). The promise and perils of alternative forms of data representation. *Educational Researcher*, *26*(6), 4–11.

Portes, P.R. (1996). Ethnicity and culture in educational psychology. In D.C. Berliner & R.C. Calfee (Eds.), *Handbook of educational psychology*. New York: Macmillan.

Robinson, D.H. (2004). An interview with Gene V. Glass. *Educational Researcher*, *33*(3), 26–30.

Smith, L.D., Best, L.S., Stubbs, D.A., Archibald, A.B., & Robeson-Nay, R. (2002). Constructing knowledge: The role of graphs and tables in hard and soft psychology. *American Psychologist*, *57*(10), 749–761.

Tucker, C.M., & Herman, K.C. (2002). Using culturally sensitive theories and research to meet the academic needs of low-income African American children. *American Psychologist, 57*(10), 762–773.

Voithofer, R. (2005). Designing new media education research: The materiality of data, representation, and dissemination. *Educational Researcher, 34*(9), 3–14.

D. Design experiments

Burkhardt, H., & Schoenfeld, A.H. (2003). Improving educational research: Toward a more useful, more influential, and better-funded enterprise. *Educational Researcher, 32*(9), 3–14.

Kelly, A.E. (Ed.). (2003). The role of design in educational research. *Educational Researcher, 32*(1), 3–37.

Sandoval, W.A., & Bell, P. (Eds.). (2004). Special issue: Design-based research methods for studying learning in context. *Educational Psychologist, 39*(4), 199–260.

E. The boy turn in research on gender and education

Connell, R.W. (1996). Teaching the boys: New research on masculinity and gender strategies for schools. *Teachers College Record, 98*(2), 206–135.

Kao, G., & Thompson, J.S. (2003). Racial and ethnic stratification in educational achievement and attainment. *Annual Review of Sociology, 29*, 417–442.

Weaver-Hightower, M. (2003). The "boy turn" in research on gender and education. *Review of Educational Research, 73*(4), 471–498.

F. The teacher research movement

Anderson, G.L. (2002). Reflecting on research for doctoral students in education. *Educational Research, 7*(31), 22–25.

Anderson, G.L., & Herr, K. (1998). The new paradigm wars: Is there room for rigorous practitioner knowledge in schools and universities? *Educational Researcher, 28*(5), 12–21.

Barone, T. (2001). Science, art, and the predisposition of educational research. *Educational Researcher, 30*(7), 24–28.

Cochran-Smith, M., & Lytle, S.L. (1990). Research on teaching and teacher research: The issues that divide. *Educational Researcher, 19*(2), 2–11.

Cochran-Smith, M., & Lytle, S.L. (1999). The teacher research movement: A decade later. *Educational Researcher, 28*(7), 15–25.

Labaree, D.F. (2003). The peculiar problems of preparing educational researchers. *Educational Researcher, 32*(4), 13–22.

Mayer, R.E. (2000). What is the place of science in educational research? *Educational Researcher, 29*(6), 38–39.

Mayer, R.E. (2001). Resisting the assault on science: The case for evidence-based reasoning in educational research. *Educational Researcher, 30*(7), 29–30.

Metz, M.H. (2001). Intellectual border crossing in graduate education: A report from the field. *Educational Researcher, 30*(5), 12–18.

Metz, M.H., & Page, R.N. (2002). The uses of practitioner research and status issues in educational research: Reply to Gary Anderson. *Educational Researcher, 31*(7), 26–27.

Page, R.N. (2001). Reshaping graduate preparation in educational research methods: One school's experience. *Educational Researcher, 30*(5), 19–25.

Pallas, A. (2001). Preparing education doctoral students for epistemological diversity. *Educational Researcher, 30*(5), 6–11.

Perry, N.E. (Ed.). (2002). Special issue: Using qualitative methods to enrich understandings of self-regulated learning. *Educational Psychologist, 37*(1), 1–63.

Pritchard, I.A. (2002). Travelers and trolls: Practitioner research and institutional review boards. *Educational Researcher, 31*(3), 3–13.

Shavelson, R., & Towne, L. (Eds.). (2002). *Scientific research in education.* Washington, DC: National Academy Press.

Young, L.J. (2001). Border crossings and other journeys: Re-visioning the doctoral preparation of educational researchers. *Educational Researcher, 30*(5), 3–5.

With regard to the conceptual framework component, several areas of scholarship that influenced the development of this book include learning theories and their influence on instruction; cognitive, social, and cultural constructivist views of learning theory and teaching; the creation of functional learning environments; a critical pedagogy of place; the reconceptualized curriculum movement; the achievement–self-esteem debate; cognitive load theory used as a framework for instructional design; Sternberg's balance theory of wisdom; and computers as metacognitive tools for enhancing learning.

Conceptual Frameworks

Learning Theory and Teaching

There has been a great body of research related to learning theory and teaching. From today's perspective, it is recognized that our knowledge related to teaching and learning has been too narrowly focused and fragmented. Teaching and learning were historically studied as separate entities. The complexities of and the relationships between teaching and learning have been ignored for decades. There have been attempts made to establish connections between what we know about brain behavior relationships, but skepticism prevails with respect to the utility of such efforts. Bruer (1997) stated that the arguments directed at linking the neurosciences to education by drawing educationally relevant conclusions from correlations between gross, unanalyzed behaviors such as learning to read, learning, math, and learning languages and its link to poorly understood changes in brain structure at the synaptic level was a "bridge too far" (Bruer, 1997). The literature clearly supports the view that there is no single best method of teaching. Most would claim that a search for a best method of teaching is misguided. The process–product research conducted during the 1970s and 1980s involved the teaching of various skills such as those in mathematics, for which a large number of examples exist. However, a large amount of what is taught in schools, especially at the secondary level, involves knowledge about and understanding of issues, events, and conceptions that consist of declarative (content) rather than procedural knowledge. The rational, technical approaches to teaching represented by the process–product, behavioral, task analytic, and mastery learning paradigms have lost popularity. These approaches are viewed as too mechanistic, didactic, and structured. In response to this narrow view of learning and teaching, cognitive, social, and cultural constructivist views of learning theory and teaching have gained popularity.

Cognitive, Social, and Cultural Constructivist Views of Learning Theory and Teaching

In the 1980s and 1990s the constructivist learning theory and teaching paradigm took shape. Most of us moved another step away from behaviorism in the direction of embracing cognitive constructivism. Theorists such as Piaget, Vygotsky, Feurstein, Gardner, and Sternberg influenced the constructivist movement. This new view of learning theory and teaching came with the realization that real-life learning is intrinsically entangled with context and socially and culturally constructed situations. Learners came to be viewed as active constructors. Human learning was thought to be unique in that humans have knowledge and feelings related to how they learn. Humans learn to control their learning. Proponents of these contemporary theories believe that these approaches are superior to behavioral approaches. These contemporary cognitive theories are crafted to address the complexities of learning. Constructivists believe in a method of instruction in which learning and teaching depend heavily on creating an interactive community of research practitioners who are critically dependent on each other. In this idea of a community of learners, as developed by Brown (1994, 1997), learners are viewed as active constructors of meaning. A community of discourse is encouraged so that higher thoughts become internalized dialogues. To foster a community of discourse, classroom activities are essentially dialogic in nature and are modeled after research seminars. These learning communities are designed to facilitate interchange, reciprocity, and community. The role of the teacher in a constructivist classroom is to guide the discovery process toward forms of disciplined inquiry that would not be reached without expert guidance to push students to their upper bounds. This arrangement leads students to higher levels of thinking. Teachers also help students set goals for future research and study. Instruction relies on a wide variety of tools, aids, and techniques that are designed to enhance the mind and develop metacognitive skills. Techniques used in these classrooms include reciprocal teaching, jigsawing, and majoring. Reciprocal teaching involves group leaders asking questions, summarizing, clarifying, and asking the others to make predictions. These activities are designed to provide a "zone of proximal development," a Vygotskian term, which helps students move beyond their current level of learning with the help of others. The jigsaw technique involves dividing units of study into smaller sections and then having the students act as researchers. They share the responsibility for their learning and teaching their piece of the puzzle to others. Majoring is another technique where students are able to "major" or specialize in a subdomain of a topic of interest to them and then teach the material to others. Individual differences are also valued within a constructivist classroom environment. Nonconformity is encouraged in that the distribution of expertise and interests of the students can benefit everyone as a result of the subsequent richness of the available knowledge. There are, however, some profound challenges related to implementing constructivist teaching practices (Windschitl, 2002). Windschitl (2002) uses four frames of reference to describe the dilemmas associated with implementing constructivist instruction. These frameworks are presented along a continuum from the personal and intellectual concerns of the teacher to the structural and public concerns of the school and community. They include conceptual dilemmas, pedagogical dilemmas, cultural dilemmas, and political dilemmas. Each of these areas represent conditions that must be realized for constructivist teaching to flourish in a classroom and are best realized when teachers draw on multiple dimensions of experience.

The Creation of Functional Learning Environments

The creation of functional learning environments is another movement that has influenced current conceptual frameworks. Functional psychology developed in close conjunction with pragmatism as a philosophical movement. Dewey, James, and Mead were all contributors. Although most commonly associated with the behavioral views of B.F. Skinner, functional psychology grew out of an attempt to avoid the split between behaviorism and cognitive psychology. Focus has been given to the effects of structuring the environment to bring about behavioral changes. Phye (1997) stated that the key to functional psychology was to emphasize the adaptive relationships that are acquired between a learner and his or her environment. Functionalists view classroom learning as a relatively permanent change in behavior that occurs as a result of adaptation. From this point of view, given a responsive classroom environment, the learner is responsible for taking advantage of what the environment offers. A function is viewed as a verb, not a noun. A function is a process. Functionalism places emphasis on the adaptiveness of the behavior.

DeGrandpre (2000) argues that basic behavioral principles do provide a framework for conceptualizing how complexity and diversity emerge from human actions and experiences. Unfortunately, behaviorists have historically been constrained in their ability to provide anything resembling a complete picture of psychological experience to date. Because of this limitation, De-Grandpre states that "psychological science has yet to exploit the full implications of basic operant principles, especially for a science of meaning" (p. 721). DeGrandpre proposes that operant (behavioral) psychology has much to offer to the development of a science of meaning, a development that could bring research closer together in several areas, including behaviorism, cognitivism, and social and cultural constructivism. He goes on to state that "one reason why meaning does not rank as a primary dependent variable in psychological science is because cognitive, social, and cultural constructivist notions in psychology are believed to threaten, rightly or wrongly, the possibility of a pure science of psychology that operates independent of consideration of larger, sociohistorical forces" (p. 722). De-Grandpre redefines the process of reinforcement as one of meaning making, not as the ultimate cause of behavior, but rather as a proximal cause. In linking behavioral principles to constructivism, DeGrandpre states that the present conceptualization of reinforcement may also provide a scientific foundation for the sociocultural processes identified by the social–constructionist theorists. Making this connection explicit seems important because the common ground between operant psychology and social constructionism has been overlooked (p. 735).

A Critical Pedagogy of Place

Another conceptual framework that influenced the development of this book is a critical pedagogy of place. Gruenewald (2003) argues that "critical pedagogy" and "place-based education" are mutually supportive educational traditions and that the two can be consciously synthesized into a "critical pedagogy of place." A critical pedagogy of place challenges educators to reflect on the relationship between the kind of education they pursue and the kind of places they inhabit and leave behind for future generations. The purpose of critical pedagogy is to engage learners in the act of what Freire (1995) calls *conscientizacao*, which has been defined as "learning to perceive social, political, and economic contradictions, and to take action against the oppressive elements of reality" (pp. 4–5). Gruenewald goes on to state that "Freire advocates 'reading the world' as his central pedagogical strategy. Reading the world radically redefines conventional notions of print-based literacy and conventional school curriculum. For critical pedagogues, the 'texts' students and teachers should 'decode' are the images of their own concrete, situation experiences with the world" (p. 5). Place-based education is both similar to and different from critical pedagogy. First, like critical pedagogues, place-based educators emphasize a pedagogy that relates directly to student experiences of the world. Efforts are made to improve the overall quality of life for students and their communities. However, unlike critical pedagogues, not all place-based educators foreground the study of place as political praxis for social transformations. Gruenewald proposes that "the two most significant intersections between these traditions are place-based education's call for localized social action and critical pedagogy's recognition that experience, or situationality, has a geographical dimension" (p. 9). A critical pedagogy of place aims to help (1) identify, recover, and create material spaces and places that teach us how to live well in our total environments (reinhabitation) and (2) identify and change ways of thinking that injure and exploit other people and places (decolonization). Gruenewald says that

> a critical pedagogy of place aims to contribute to the production of educational discourses and practices that explicitly examine the place-specific nexus between environment, culture, and education. Place-based education is linked to cultural and ecological politics, a pedagogy informed by an ethic of eco-justice, and other socioecological traditions that interrogate the intersection between cultures and ecosystems. The chief implication of a critical pedagogy of place to educational research is the challenge it poses to all educators to expand the scope of their theory, inquiry, and practice to include the social and ecological contexts of our own, and others' inhabitance (p. 10).

The Reconceptualized Curriculum Movement

In *Extracting Sun-Beams Out of Cucumbers: The Retreat from Practice in Reconceptualized Curriculum Studies*, William G. Wraga (1999) examines the manifestations of a philosophy which seeks to distance theory from practice. William Pinar is cited as the most influential theorist associated with the reconceptualized curriculum movement. This movement is characterized by emphasizing a shift away from curriculum development toward curriculum understanding, an acceptance of life experiences as the subject of curriculum inquiry, and a separation of theory from practice. Wraga describes and evaluates the views of the reconceptualized curriculum theorists and compares their views to Dewey, who emphasized the connections between theories and practical events.

Pinar (1991) stresses the need for reconceptualized curriculum theorists to distance themselves from their constituencies (practitioners) and practical concerns. By attributing the problems identified to unsolvable social–political–cultural differences, Wraga claims that these theorists abrogate responsibility to resolve them. Their focus is directed toward conceptualization, contemplation, and criticism rather than application. They believe that by separating themselves from practitioners, they free the practitioners from conventional thinking and provide opportunities for a wider, more creative exploration of new ideas.

Wraga (1999) takes strong issue with reconceptualized curriculum theorists' claims that their thinking is based on Dewey's educational theory. He describes a number of inconsistencies between the views of Pinar and Dewey. Dewey saw inherent elitism in the theory–practice split. Dewey had a strong commitment to scientific methods of discovery and exploration. Dewey and other scholars recognize a polarization between theorists and practitioners that parallels that between the humanities and the sciences. The reconceptualists recommend that practitioners "seek wisdom" from theorists, rather than expecting theorists to address practical problems. In contrast, Dewey viewed theoretical knowledge to be relevant only when it could be applied. It is only the practical that makes the theoretical possible! Dewey was committed to science as the method for solving problems and promoting growth. He believed that research and theorizing were valuable only if they could be practically applied. This represents a clear repudiation of reconceptualists' thinking. Dewey's view is certainly contrary to the reconceptualized curriculum theorists' "exaltation of theory over practice."

Wraga (1999) examined the theory–practice dichotomy within professional schools of education at large land-grant universities. In an effort to elevate the status and effectiveness of education schools, many became a part of large research-based universities. Education faculties took on a more scholarly approach and disassociated themselves from the practical in an attempt to gain prestige. Yet most academicians remained unimpressed and many practitioners felt alienated from these efforts. Wraga sees this separation of theory from practice as the antithesis of the mission of American education, which historically has had a practical bent. In the United States, education has been seen as a means to address inequities that thwart elitism by replacing aristocratic with democratic thinking that emphasizes the application of knowledge to solving practical problems. To a large degree, land-grant universities were developed to address this pragmatism.

It could be argued that some recent proposals for educational practices that are based on reconceptualized curriculum theorizing represent a paradox. Some of the reconceptualized curriculum theorists fail to recognize that they have, ironically, adopted the views of more traditional thinkers. Some impose a predetermined view of society on curriculum, failing to address local realities or "place," as well as ethnicity and culture.

Wraga's (1999) criticism of reconceptualized curriculum theory shares a few common grounds with Windschitl's (2002) criticism related to the implementation of constructivist teaching practices. Both (the reconceptualized curriculum and constructivist teaching practices) are theoretically anchored. However, there is a huge difference between the reconceptualist's view, which has no mandate toward solving problems in practice, and the constructivist's teaching view, which is centered on practical applications. The basic problem for the constructivist teacher, according to Windschitl, is the difficulty in moving from the theoretical to the practical. As opposed to the call for a separation between theory and practice, we need the reconceptualized curriculum theorists to find and nurture a set of common grounds. One would assume that theorists and practitioners would attempt to define and address a set of common goals related to solving problems in education. However, many reconceptualized curriculum theorists hold an us-versus-them attitude toward practitioners with their own self-justification of thinking being perceived as having paramount importance.

Reconceptualized curriculum theorists conceptualize and criticize but offer few practical solutions. Problems are perpetuated. They not only alienate themselves from practitioners, but they open the doors for others to assume power to address these problems. Many critics have commented on policy positions that are recommended by academicians. At times, they are seen as pontificating from "glass towers," with little connection to the feasibility of putting their positions into practice. In the real world, theory for the self-satisfaction of theorists is a narcissistic approach likened to "art for art's sake" or "form without function."

The Achievement of Self-Esteem Debate

Another conceptual framework that has influenced current educational practices is the assumption that high self-esteem in children will cause many positive outcomes and benefits throughout their lifetime. Baumeister, et al. (2003) critically examines this assumption. He addresses the complexities of studying the effects of self-esteem. It is hard to obtain objective measures of self-esteem. It is a heterogeneous category composed of different types of individuals and different types of self-esteem. Baumeister's meta-analysis of the research findings related to self-esteem indicates that there are only modest correlations between self-esteem and school performance. The evidence does not support the notion that high self-esteem leads to good school performance. Instead, high self-esteem is believed to be partly the result of good school performance. With the exception of a link to happiness, most of the effects of self-esteem to other factors were reported to be modest. In sum, self-esteem was not found to be a major predictor or cause of anything, with the possible exception of happiness. Overall, the research findings suggest two major benefits of high self-esteem—enhanced initiative and pleasant feelings. As a result, Baumeister, et al. proposes that self-esteem should be used in a limited way as one of a cluster of factors to promote positive educational outcomes. Using self-esteem as a reward rather than an entitlement appears to be more appropriate. In particular, Baumeister, et al. proposes, "Success in modern society depends on lifelong learning and improvement—academically, socially, culturally, and occupationally. We encourage linking self-esteem to learning and improvement" (p. 39). Taken together, the evidence does not support the notion that high self-esteem leads to good school performance. As a result of these findings, it is recommended that the development of high self-esteem is best viewed as a reward for achievement. Focusing on self-improvement and comparing students' growth relative to themselves is believed to be conducive to both the happiness of the individual and the betterment of society.

Cognitive Load Theory Used as a Framework for Instructional Design

Fred Pass, Alexander Renkl, and John Sweller (2003) use cognitive load theory (CLT) as a general organizing framework in which to investigate cognitive processes and instructional designs. Examining the structure of information simultaneously along with the cognitive architecture in which the information is situated enables CLT theorists to generate unique, effective instructional designs.

Element interactivity is considered to be a critical feature of cognitive load. Cognitive architecture is used as a framework in which to explain the interactions taking place among working memory, long-term memory, and element interactivities across the memory systems. Working memory (sometimes referred to as short-term memory), in which all conscious cognitive processing occurs, is limited in capacity. Long-term memory is not limited. It allows for the expansion of processing ability by storing schemas. It consists of constructs that combine multiple elements into a single one with a specific function.

Three types of element interactivity are believed to be at work with respect to cognitive load. *Intrinsic cognitive load* describes the demands on working memory related to the representation of domain-specific (content) knowledge. For deep understanding to occur, simultaneous processing of all essential elements must occur. Cognitive load can also be imposed in the manner in which new material is presented and the types of activities involved related to how knowledge is presented. *Extraneous cognitive load* is unnecessary and takes up valuable working memory space. It interferes with schema acquisition because the space within working memory must be used for irrelevant cognitive activities. *Germane cognitive load* is influenced by the instructional designer. If the manner of presentation is relevant, it enhances learning. Intrinsic, extraneous, and germane cognitive loads work in an additive fashion. The total load cannot exceed the capacity of working memory. Given that intrinsic load is a fixed entity, only reducible by constructing new schema and automating previous schema, it is necessary to reduce extraneous and increase germane cognitive loads to make the best use of the limited resources associated with working memory. When working memory demands are reduced, opportunities for new learning are enhanced. From a CLT point of view, it is recommended that instructional designers direct their efforts to the reduction of extraneous cognitive load so that more working memory resources can be used for intrinsic and germane cognitive loads.

CLT is congruent with the cognitive scientist's views of knowledge representations. From a cognitive science perspective, knowledge representations consists of content knowledge structures (domain-specific knowledge structures), content procedural knowledge structures (procedural knowledge structures that are connected to a discipline; e.g., the periodic table of a chemist), and procedural knowledge structures (general problem solving skills). As we learn and develop expertise in a given knowledge domain, the content knowledge structures are used to think and solve problems—the content becomes the process for the mature (expert) learner. The expert has an advantage compared to the novice because the expert has automatized the content procedural and procedural knowledge components of the memory system. The expert has freed up his or her limited working memory space so that the contents can be used to think and problem solve.

The following connections can be made between CLT and the three cognitive science–based components of the knowledge representation system. Content knowledge is similar to what Pass, Renkl, and colleagues (2003) refer to as intrinsic cognitive load. Extraneous cognitive load and germane cognitive load appear to be congruent with the procedural knowledge components (content procedural and procedural knowledge components) of the cognitive science–based knowledge system.

Initial research efforts related to CLT were not related to the development of a learner's expertise. Emphasis was given to the design of instructional techniques geared to reducing extraneous cognitive load. Examples included goal specificity, worked examples, completion tasks, split-attention tasks, redundancy procedures, and modality effects. Instructional techniques employing variability and prompting imagination were used to replace extraneous cognitive load with germane cognitive load. In the late 1990s, intrinsic cognitive load was seen as a property of task–subject interactions open to instructional control. Here the emphasis was to design instructional techniques that facilitated the transition from novice to expert. An expertise reversal effect was documented. Instructional techniques that work with novices often lose some of their effectiveness with more experienced learners.

Instructional designs should be altered as learners' knowledge increases. Since schemes held in long-term memory are related to characteristics of working memory, how do these relationships affect instructional design? Van Merrienboer, Kirschner, and Kester (2003) stated that it is important to present realistic tasks to novices even in complex problem solving situations in which cognitive load is very heavy. They suggested a form of scaffolding in which intrinsic cognitive load is decreased by simple-to-complex sequencing. They recommended that we begin with worked examples, followed by completion problems and finally a set of authentic problem solving activities. Renkl and Atkinson (2003) described a fading procedure. The timing of essential information presented was considered to be critical. They suggested that "overarching supportive information" be presented first in order to use it to construct schema. Procedural information should only be presented when required. The role of worked examples used as a technique to reduce cognitive load should change as expertise increases. The fading technique has much in common with scaffolding. Both scaffolding and fading techniques appear to be congruent with Vygotsky's view of knowledge development and the zone of proximal development. Kalyuga, Ayres, Chandler, and Sweller (2003) reviewed research related to the consequences associated with different levels of expertise. They found that instructional designers often overlook the level of expertise of the learner(s). Many instructional designs are geared to novices and require modifications as a function of increasing expertise (the expertise reversal effect). In sum, we must be careful to consider what we know about the expertise reversal effect when we are called on to design learning environments for learners with different levels of expertise.

Several other studies in the area of CLT include Gerjets and Scheiter's (2003) work with learner–driver instructional decisions. As previously noted, as the level of expertise increases, decreasing instructor control and increasing learner control becomes important. Mayer and Moreno (2003) examined CLT within the context of multimedia learning when cognitive overload is often significant. They emphasized the importance of the need to measure cognitive load. Brunken, Plass, and Leutner (2003) recommended a dual-task technique for this measurement. Paas, Tuovinen, Tabbers, and Van Gerven (2003) provided a conceptual and practical overview of issues related to CLT measures. CLT, which is grounded in cognitive psychology, applied to the improvement of instructional design represents the antithesis of the reconceptualized curriculum theorists' view that separates theory from practice. Here practical outcomes, including measured results, are used to substantiate the theoretical.

Sternberg's Balance Theory of Wisdom

Robert Sternberg (2001) advocates that a "balance theory of wisdom" be incorporated into the school curriculum. Wisdom is defined as "the power of judging rightly and following the soundest course of action, based on knowledge, experience, understanding, etc." Approaches to the systematic study of wisdom in the past have been philosophical, implicit theoretical, and explicit theoretical. Philosophical theorists view wisdom as contemplative life in search of truth. The implicit–theoretical approach is culturally oriented in that wisdom is viewed as a search for an understanding of people's beliefs. Those associated with the explicit–theoretical perspective view wisdom as expert knowledge about life that is associated with good judgment and/or advice. Wisdom includes factual and procedural knowledge, contextualism, relativism, and awareness of uncertainty. Some theorists see wisdom as a stage that is beyond Piaget's formal operational stage of development. Wisdom has also been viewed as evolutionary, a cultural acquisition of values acquired over time.

Sternberg (2001) stated that knowledge is necessary to make judgments in life that are both explicit and tacit in nature. There is a formal body of knowledge (domain-specific knowledge) that is complemented by a social organization for the discovery and transmission of knowledge. Explicit knowledge is what is taught in schools directly and corresponds to domain-specific (content) knowledge. Sternberg claims that field knowledge of the tacit nature is crucial to the development of wisdom, and this is what he emphasizes in his balance theory of wisdom. Tacit knowledge is action oriented, procedural, and relevant, and it allows individuals to achieve the goals they value with or without help from others. The emphasis is on knowing "how" rather than knowing "that." Although help from others is not always necessary, the constructivist conceptualization of scaffolding is believed to be significant in the acquisition of wisdom. Context is also believed to be of great importance. From Sternberg's perspective, mediated learning experiences are likely to be more valuable than direct instruction. Wisdom is a form of practical intelligence. A balance theory of wisdom combines tacit and explicit knowledge representations as being mediated by values toward goals that benefit the common good by achieving a balance between intrapersonal, interpersonal, and extrapersonal interests, over both the long and short term, balancing adaptation and shaping of existing environments, and selecting new environments. A wise individual seeks outcomes that are not only good for him or her, but also for the common good. The focus is on the wider picture. It is an "us" view rather than a "me" view.

Values are believed to be an integral part of wisdom, in particular universal human values such as respect for life, honesty, fairness, and enabling people to maximize their potential. However, the inclusion of values within the conceptualization of the wisdom construct often confounds how wisdom is measured. Yet Sternberg (2001) claims that there is a need to include values within the conceptualization of wisdom and in doing so, the focus should be on assessing the process of thinking to determine if wisdom has been displayed. He has elaborated this process in his descriptions of the "metacomponents of thought," which include (1) recognizing a problem, (2) defining its nature, (3) representing information about it, (4) formulating a strategy to solve it, (5) allocating resources toward the solution, (6) monitoring the solution, and (7) evaluating feedback about the solution. The basic idea is that the development of wisdom depends on encoding relevant new information into a context of understanding, comparing new information to old information, and integrating new and old information. Sternberg's description of the development of wisdom is congruent with cognitive load theory. Encoding relevant new information into a context of understanding reflects maximizing intrinsic and germane cognitive load and the integration of information is parallel to creating schema. Sternberg emphasizes the importance of using formal knowledge structures to make wise judgments and decisions.

With the balance theory of wisdom, Sternberg (2001) has defined seven sources of individual differences: goals, responses to environmental contexts, interests, balancing of short- and long-term perspectives, acquisition of tacit knowledge, utilization of tacit knowledge, and values. He claims that the sequential development of tacit knowledge and values explains why wisdom is often associated with maturity. He also describes relationships between wisdom and knowledge; analytical, creative, and practical intelligence; and other aspects of intelligence, yet he articulates why these constructs are not the same as wisdom. To describe wisdom, more emphasis is given to tacit knowledge than formal knowledge. Emphasis is given to real-world situations, rather than what is typically measured in academic settings. Wise thinking entails thinking creatively to generate novel and appropriate solutions involving balancing of interests. Sternberg describes wisdom as a form of practical thinking with its emphasis on balances for the common good. Finally, he also connects wisdom to social, emotional, interpersonal, and intrapersonal intelligences, but sees wisdom as being different from intelligence with respect to a learner striving for a goal toward a common good. He likens this to the Chinese conception of intelligence in contrast to the American conception. The difference may be likened to a more collectivistic perspective compared to an individualistic worldview.

Sternberg (2001) acknowledges that his theory of wisdom does not contain a specification of "correctness" of values, contents of wise thinking, or prescriptions of wise behavior. Addressing some of his critics, he stresses that wisdom is not about "right" answers; rather, wisdom refers to reflective responses that balance considerations with an emphasis on the common good. He claims that we should not attempt to provide definitive answers to complex and unresolved questions. There are believed to be few, if any, right solutions to complex problems.

Because wisdom is not objectively defined, it is difficult to measure. But Sternberg (2001) states that doing so is important. In studying practical intelligence, Sternberg and his associates have attempted to develop assessments that measure tacit knowledge, one of the underlying foundations of wisdom.

Unlike the reconceptualized curriculum theorists' split from the practical, Sternberg (2001) makes an effort to describe how his balance theory of wisdom could be included in a wisdom-related curriculum. There are several reasons he feels that schools should make an effort to include the development of wisdom in their curriculum plans. First, he stresses that the emphasis on knowledge alone is not sufficient. Second, the development of wisdom is associated with deliberative and considered thinking that includes values in judgment and decision making. Third, wisdom is the "avenue to a more harmonious world." Finally, given that individuals are part of a community, there are likely to be benefits associated with encouraging the development of wisdom, with emphasis being given to thinking "rightly, soundly, and justly" on behalf of their community and the common good. According to Sternberg, the development of wisdom offers a greater chance for the establishment of happiness and success.

Sternberg (2001) describes a set of principles related to teaching wisdom based on his balance theory of wisdom. The emphasis is on how to think rather than what to think. There is no place for indoctrination. He acknowledges that good instruction already encompasses many of his principles. He also offers procedures to follow in teaching wisdom. These include incorporating the classics into the curriculum; class discussions emphasizing the development of dialogue and dialectical thinking; studying values; emphasizing critical, creative, and practical thinking related to the pursuit of common goals that benefit not only individuals but others, realizing that outcomes matter; and encouraging teachers to serve as role models of wisdom. Students must be encouraged to actively participate in constructing their knowledge structures, but not from a single perspective. The emphasis must be on continuing constructions and reconstructions from the point of view of others in order to have a balanced rather than egocentric understanding. Sternberg describes lessons incorporating wisdom as being different from current instructional practices. For example, in a history class, lessons incorporating wisdom would differ greatly from current practices. Propagandistic and ethnocentric views would be eliminated. Science would not be presented as facts that are final, rather as midpoints of evolving discoveries. Literature instruction would reflect a balanced perspective of contexts related to time and place of writing, not just current standards. Foreign languages would be taught within a cultural context. Most significantly, the curriculum would be more integrated. Sternberg's views related to incorporating the balance theory of wisdom into the curriculum are a mandate for awareness of culture and ethnicity as well as place.

Sternberg (2001) and his associates have developed an "infused curriculum for teaching wisdom" and have set up a research project to study the outcomes associated with three comparative conditions. The first (the experimental) condition incorporates the teaching for wisdom curriculum. The second (the control) condition involves a critical thinking–skills curriculum. The third (another control) condition includes the regular curriculum.

As might be expected, there have been several reactions to Sternberg's theory. Keith Stanovich (2001) essentially aligns himself with Sternberg as a cognitive scientist and "welcomes" the call to teach for wisdom. He claims that Sternberg's emphasis on wisdom, like his (Stanovich's) emphasis on rationality, are unified by their focus on aspects of cognition that have been underexamined, such as goals and beliefs of the learner, thinking dispositions, values, morals, learning styles, and the evaluation of cognitive norms. Diane Halpern (2001) agrees that children can be taught to think from multiple perspectives. She, however, understands wisdom as "critical thinking within a system of values." Deanna Kuhn and Wadiya Udell (2001) applaud Sternberg's intent but see his goal as "overly bold." They suggest that perhaps the goal should be to teach the tools for wisdom, to focus on the means, or thinking, rather than make efforts to teach wisdom itself. David Perkins (2001) believes the educational application of Sternberg's theory will have positive results. He addresses two potential criticisms. The first criticism that there is a lack of solutions to problems Perkins dismisses, stating that theories do not need to offer such prescriptions. He claims that the balance theory and intervention's focus on detached judgment fail to address potential blind spots adequately. Scott Paris (2001) is the most critical. While he acknowledges strengths in Sternberg's process-based emphasis of reasoning that is integrative, intelligent, and wise, he doesn't see it as a "marketable" approach. Sternberg (2001) has addressed these critiques and continues to argue the value of teaching for wisdom. Finally, it should be noted that Kuhn and Udell claim that to maximize the implication of this theory in education, the focus should be on the process, or thinking, rather than teaching wisdom itself.

Computers as Metacognitive Tools for Enhancing Learning

There has been an expanded interest in the use of computers and multimedia as metacognitive tools for enhancing learning. Computer-based and multimedia learning environments have become ubiquitous. It is probably fair to say that the effectiveness of these computer-based multimedia environments will only be achieved if learners learn how to regulate their learning. These metacognitive self-regulatory processes include a complex set of interactions among cognitive, motivational, affective, and social processes.

For the most part, researchers have used cognitive theories (e.g., J. Anderson & Labiere, 1998) or constructivist models of learning and instruction (e.g., Cognition and Technology Group at Vanderbilt, 1990; Collins, Brown, & Newman, 1989; Greeno, 1998; L.B. Resnick, 1991; Rogoff, 1997) to describe the learning process within computer-based and multimedia learning environments. Given the complexities of these learning environments, efforts have been made to extend these cognitive and constructivist frameworks by adding the study of metacognition and self-regulated learning to the mix. A sample of these efforts is presented in a recent special issue of *Educational Psychologist* (Azevedo, 2005a, 2005b). It should be noted that these frameworks are in their infancy with respect to their explanatory adequacy.

A set of characteristics described by Lajoie (1993) has been used as a framework to study the use of computers as metacognitive tools. According to Lajoie, computers can be used to

assist learners to accomplish cognitive task by supporting cognitive processes, share cognitive load by supporting lower level cognitive skills so that learners may focus on higher level thinking skills, allow learners to engage in cognitive activities that would be out of their reach otherwise because there may be no opportunities for participating in such tasks . . . and allow learners to generate and test hypotheses in the context of problem solving.

According to Azevedo (2005a, 2005b), questions have been raised with respect to the educational potential of computer and multimedia learning environments because of the limited learner gains that have been documented in these environments. It is likely that these learners failed to use key metacognitive and self-regulatory skills necessary to regulate their learning activities.

Self-regulated learning (SRL) has become a guiding theoretical framework related to the study of using computer-based and multimedia learning environments as metacognitive tools for enhancing student learning. According to Azevedo (2005a, 2005b) there is a great deal of research related to addressing whether students regulate their learning with hypermedia and whether SRL fosters the learning of complex and challenging domain-specific topics. What is needed is more detailed information related to the how the four phases of SRL (Pintrich, 2000a, 2000b; Zimmerman, 2000) (planning, monitoring, strategy use, and handling of task difficulty, demands, and interest) mediate the learning of complex topics within computer-based and hypermedia learning environments. Researchers have begun to examine the dynamics of the SRL processes (cognitive, motivational/affective, behavioral, and contextual) during the planning, monitoring, control, and reflection phases of the process.

Unfortunately little emphasis has been placed on the development of metacognitive knowledge and skills as critical goals for learning in the national curricular standards. Yet according to White and Fredericksen (2005), "Research has shown that metacognitive expertise is needed in developing knowledge through inquiry . . . and is critical in transferring one's capabilities for learning in one domain context to learning in new domains, as well as taking charge of one's own learning." As technology advances, we will likely reach a point where we will work with software advisers and assistants throughout our school, work, and personal lives. Acquiring a common language of metacognition will be center stage with respect to the distributed models of expertise collaborative process.

It is well documented (Graesser, McNamara, & VanLehn, 2005) that most students have not acquired the metacognitive skills related to the engagement of deeper levels of comprehension that require explanatory reasoning. Given that these metacognitive skills are not routinely taught by teachers, a case can be made for the design and use of computer-based multimedia learning environments that are designed to facilitate explanation-centered learning through the use of strategies of inquiry and metacognition. Graesser et al. (2005) describe three computer-based systems (Point & Query, AutoTutor, and iSTART) designed to enhance the development of deep comprehensive scaffolding strategies.

With the growing amount of information now available online, increased attention is being paid to online inquiry: asking questions and searching online libraries and other information sources. Metacognitive skills are believed to be important to the complex practices related to reading, accessing, and synthesizing online information. These metacognitive skills are reported (Quintana, Zhang, & Krajcik, 2005) to be weak in novice learners. Computer-based and multimedia learning environments can help make the implicit nature of metacognition (task structures, the importance of planning and reflection, the space of activities that learners use to monitor the strategies that regulate different activities) more explicit to novice learners.

J. R. Anderson (1993) defines cognitive tutors as computer-based instructional systems that use cognitive models (fine-grained representations of successful and unsuccessful strategies employed by learners) to track students through complex problem spaces. Positive outcomes associated with the use of cognitive tutors have been documented within authentic classroom environments and laboratory contexts. There is evidence (J. R. Anderson, Corbett, Koedinger, & Pelletier, 1995) that training time can be reduced by 50 percent and that learning outcome measures can be increased by one standard deviation or more. Cognitive tutoring systems have been used to teach basic skills and complex domain-specific content. The U.S. Department of Education has recommended the use of cognitive tutoring systems in some content areas (mathematics). Some questions remain with respect to the provision of immediate or delayed feedback, but overall the models appear to be highly regarded (Mathan & Koedinger, 2005).

Computer-based multimedia learning environments represent positive attempts to create ways of engaging a learner's metacognitive processes. SRL and social cognitive research has been used as a theoretical framework for most of these attempts. Taken together, the findings appear to hold considerable promise. A number of metacognitive processes (forethought phase processes such as task understanding, goal setting, and planning; performance phases processes such as attention focusing and monitoring, generating questions, self-explanation and elaboration, and collaboration; and self-reflective phase processes such as self-evaluative judgments and adaptations) have been reported (Zimmerman & Tsikalas, 2005) to enhance learning. However, relatively little attention has been given to the role of motivational beliefs associated with SRL. According to Zimmerman and Tsikalas (2005), "Self-reliance represents the most demanding criterion of self-regulatory effectiveness of computer-based multimedia learning environments."

Politics and Policies

In addition to the conceptual frameworks described here (learning theories and their influence on instruction; cognitive, social, and cultural constructivist views of learning theory and teaching; the creation of functional learning environments; a critical pedagogy of place; the reconceptualized curriculum movement; the achievement–self-esteem debate; CLT used as a framework for instructional design; Sternberg's balance theory of wisdom; and the psychology of school subjects), current politics and policies also strongly influenced the knowledge structures used to frame this book. Recent changes related to school reforms, accountability systems, and high-stakes testing implications of the requirements associated with the NCLB, and school choice initiatives have been described and critically evaluated by educational researchers.

School Reforms

At any given time, socially and politically constructed policies and practices within the field of educational psychology affect the discourse of the discipline. Comprehensive school reform efforts marked the latter half of the twentieth century in American schools (Borman, Hewes, Overman, & Brown, 2003). Yet the cycle of reforms seems to move from one fad to another with little evidence of national progress. It seems as if after each new reform is widely disseminated and implemented, the research that follows is sometimes too late as schools have already moved onto the next "innovation." However, the tide may be changing. Borman and colleagues (2003) stated that the "recent national reform and political movements . . . may halt this frustrating cycle. Indeed, for the first time Congress and other educational policy makers are making some funding sources available only to schools that implement educational reforms with high-quality evidence of effectiveness" (p. 125). The Comprehensive School Reform Program (CSRP) provides grants to schools to adopt proven comprehensive reforms. The CSRP focuses on reorganizing and revitalizing entire schools rather than on implementing a number of specialized, potentially uncoordinated school improvement initiatives. In general, the funding has been targeted at the schools most in need of reform and improvement, namely high-poverty schools with low student test scores. The overall effects of CSRP are statistically significant and appear to be greater than the effects of other interventions that have been designed to serve similar purposes. Clearly support for CSRP models that focus on early interventions and prevention may save schools investments in the costly remedial practices of special education referrals and retentions in grade, which alone can offset the costs of implementing the models. The models meeting the highest standards of evidence have been well researched and have shown that they are effective in improving achievement among many schools and children from varying contexts.

Accountability Systems and High-Stakes Testing:
Implications of the Requirements Associated with the NCLB

In January 2002, with the reauthorization of Title I as the NCLB, the CSRP and Title I came together under the same legislation. CSRP has since become a significant component of the growing federal movement to support scientifically based efforts to reform schools across the nation. "Like a mantra, the No Child Left Behind Act repeats phrases such as 'scientifically based research' more than 100 times" (Borman et al., 2003, p. 163). Clearly NCLB sets demanding accountability standards for schools, districts, and states with measurable adequate yearly progress objectives for all students and subgroups of students (Linn, Baker, & Betebenner, 2002). Schools that fail to meet improvement targets must adopt alternative instructional approaches and/or programs that have been shown to be effective through scientifically based research. In describing the impracticality of the accountability requirements of NCLB, Linn and colleagues (2002) state,

> One can agree that schools should improve and that holding schools accountable will contribute to improvement, but still conclude that the goal of having 100% of students reaching the proficient level or higher . . . is so high that it is completely out of reach. Furthermore, having a goal that is unobtainable no matter how hard teachers try can do more to demoralize than to motivate greater effort. Goals need to provide a challenge, but not be set so high that they are unachievable (p. 12).

Furthermore, they explore the volatility of results from year to year due to changes in staff and students within a school. They propose alternatives such as the use of index scores, composites across grades, and rolling averages. There are also potential advantages of working with scale scores and monitoring changes in average scores over time in terms of standard deviation units which could be another alternative as well.

School Choice Initiatives

School choice is another movement associated with some of the current trends in politics and policies. Although school choice was first proposed in 1962 and only a handful of liberal thinkers supported voucher plans in the 1970s, research on school choice has greatly expanded in the past twenty years (Fowler, 2003). Overall, it is probably fair to say that the literature is problematic. A high percentage of the people who publish articles and books related to school choice either passionately support or passionately oppose such policies, usually for ideological reasons. Those who support it feel that school choice can dramatically improve education by subjecting public education to much needed market pressures, thereby raising student achievement, increasing parent involvement, providing for diverse educational needs, and building more cohesive school communities. Those who oppose school choice view it as a social threat to public education, and by extension to American democracy. "They commonly point out the many ways that markets can fail as well as how inappropriate they are for producing public goods like education. They fear that competitive educational markets will favor those who possess abundant financial and cultural capital, increasing stratification by race and class. Moreover, they fear that competition could lead to a variety of 'choice' schools that serve those children who are relatively easy (and cheap) to educate while traditional public schools would be transformed into dumping grounds where teachers struggle with those who are most difficult to educate: the poor, the disabled, and the children with behavior problems" (p. 34). Fowler concludes by stating that "the question is not whether we should have school choice, but rather what type of school choice policies should we have? In order for policy scholars and policy makers to be able to answer that question, we need a more mature school choice literature" (p. 38). Additional research is needed on charter schools. More integrative research efforts are needed as well as research that is more balanced on a variety of issues related to school choice.

Methodological Issues: Disciplined Methods of Inquiry

Finally, methodological issues, or disciplined methods of inquiry, is another organizational structure that was used as a framework in the design of this book. The methodological issues specifically addressed include the following: scientific research in education and the case for evidence-based reasoning in educational research, alternative forms of data representation, and the teacher research movement.

Scientific Research in Education: The Case for Evidence-Based Reasoning in Educational Research

As stated earlier, the NCLB requires federal grantees to use their funds on evidence-based methods (Feuer et al. 2002). These initiatives pose a rare opportunity and great challenge to the field in determining the most effective means of stimulating scientific educational research. Feuer and colleagues (2002) propose that the primary emphasis should be on "nurturing and reinforcing a scientific culture of educational research" (p. 4). Some are concerned, however, that the narrow definitions of "research" or "science" might

trivialize rather than enrich our understanding of education policies and practices, and that the "splendors of unfettered scholarship will be eroded by
creeping tides of conformity and methodological zealotry" (Feuer et al.,
2002, p. 4). In addressing the controversial issues regarding educational research methodology, the National Research Council (NRC) in 2002 articu-
lated the nature of scientific research in education and offered a framework
for the future of educational research. The NRC report contains two major
points.

> First, it dispels the myth that science is synonymous with a particular method.
> Although method is key to science, method does not uniquely define science
> and choices of method are often highly nuanced. Second, specifically with re-
> spect to developing a common research culture, the report implicitly cautions re-
> searchers against organizing themselves exclusively according to common
> methods. The questions drive the methods, not the other way around (p. 8).

Alternative Forms of Data Representation

Interestingly, federal politics and policies are demanding more "scientific
research" in education and the use of evidence-based practices even as educational researchers are slowly expanding their traditional conceptions of
knowledge to include explorations of alternative forms of data representation
(Eisner, 1997). Traditionally, our view of knowledge was associated with
matters of verification and "truth." Concerns for verification, truth, and pre-
cision led researchers away from an experiential conception of understanding
and toward a verificationist conception of knowledge. As a result, the idea
that knowledge as a process, a temporary state, has been threatening to many.
If one steps out of academia and considers culture at large, one can list a number of ways to convey what is known including stories, pictures, diagrams,
maps, theater, demonstrations, and poetry. However, the notion of research in
academia has been confined to one's conception of meaning, one's view of
cognitions, and one's beliefs about the forms of consciousness that are said to
advance human learning. Research can take a variety of forms including those
that reflect the forms of the arts and humanities or those of the natural and social sciences. Eisner purports that the forms of data representation should be
open to invention. Ultimately, the value of research is determined by the judgment of a critical community. Historically, the discussions of qualitative research methods were almost always reduced to doing ethnographies associated with the disciplinary traditions of cultural anthropology. Ethnography
was eventually recognized as a respectable discipline in the 1960s: It was a
teachable and learnable method, and it had technical language and scholarly
standards associated with its use. However, the door has now been opened to

other alternative forms of data representation as well. A defining moment came with the realization that qualitative research methods were not the monopoly of ethnographers, but were also used by sociologists, clinical psychologists, writers, and other scholars in the arts and humanities. At that point, there was the realization that research methodologies (i.e., disciplined methods of inquiry) did not belong to science alone. The door was then opened to questions about what constitutes legitimate forms of inquiry in education. As a result, the field of educational research has come a long way since the late 1960s and early 1970s. Since the late 1980s qualitative research as a category in the AERA programs has been the fifth- to sixth-largest classification for papers presented at its annual meetings. There are several advantages to broadening the conception of research to include alternative forms of data representation. Alternative forms of data representation can provide a sense of particularity that abstractions cannot render, which then allows for more authenticity. Furthermore, alternative forms of data representation promise to increase the variety of questions that we can ask about the educational situations we study. Our capacity to wonder is stimulated by the possibilities that new forms of representation suggest. Alternative forms of data representation also take advantage of individual researchers' aptitudes. Neither the literal nor the quantitative are everyone's cup of tea (Eisner, 1997).

The Teacher Research Movement

The teacher research movement is one form of alternative research that has been receiving more attention within the field of education. The terms *teacher research, practitioner research,* or *insider research* are given to research that is done by school practitioners (G. Anderson & Herr, 1998). There has been resistance within the academic community to legitimate practitioner research as universities have traditionally valued basic research and theoretical knowledge. Academics have been comfortable with practitioner research as a form of "local knowledge" that can lead to changes within the practice setting. However, they are less supportive when it is presented as public knowledge with epistemic claims that extend beyond the practice setting. The conception of insider research by academics as "practical inquiry" focuses on the improvement of practices and gives it a secondary status to real research. This creates a sort of dualism between formal knowledge and practical knowledge. Practitioner researchers face additional hurdles. Even qualitative researchers have serious reservations about the validity of practitioner research. Furthermore, many teachers may not have the time and/or the training to do research.

Additionally, the teachers' workplace has not been conducive to research and there are few incentives for teachers to engage in and disseminate their research findings. Rarely is research cited that has been generated from teachers' classrooms by teachers themselves. In contrast to traditional academia, there is a professional culture of school that has traditionally valued applied research and narrative knowledge. Some scholars place value on insider researchers as they have unique opportunities to document the hidden transcripts within educational institutions, which have been only partially accessible to researchers in the past. Furthermore, as many teachers today are working to obtain master's degrees and doctoral degrees, it seems that the time is ripe for such advances in an expanded, more inclusive view of the methods of discovery. Some schools are encouraging teachers to meet together and design and implement collaborative research projects. Some education research textbooks now include practitioner research descriptions. More and more journals are being created that deal exclusively with practitioner research. While there is a long way to go before practitioner research is considered a legitimate method of discovery, we are on the verge of seeing an outpouring of practitioner inquiry that will force redefinitions of what "counts as research" (Anderson, 1998). Practitioner researchers (insider researchers) will also need a set of acknowledged criteria so that their research can gain ground when compared to that conducted by outsider researchers. As a result, there will have to be rigorous efforts made to encourage greater collaboration between academics and school professionals. Colleges of education will need to rethink the ways they train students and produce knowledge for school practitioners. As a result, the benefits of practitioner research can be realized by reconceptualizing the work of school practitioners as intimately linked to ongoing inquiry. Schools can then be restructured into collective, evidence-based, inquiry-oriented, professional, organizational learning environments and so can tutoring programs.

4

Tutoring and the Advancement of Learning

In the first half of chapter 4, we introduce a cognitive science perspective to the study of tutoring. As the outline of chapter 4 shows, we begin with a discussion of three models of instruction (tutoring, mastery learning, and personalized systems of instruction). Emphasis is given to the commonalities across the three models (e.g., their emphasis on continuous assessment, remediation, encouragement, and support) rather than the differences. A special effort is made to relate contemporary developments reported in the cognitive science literature to John B. Carroll's (1963) original behaviorally based model of tutoring and mastery learning. Particular attention is given to possible instructional correctives and the special problems related to the application of these models to atypical and/or nontraditional learners.

Cognitive scientists claim that the major differences in the learning characteristics between novice and expert human learners are found primarily in the cognitive mediation differences of attention, cognitive-style expectancies, and memory organization. Individual differences among learners are broken down further into biological differences (attention, maturation stages, and temperament) and psychological differences (knowledge, language, memory organization, mood, attitudes, personality, cognitive-style expectancies, and motivation). Although biologically determined differences cannot be modified, we can modify many of the environmentally determined psychological individual differences. Most of the individual difference characteristics of interest to a cognitive scientist are believed to be learnable.

In the second half of chapter 4, we describe the 2 sigma effect and the search for methods of instruction to yield a 2 sigma effect. Barriers to reaching the 2 sigma level of performance are also described. Special attention is given to recommendations related to the improvement of teaching higher

mental processes and better use of multimedia learning and instructional technologies. The final sections of the chapter contain detailed reviews of what
we know and don't know about a social learning perspective, mentorship, the
development of expertise, and constructivist teaching practices.

Outline of Contents Related to Tutoring and the Advancement of Learning

Three models (views) of instruction
    Mastery learning
    Personalized systems of instruction (PSI)
    Tutoring

*Individual differences and the learnable aspects of human thinking and prob-
lem solving*
    Behavioral views
    Gestalt views
    Piagetian and neo-Piagetian developmental views
    Cognitive science (information processing) views

A cognitive science model of mastery learning, PSI, and tutoring
    The advancement of learning

The 2 sigma effect and the search for methods of instruction
    Barriers to reaching the 2 sigma level of performance
    Improvement of teaching
    Improvement in the teaching of higher mental processes
    Improving instructional materials and educational technologies (multi-
        media learning)

A social learning perspective
    Components of social learning theory
    Reciprocal determinism and the self-system of human agency
    Social learning theory and education

Mentorship
    Issues related to mentorship
    Methodological issues
    Theoretical models
    L. S. Vygotsky's theory of cognitive development

A cognitive science–based expert–novice view
    Do rewards undermine intrinsic interest?

Constructivism
   Constructing a room for two
   Cultural, social, and cultural constructivism
   A reaction to Bruner's views of constructivism
   A postmodern–neomodern perspective
   Always question authority

THREE VIEWS OF INSTRUCTION

Three models of instruction have prevailed (i.e., mastery learning, PSI, and tutoring). In what follows, we attempt to relate theory to practice. An effort is made to focus on the commonalities across these three models of instruction (e.g., their emphasis on continuous assessment, remediation, encouragement, and support) rather than the differences. Trends and existing knowledge related to the effectiveness of each of the models are presented.

An effort is made to relate contemporary developments reported in the cognitive science literature to John B. Carroll's (1963) original behaviorally based model of mastery learning. Particular attention is given to the possible instructional correctives and the special problems related to the application of mastery learning, PSI, and tutoring procedures to the atypical and/or nontraditional learner. Those cognitive science components requiring particular attention in the design and implementation of mastery learning, PSI, and tutoring instruction are presented.

Specific attention is given to the learnable aspects of human thinking and problem solving. The overall thesis is that most of the cognitive science components are learnable. Therefore when we are called on to design mastery learning, PSI, and tutoring learning environments, we should attempt to include instructional procedures having potential for the modification of the cognitive components presented in the cognitively embellished behaviorally based mastery learning model described in the sections that follow. Much of what is presented in this section and the two following sections closely parallels what was presented in a book published by three of the four authors in 1998 (Morgan, Ponticell, & Gordon, 1998).

Mastery Learning

John B. Carroll (1963) proposed that degree of learning is a function of the ratio of two quantities: (1) the amount of time a learner spends on the learning task and (2) the amount of time a learner needs to learn the task.

$$\text{Degree of learning} = \frac{\text{Amount of time spent on a task}}{\text{Amount of time needed to learn the task}}$$

Figure 4.1. Carroll's Model of Mastery Learning

Carroll's model of mastery learning is depicted in figure 4.1. This model has served as a behaviorally based theoretical anchor for much of Benjamin Bloom's (1968, 1974) work related to mastery learning instruction. Carroll's formulation implied that allowing sufficient time to learn a task (i.e., permitting the numerator of the ratio to be larger) and improving instructional conditions (i.e., decreasing the denominator) should enable most students to reach a criterion of mastery. Mastery learning is an educational procedure in which a learning hierarchy is developed and learners are required to master each unit of the hierarchy prior to beginning a subsequent unit. Mastery usually is determined by end-of-unit tests that learners must pass.

Bloom (1971, 1976) and others (Block, 1971; Block & Burns, 1976) have argued that mastery learning research supports the claim that mastery learning strategies can raise the achievement levels of approximately 80 percent of students to levels achieved by the upper 20 percent under nonmastery conditions. These findings apply to many academic content areas (e.g., reading, writing, and math) in addition to different types of thinking and problem solving situations. From these reviews, it seems that most investigators recognize that the tutoring and mastery learning research findings confirm the achievement claims.

The time claims, however, require further investigation. Most tutoring and mastery learning theorists acknowledge that during the initial learning sequences, extra time must be provided to less able learners. However, this extra time is viewed as a temporary "crutch" that becomes less and less necessary with practice (Bloom, 1976).

A number of critics of mastery learning instruction (L. Anderson & Burns, 1987; Buss, 1976; Greeno, 1978; Guskey, 1987; Guskey & Gates, 1986; Mueller, 1976; Resnick, 1977; Slavin, 1987a, 1987b) have argued that in regular nonmastery instructional situations in which time is held constant for all learners, individual differences among students are reflected primarily in differences in achievement outcomes. If all students are restricted to learning a lesson in a certain amount of time, then a normal distribution of high, average, and low achievement scores will probably be observed. However, if achievement outcomes are held constant in mastery learning instruction, then individual differences among learners will be reflected by differences in the time needed to learn.

Another way of stating this is that the assumption of stability in individual differences among students is directly related to the assumption of a time–achievement trade-off. To bring less able learners up to the desired mastery level, additional time must be provided for both learners and instructors. Since individual differences among learners are assumed to be relatively stable, critics claim that these time costs remain relatively constant throughout mastery learning instruction. Time is traded for increased achievement of less able students, and time inequality is traded for achievement equality. Thus there may be a Robin Hood effect associated with the use of mastery learning approaches to instruction. Mastery learning may help slower-learning students at the expense of faster-learning students. The important educational resources of instructor time and attention may be used to benefit the slower learners at the expense of faster ones.

From the results of numerous investigations (Block & Burns, 1976), we know that mastery learning programs when compared to traditional approaches to instruction produce positive gains in academic achievement and student attitudes. There is considerable evidence indicating that the effectiveness of the mastery approach depends on the length of the training program and the type of outcome measures used. Robert Slavin (1987a) found that training programs lasting four weeks or longer yielded more positive findings than training programs lasting less than four weeks.

It should be noted, however, that standardized achievement outcome measures yield much weaker results than performance- and/or curriculum-based outcome measures (Slavin, 1987b) and that group-based mastery learning approaches appear to be extremely difficult to carry out with success in large-scale training projects such as inner city schools (Brophy, 1988).

PSI

Although mastery learning and PSI approaches were derived from different theoretical perspectives, they are similar in many ways. Bloom's (1971) learning for mastery strategies evolved from Carroll's (1963) theory of school learning and has had its major impact on elementary and secondary school educators. In contrast, the PSI strategy developed by Fred Keller (1968) evolved from Skinnerian behavioral psychology and has had its major impact on the thinking of university and college educators.

The basic components of PSI include self-pacing, the use of human tutors and proctors, the mastery requirement, immediate feedback, and frequent testing over relatively small units. Advocates of PSI assume that traditional instructional procedures do not encourage an adequate number of learner responses or provide learners with personalized opportunities for reinforcement to occur. Keller (1968) proposed that subject matter be divided into brief instructional units, enabling students to study at their own rate, progressing to the next unit when mastery (80–90 percent correct score) was achieved. Students who do not master an instructional unit the first time are provided with additional time and individualized (i.e., personalized) tutoring until mastery is achieved.

The meta-analysis of PSI by James A. Kulik, Chen-Lin C. Kulik, and Peter A. Cohen (1979) indicated that when compared to traditional instruction, PSI produces superior student achievement, considerably less achievement variation, and higher student evaluations. In addition, PSI procedures were found to be unrelated to increased study time or course withdrawals.

Considerable disagreement exists over the respective contributions of each of the basic components (self-pacing, the use of human tutors and proctors, the mastery requirement, immediate feedback, and frequent testing over relatively small units) to the overall effectiveness of the PSI approach to instruction. For example, J. F. Calhoun (1973) found that all of the components make important contributions. However, James H. Block and Robert B. Burns (1976) reported that the mastery requirement produced the strongest effects. Finally, it should be noted that the Robin Hood effect, cited previously as a potential problem with mastery learning instruction, does not manifest itself with PSI since students work independently (Calhoun, 1973). Since students work independently with PSI, instructor time and attention are not used to benefit slower learners at the expense of their faster peers.

In sum, PSI gets generally favorable marks when compared with traditional instructional methodologies. It appears to be easily adaptable to a wide variety of instructional situations and has few, if any, empirically demonstrated negative side effects.

Tutoring

In their book *Centuries of Tutoring: A History of Alternative Education in America and Western Europe,* Edward E. Gordon and Elaine H. Gordon (1990) reported that large group–based schooling has dominated the twentieth century, but individual and small-group tutoring approaches to instruction are still important. Peer tutors, after-school remedial programs, home-bound instruction, and the home schooling movement are modern expressions of tutoring. A child's education is a highly personalized process, supported by the family, and guided through the assistance of literate teachers. At their best, tutors remained the best equipped to assess individual differences among their students and engineer stimulating learning environments.

In the nineteenth and twentieth centuries, tutoring became an actual part of schooling. Some of the most important Western philosophers developed educational theories based on their practical experience as tutors. Their tutorial philosophy led to the development of many of our modern educational principles such as continuous assessment, remediation, encouragement, and support—the same principles held by advocates of mastery learning and PSI instruction.

A review of the literature indicates that tutoring usually produces positive results. L. F. Annis (1983) reports that tutoring procedures appear to produce positive effects on both tutees and tutors. Summaries of research on tutoring (Cohen, Kulik, & Kulik, 1982; Gage & Berliner, 1992; Mathes & Fuchs, 1994; Shanahan, 1998; Wasik & Slavin, 1993) have indicated that these positive effects have been consistently found on measures of achievement and on affective measures of self-esteem and intrinsic interest in the subject matter being taught. In addition, the results from numerous cross-age peer tutoring studies conducted with learners across the life span have yielded positive findings (P. Lippitt, 1969; P. Lippitt & Lippitt, 1970; R. Lippitt & Lippitt, 1968). A detailed description and critique of tutoring research is presented in chapter 5. In sum, tutoring appears to be a very powerful technique for enhancing student learning across a wide sample of different types of students and content areas.

INDIVIDUAL DIFFERENCES AND THE LEARNABLE ASPECTS OF HUMAN THINKING AND PROBLEM SOLVING

Cognitive scientists (Brown, 1978; Bruer, 1993a, 1993b; Case, 1985; Glaser, 1984, 1990) claim that the major differences in the learning characteristics between novice and expert human learners are found primarily in the cognitive mediation differences of attention, cognitive-style expectancies, and memory organization. It is argued here that these cognitive mediation differences, the study of individual differences and the learnable aspects of human thinking and problem solving, appear to be of particular relevance to advocates of mastery learning, PSI, and tutoring instruction.

Behavioral Views

The behaviorists have viewed individual differences in terms of biological differences and learnable habits. Thinking has been viewed as a change in habit strength, problem solving as related to trial-and-error application of existing habits, and creativity as an accidental combination of two or more previously acquired stimulus–response (S–R) chains. In terms of instruction, the accumulation of experience, not the remodeling of experience, has been considered to be of primary importance. From this point of view, instruction involves setting up instructional situations to help learners acquire successful learning habits. The greater the number of acquired habits, the greater the adaptive problem solving behavior and intelligence of the learners.

Gestalt Views

Gestaltists have focused their attention on individual differences in perception, both biological and psychological. The relationships among attention, perception, learning, and memory have been viewed as particularly important. There is considerable evidence (Bower & Hilgard, 1981) to suggest that most of our perceptions of environmental events are learned. In the process of learning, we develop memories and our memories set up expectancies, stereotypes, and biases that affect the way in which we perceive environmental events. These learned perceptual templates (expectancies) have a great deal to do with stimulus input, and they may facilitate or retard learning.

Gestaltists have viewed stimulus–response associations as mere by-products of perceptual chunks. They have described two kinds of problem solving: productive (creative–insightful) and reproductive (application of S–R habits, simple trial and error learning). From a gestalt point of view, the primary difference between the novice and the expert learner is considered to be in their learned perceptual templates, which create learning expectancies and in turn differentially affect stimulus input and memory organization.

Piagetian and Neo-Piagetian Developmental Views

For Piagetians and neo-Piagetians (Brown, 1978, 1994; Case, 1985), individual differences are cognitive and have to do with differences in schematic representations. These master cognitive templates (schematic representations) serve as logical problem solving components. Thinking and problem solving are seen in terms of assimilation and accommodation. All thinking is believed to be creative. In addition, the neo-Piagetians focus on the development and use of executive processes (i.e., self-controlling processes). They consider equilibrium to be the major type of adaptive problem solving and look at perception as a gestaltist would, viewing individual differences as differences in cognitive expectancies and style (field dependence–field independence; internal and external locus of control).

Novice and expert learners differ with respect to the number of bits of information they can attend to without support from the perceptual field. With age and experience the number of things a person can attend to remains the same $(7 + 2)$, but the bits of information become more cognitively differentiated and sophisticated. From a neo-Piagetian perspective, what develops is attention, and one learns when one is able to acquire a rule (usually a verbal rule) relating new learning to existing cognitive structures. To facilitate learning, a neo-Piagetian would attempt to teach the novice the memory and metamemory (knowing what you know) strategies (e.g., rehearsal and other active engagement strategies) used by expert learners.

Information Processing (Cognitive Science) Views

Those individuals associated with the information processing (cognitive science) camp (Bruer, 1993a, 1993b; Glaser, 1978, 1982, 1984, 1986, 1990; J. Levin & Pressley, 1983; Pressley & Levin, 1983) view individual differences in terms of fixed (attention limitations) and flexible (instructional manipulations) control structures. They are concerned essentially with the description and facilitation of the thinking and problem solving processes. They do not specifically address creativity. They provide detailed task analytic descriptions (computer simulation models) of the expert learner's assimilation processes and construct models to facilitate the acquisition of knowledge among novices.

Individual differences are viewed as the fixed biological control structures of attention, maturational stages, and temperament. Manipulatable, flexible psychological control structures comprise differences in knowledge, language, memory organization, mood, attitudes, personality, cognitive-style expectancies, and motivation. These flexible control structures are what we attempt to modify to enhance the quality and organization of instruction. For the most part, the neo-Piagetian and the information processing theorists are closely aligned in their mutual focus on strategy–training procedures directed at the novice learner.

A COGNITIVE SCIENCE MODEL OF TUTORING, MASTERY LEARNING, AND PSI

Given the recent advances with respect to the cognitive science perspective, it is our view that it is desirable to embellish the behaviorally based mastery learning model originally proposed by Carroll (1963) to include a number of cognitive variables. An embellished cognitive science model of mastery learning, PSI, and tutoring instruction is presented below:

Degree of learning = Time spent (willing or allowed)

Time needed (aptitude, i.e., individual differences) + (quality of instruction × ability to understand instructions)

Where: *Student aptitude* would consist of the biological differences of attention, temperament, and maturational stages of development and the psychological differences of existing knowledge and language templates, memory organization, mood, attitudes, personality, cognitive-style expectancies, and motivation.

Quality of instruction would be viewed as the ability of the teacher to organize instruction, to give it meaning, and to set up problem solving situations which enhance critical thinking.

Ability to understand instructions would consist of the same components as *quality of instruction*.

From a cognitive scientist's perspective, individual differences in student aptitude would consist of differences in attention, temperament, maturational stages of development, existing knowledge and language templates, memory organization, mood, cognitive styles, attitudes, personality, cognitive-style expectancies, and motivation. Quality of instruction would relate to the ability of the instructor to organize instruction—set up situations that enhance meaning and contribute to the development of critical thinking and problem solving skills.

It is recognized that we are unable to modify biological differences in temperament and maturational stages. But most of the other components listed in the embellished cognitive science model can be modified. We can enhance knowledge and language templates. It is generally accepted that how efficiently we learn depends to a great extent on what we already know.

From a cognitive science perspective, a major constraint on novice learners is that their knowledge base and ability to use language to code and store information is very limited. There is a literate bias in schooling that is viewed as enhancing our thinking and problem solving behaviors. The assumption is that this literate bias allows the expert learner to interpret environmental events in a different way than the novice learner.

It is further assumed that the learner with an internally controlled, field-independent cognitive style interprets his or her environment in a way that differs from the externally controlled, field-dependent learner. For example, the internally controlled learner would attribute successes to effort, persistence, and hard work while the externally controlled learner would be more likely to attribute success to luck. Negative attitudes, low expectancies, and bad moods constrain cognitive performance. Again, the point is that knowledge and language templates, cognitive styles, attitudes, expectancies, and mood can be modified by the instructor.

WHAT MATTERS?

Much of what is presented here is derived from the field of cognitive information processing, a field replete with overlapping ideas and concepts expressed in multiple terms. There are practitioners who would claim that the field is too complex and the instructional procedures derived from it too cumbersome to use. While most of us may agree that teachers should utilize cognitive information processing principles in the curriculum and instructional designs they create for all learners, we may not think that this complex theory of learning and instruction can be directly applied to pragmatic tutoring situations.

Should tutors be expected to monitor and shape the cognitive information processing capabilities of learners? Can a novice learner's attention, cognitive-style expectancies, and memory be modified? The research evidence from a cognitive science perspective (e.g., Bransford, Sherwood, Vye, & Rieser, 1986; Bruer, 1993a, 1993b; Foster, 1986; Glaser, 1978, 1982, 1984, 1986, 1990; Glaser & Takanishi, 1986; Greeno, 1989; Pressley & Levin, 1983; Shuell, 1986; Weinstein & Marges, 1986), together with the effective teaching and learning productivity perspectives (e.g., Good & Brophy, 1987; Walberg, 1984; Wang, Haertel, & Walberg, 1990), indicates that they can. Several common factors that emerge within the context of the research literature supporting the use of mastery learning, PSI, tutoring, and cognitive science models of instruction appear to be particularly important to tutors.

Time Actively Engaged in a Learning Task

The amount of time that learners actively engage in a learning task (i.e., the concept of academic learning time) is important (Fisher et al., 1978; Stallings,

1980). From a cognitive science perspective, the performance of a task becomes more automatic with repeated exposure to small, meaningful components of the task consistently presented over a period of time (Myers & Fisk, 1987). Learning is enhanced by instruction that breaks down complex tasks into small, meaningful components that are individually taught.

Connect Small Competency Units to Existing Knowledge

From a cognitive science perspective, knowledge might be viewed as organized in schemas (i.e., hierarchical structures or networks of concepts, components, and interrelationships). Increasing a learner's ability to develop more elaborate schemas, accessing them more easily, and automatizing problem solving learning procedures enhances learning.

Instruction that facilitates students' relating new information to old is useful. New information is more readily learned when it is organized and presented within a conceptual structure, using associations, advance organizers, topic headings, and mnemonics. It is important to teach the prototype first (i.e., concepts, rules, and principles), then variations, including real-world examples and applications. It is also important that learners see the alignment among goals, content, instructional tasks, and evaluations.

Provide Continuous Feedback and Assessment

Research indicates that learning is enhanced by detailed and specific feedback, not only on the correctness of a learner's responses but also on the appropriateness of a learner's learning strategies (Brophy, 1981; Guskey & Gates, 1986; Walberg, 1984; Wang et al., 1990). In addition, feedback is important not only on total performance but also on specific task components, so that the learner can discover sources of error. Continuous assessment that is integrated with instruction enhances the learner's ability to identify useful problem solving strategies.

Teach Metacognitive (Learning How to Learn) Strategies

Research indicates that effective learners use mental models to conceptualize task demands, methods for accomplishing the task, and relationships to the task domain (e.g., Brainin, 1985). The best problem solvers are those who develop detailed mental representations of a "problem space" before attempting a solution (Norman & Rumelhart, 1981).

Marlene Scardamalia and Carl Bereiter (1983) have found that learners can be explicitly taught to use learning models and thinking skills. It is important to find out from learners the models they already use in everyday work or life situations. Learning is enhanced when these existing models are elaborated and refined through the instructional process. Effective task analysis enables the learner to identify the development of individual learning models. In addition, using learners' existing models, providing examples and counterexamples, and structuring situations in which models are applied and tested enables learners to identify "good" models.

Attempt to Establish Motivational Links

Researchers have found that learners use two kinds of knowledge to learn task knowledge and motivational knowledge (C. Ames & Ames, 1985, 1989; R. Ames & Ames, 1984; Winne, 1991). Motivational knowledge influences students' involvement in learning and stimulates feelings learners associate with the learning experience. Several motivational factors appear to be important: a stress-free learning environment; academic aspirations; a learning culture that emphasizes academic achievement and work-related performance, accessibility, and cohesiveness among the participants; and the individual's value for persistence (Gordon, Morgan, & Ponticell, 1994).

It was argued above that individual differences in cognition (knowledge and stylistic) and perception can both constrain and facilitate learning. Our view is that individual differences, especially the cognitive bases of differences of the novice learner and instructional task, appear to have a valid place in the psychology of learning as it relates to mastery learning, PSI, and tutoring instruction. A great deal of research in a number of areas of cognitive science (e.g., expert–novice comparisons, cognitive strategy training, critical thinking, and performance outcome–based assessment) considered to be relevant to the implementation of mastery learning, PSI, and tutoring instruction has been conducted (Bransford et al., 1986; Bruer, 1993a, 1993b; Foster, 1986; Glaser, 1978, 1982, 1984, 1986, 1990; Glaser & Takanishi, 1986; Greeno, 1989; Pressley & Levin, 1983; Shuell, 1986; Spady & Marshall, 1991; Weinstein & Marges, 1986).

The findings related to research on cognitive strategy training, metacognitive processes, and computer simulation of expert performance may provide us with teachable cognitive process variables that could supplement and perhaps replace traditional intelligence tests in the successful matching of student's individual differences and educational treatment approaches. Detailed cognitive task analyses of instructional sequences have been conducted and continue to be conducted. It is expected that the training of metacognitive skills and problem solving strategies may help novice learners master the intellectual skills and the content used by the experts. The identification of these individual differences in cognitive information processing capacities could be utilized to design instruction that compensates for a particular deficiency by providing for learners what they cannot provide for themselves. Such information could be used to capitalize on the learner's strengths and would appear to be particularly valuable for diagnosing reasons for current learning difficulties and in suggesting mastery learning, PSI, and tutoring instructional procedures (prescriptions) for overcoming them.

What we are proposing here is a cognitively embellished model of tutoring, mastery learning, and PSI instruction. Instruction should be directed at modifying student attention, cognitive expectancies, and memory. Cognitive information processing is enhanced when learners are actively engaged in the learning task, discuss, rehearse, analyze, problem solve, use graphs to represent experience, and share observations, understandings, and knowledge.

When we are called on to design mastery learning, PSI, and tutoring environments, we should attempt to include instructional procedures having potential for the modification of cognitive learning components (e.g., attention, knowledge and language templates, cognitive strategies, attitudes, expectancies, and mood). We know that mastery learning, PSI, and tutoring instructional systems work. The three instructional systems have been carefully tested in highly controlled laboratory, field experimental, and applied settings. What is now needed is a greater focus on and appreciation for attempts to relate recent findings reported in the cognitive science literature to these behaviorally anchored models in support of a tutoring revolution.

THE ADVANCEMENT OF LEARNING

A primary goal of many educational researchers is to design evidence-based instructional procedures. Well-developed theories of learning and development are needed to ground the evidence-based research activities. Even though substantial advances have been made in learning and development, the schools do not appear to be utilizing our new discoveries.

Brown (1994) reviewed the advances that were made in learning and development since the beginning of the cognitive revolution (30 years ago). According to Brown, even though progress has been made in terms of research, many of our most useful findings have been ignored by the policy makers. When Brown began her quest for knowledge, her initial experiences with learning theory were based on behavioral approaches associated with the experimental analysis of behavior. The cognitive revolution had not yet begun. At the time, the main players in educational research were Hull, Spence, Tolman, and Skinner. The main principles of learning that were developed by these theorists were derived from the study of rats and pigeons studied in highly controlled learning environments. It was expected that these behaviorally based principles of learning would be generalizable to all species across all conditions and/or environments. Although much was established about the learning behavior of animals in laboratories, very little was determined about the learning behavior of animals and humans in their natural (less controlled) learning environments. Of course, it could be argued that school environments as they exist today are very unnatural environments.

During the first half of the twentieth century, the field of developmental psychology was also dominated by the behaviorists in spite of the work of cognitively based researchers such as Binet, Baldwin, and Piaget. Not only the theories but the methods under which children were studied were greatly influenced by the behavioral school of thought. Brown's (1994) critique of behavioral methods included the notion that many of the tasks which were designed to study learning in children were unsuitable and/or inappropriate. Children were viewed as being incapable of inferential reasoning, insight, and logic. These behaviorally based research efforts had a tremendous impact on education. Educational researchers focused their efforts on external factors such as the manipulation of rewards and punishers to bring about desired behaviors. Children were considered to be limited in their attention and easily bored by new learning tasks. In experimental settings that were originally designed to study animal potential, children performed poorly and consequently were described as inept, lacking reason, and limited in their ability to classify, be insightful, and transfer information and/or sets of problem solving and thinking skills from one problem solving situation to another. Given these findings, school schedules were designed to allow children to work for short periods of time on mastery of decontextualized skill building activities. The problem at midcentury was that even though the behaviorists made many important contributions (behavior management and token economies), most educational researchers adapted behavioral (external) approaches and disregarded the important factors of content, context, and development. Even today, the contemporary use of behavioral objectives and high-stakes standardized tests continues to reflect the behavioral theories that were center stage fifty years ago. Today the educational research emphasis has shifted from behavioral views of learning theory and teaching to cognitive, social, and cultural constructivist views of the overall learning process.

Fortunately, our knowledge of cognitive science has helped us change our passive views of the learning process. Children are now regarded as active, introspective, metacognitively (and to some degree biologically) predisposed to learn specific things. Environments that foster meaningful learning are described by many as communities of learners (COLs) and researchers. Instead of continuing to study how children memorize words and pictures (discrete stimuli), Brown (1994) focused her efforts on studying how children learn to comprehend and self-monitor. Developing strategies (like questioning, clarifying, and summarizing) that facilitate comprehension is often difficult for children. In order to help facilitate reading comprehension, Brown developed an instructional program called reciprocal teaching (RT). Thus a COL was developed. In a COL, students are responsible in part for designing their curriculum and are encouraged to play the roles of researchers and teachers. How? In its most basic form, RT resembles a small reading group made up of five or six participants. The group leader (i.e., the teacher) attempts to help the group members develop comprehension and monitoring skills by questioning, summarizing, and clarifying the material being studied. By raising questions, summarizing arguments, and clarifying problems contained in the reading assignments, the leader helps each group member develop comprehension and monitoring skills. Through RT, children of varying abilities can be supported by provoking Vygotsky's zones of proximal development within each child. Even if some children are not yet proficient at joining in, RT in the form of reading groups can help each learner acquire meaning, applicability, and importance. In conjunction with RT, a jigsaw method of instruction may be used that requires children to share the responsibility for teaching and learning by dividing a lesson into five or six subunits; each group conducts research and shares its knowledge with others. To complete the puzzle, all the pieces (subunits) are needed. Using jigsaw, children are encouraged to focus on whatever topic was chosen within the perimeters of the unit and thereby acquire specific knowledge within that area. Children apparently sustain considerable engagement and excitement over what they have learned.

Within these learning communities, performance is center stage. When they are encouraged to teach (perform) their specific units to others, children are inclined to reach better coherence and higher stages of understanding, and they acquire the ability to explain and interpret the material assigned. By encouraging learners to teach others what they know, they are likely to plan, prepare, practice, and reflect. Creating a positive teaching and learning environment, setting goals, and nurturing learners to achieve higher levels of thought are the teacher's primary objectives. Outsiders are often included in these learning communities. Since increasing the ratio of adults to children in classrooms is often challenging, other students and peers are used as learning resources. Efforts are made to include adult experts within the COL environment whenever possible in order to reduce the possibility of the COL groups becoming stagnant.

A set of learning principles is required in order to provide a conceptual framework in which to situate our research efforts and applications. According to Brown (1994), many of the conceptual frameworks developed by progressive educators were too vague. Brown made an effort to develop useful pathways of intelligent inquiry. In order to ensure best practices, learning outcomes need some degree of specificity, documentation, and systematic, ongoing evaluation. Brown warns us not to separate questioning and summarizing from understanding, two strategies that are believed to be keys to comprehension.

According to Brown (1994), academic learning is "active, strategic, self-conscious, self-motivating, and purposeful." Metacognition (having insight into your own strengths and weaknesses) is not a new idea. Pioneers like Binet, in an attempt to remediate curriculum for atypical learners, developed mental orthopedics in an attempt to help atypical learners understand their strengths and weaknesses. The goal was to increase study habits, effort, attention, reasoning, and self-criticism skills in atypical learners. Unfortunately, instructions on how to operationalize the program were unclear: active learning must be vigorously nurtured. Brown claims that the behaviorists did not necessarily discourage the study of the mind and cognition; they just neglected to pursue and/or encourage cognitively focused research.

In terms of the zone of proximal development (ZPD), Brown (1994) asserted that children enter school at different levels of learning and development (some are more ready than others). Within the ZPD, learning takes place somewhere between the lower and higher bounds of a learner's potential. The goal is to assess the level and then teach beyond it. According to Brown, teachers need to guide the learning process (i.e., guided discovery learning), as well as recognize and find value in individual differences. The goal is to identify unique talents and then utilize them to teach math, science, reading literacy, and anything else that is valued and considered important by a society of learners. Brown asserts that all learners vary in the amount of work they can handle, at what age they are capable of handling it, in the amount of work they can complete, and in the amount of time needed to complete the work. Efforts are made to encourage children to externalize and share internalized information and to think through discussion and dialogue.

Brown (1994) also asserted that research practices within and between COLs must be sustained and expanded. The creation of COLs provides support for the development of deep conceptual content and the use of authentic assessment procedures that are aligned with the curriculum. Many school reform programs are uni-educational and don't account for varying levels of development. We need to question and critique why we teach certain domain-specific subjects when we do. Our reasons are based on antiquated developmental theories that lack empirical verification. In sum, our traditional behaviorally based perspectives related to the age when children are capable of learning to perform certain types of tasks need to be revised based on current cognitive research. Academic practices must be redesigned based on the principles that underlie disciplinary understanding. In order to set age-appropriate goals, an evidence-based understanding of the growth of a child's thinking in a content domain must be acquired.

THE 2 SIGMA EFFECT AND THE SEARCH FOR METHODS OF INSTRUCTION

Bloom (1984, 1995) described three methods of instruction: (1) conventional—situations in which you have about thirty students per teacher and periodic formative tests are given for grading the students, (2) mastery learning—situations in which you have thirty students per teacher and some formative tests are given along with additional tests to assess mastery, and (3) tutoring—situations in which a student learns a subject via a tutor on a one-to-one or (at most) one-to-three basis followed by formative tests, feedback, corrective procedures, and follow-up tests to assess mastery. Comparing the three methods of instruction, Bloom found that the average student under the tutoring condition scored about two standard deviations (2 sigma units) above the average control group class, while the average mastery learning subject scored about one standard deviation (1 sigma unit) above the average control group subject. Under conventional instruction, only about 20 percent of students reach the highest summative levels of achievement, but under the tutorial instruction, 90 percent reached the highest summative level and around 70 percent of the mastery learning students reached the highest summative level.

According to Bloom (1984, 1995), most students have the potential to reach the 2 sigma level when tutored. But the tutorial method is impractical and too costly to be applied to large numbers of students, so the question becomes, How do we attain these high levels of achievement using conventional, less costly group-based methods of instruction?

Barriers to Reaching the 2 Sigma Level of Performance

Bloom (1984, 1995) contrasted a set of alterable variables (quality of teaching, use of time, formative testing, rate of learning, and home environment) with more stable variables (teacher characteristics, measures of intelligence, measures of academic aptitude, personality characteristics of students, and socioeconomic status). The alterable variables differ in terms of how much each can affect learning. It is assumed that the 2 sigma effect is probably a result of combining two or three alterable variables. Although the combination of some variables has shown that achieving a 2 sigma effect is possible, exceeding the 2 sigma effect has not yet been attained. The research conducted by Bloom (1984, 1995) provides support for this view. However, trying to systematically examine and document the effects of more than one variable at a time can be complicated. How can students learn more effectively without having to greatly alter the basic conventional instructional programs? Mastery Learning when used in conjunction with conventional approaches to instruction has been found to increase the time spent on learning (Bloom, 1984, 1995). By combining some of the components of tutoring, students achieve a 1.6 sigma effect (standard deviation) compared to control group participants on summative examinations.

Improvement of Teaching

Teachers frequently direct their teaching and explanations toward some students and disregard others, and consequently 80 percent of students are reported to perform poorly in situations in which conventional instruction was used in contrast to what they could accomplish in situations in which tutoring was used as the means of instruction. In conventional instructional situations, many teachers encourage the participation of some students while discouraging the participation of others. According to Bloom (1984, 1995), students in the bottom third of the distribution receive the least amount of encouragement while those in the top third receive the most. Under one-to-one tutoring, students can receive more encouragement and reinforcement as long as the tutor remains actively involved with the student. To promote a more balanced treatment of students, Bloom recommended a number of teaching procedures that are likely to bear fruit: (1) look for explicit encouraging statements, (2) actively engage several students at the same time, (3) randomly choose a small group of students and ask them to provide feedback, and (4) supply additional advance organizers to enhance clarification. The goal, according to Bloom, is not to alter the teacher's method of instruction but to raise the teacher's self-awareness of the learning process. Increasing the teacher's level of awareness is expected to facilitate equal treatment of students. The results of a series of studies conducted by Bloom (1974, 1976) comparing experimental and conventional methods of instruction groups indicated that higher levels of sigma were acquired by (1) enhancing cues and participation (1.5); (2) combining cues, participation, reinforcement, and mastery learning (1.7); and (3) combining tutorial and mastery learning techniques (2.0).

Improvement in the Teaching of Higher Mental Processes

According to Bloom (1974, 1976), while countries such as Israel, Malaysia, and South Korea encourage the development of general problem solving skills, analytic skills, and creativity, many policy makers and teachers in the United States emphasize content. Bloom claimed that if the development of thinking and problem solving skills became more central in teaching, these higher mental processing skills (HMP) could be learned. The results of four frequently cited studies provide support for Bloom's claim. Tenenbaum (1982) found that when cue participation reinforcement was combined with mastery learning instruction, students on the HMP part of the summative examination performed 1.7 sigma units higher compared to a control group. In two separate studies in which HMP teaching was combined with mastery learning, the students on the HMP's part of the summative examination scored 2.0 (T. Levin, 1979) and 1.3 (Mevarach, 1980) higher compared to the low mental processing groups. In a study conducted by Burke (1984), it was found that when tutoring and mastery learning procedures were combined, the participants scored two standard deviation units higher on a combined part of a summative examination compared to the control group participants. Given what is described above taken in combination with the findings reported in recent meta-analyses (Cohen et al., 1982; Mathes & Fuchs, 1994; Shanahan, 1998; Wasik & Slavin, 1993) related to tutoring, a strong case can be made for the notion that educational researchers must continue to make an effort to find group-based methods of instruction that are as effective as costly tutorial learning instructional programs.

Improving Instructional Materials and Educational Technologies (Multimedia Learning)

In *Engines for Education,* Schank and Cleary (1995) connect cognitive science and technology and relate this connection to education and implications for effective structural change. It is Schank's belief that school reformers are headed in the wrong direction by focusing their efforts on policy issues and market-driven (business) approaches to educational reforms. He believes that today's schools are organized around yesterday's ideas associated with behaviorism and teacher-controlled instruction. He criticizes the economic focus of policy makers. A case is made for the view that it would be better and more effective to focus our efforts on the development and use of technology and our knowledge of cognitive science. These efforts may yield a 2 sigma effect. Through the combined use of individualized tutoring and technology, we may find that students can move two standard deviations in academic achievement (a 2 sigma effect) as opposed to a one standard deviation effect with a mastery learning approach. By trying to create an index of possibilities through the use of technology, Schank believes that the standard student–teacher ratio of twenty-plus novices (students) to one expert (teacher) can be converted to thirty experts (teachers) and one novice (student).

The plan would be for a student to be exposed to the views of many (30 in this instance) experts. A series (30) of computer-presented case-based views would be presented to the learner using video interactive technologies. For example, a student who was interested in the origins of the social, political, and economic tensions in the Middle East would have access to thirty or so video-presented expert views. These video presentations could include news clips from CNN news and interviews with world leaders and policy makers from the *Charlie Rose Show*. We need to develop highly generative and easily accessible indices connected to video-based archival materials that expose a student to the contrasting views of many experts on a selected topic. According to Schank and Cleary (1995) and many others (Azevedo, 2005a, 2005b; Mayer, 1997, 2001; Mayer, Moreno, Boise, & Vagge, 1999), this video-based, case-based, instructional plan has great potential for yielding a 2 sigma effect. This plan may be a means of using technology to yield what would only be obtainable (a 2 sigma effect) with one-on-one tutoring instruction.

Schank's viewpoint can be contrasted with the perspective Hirsch (1987) describes in his book *Cultural Literacy: What Every American Needs to Know*. He engenders a requisite standard core of knowledge for every educated person. Hirsch expresses great concern regarding Americans' cultural illiteracy and believes that a common, shared knowledge base should serve as the foundation for communication with one another. He believes that this standard core of knowledge is necessary in order for people to share information, ideas, and thoughts. To this end, Hirsch has created a series of books containing what he believes to be this core knowledge. He believes that the inequities of public education can be eliminated by focusing our educational efforts on establishing and developing within all people this standard core knowledge; subsequently the difference between socioeconomic groups will be diminished and educational opportunities will be equalized.

Schank and Cleary (1995) criticize Hirsch's (1987) definition of an educated person. Hirsch claims that the difference between the schooled and the unschooled mind is about two hundred pages of knowledge. According to Hirsch, there is a basic set of facts that constitute what an educated person knows. Schank opposes this position to some degree by pointing to the necessary context and background knowledge structures needed to make learning useful and meaningful. While Schank accepts the acquisition of knowledge as a necessary component of schooling, he claims that learning a basic set of facts is likely to be meaningless and useless without the provision of organizing knowledge frameworks (contexts).

Schank and Cleary (1995) disagree with Hirsch (1987) on the grounds that facts learned in isolation without links to existing knowledge structures and contexts are limited in meaning and not very useful. From a cognitive science perspective, the rote memorization of isolated facts must be supported through the acquisition of organizational schematic structures (knowledge frameworks). Schank makes a strong case for the use of technology in our schools. By individualizing education through the use of technology and increasing the ratios of experts and novices, Schank contends that meaningful contextual knowledge will be created. He emphasizes the use of case-based rather than rule-based instructional procedures. He uses the expert–novice views of the cognitive scientists to ground his recommendations for school reform. Schank emphasizes the need for and benefit of student-generated questions. In generating questions, students become actively engaged in the learning process. Generating questions is more difficult than generating answers. Learning is more authentic in question-generating situations.

Schank and Cleary (1995) claim that the solution to many of the problems facing education today is technology. Through the application of technology, we can recreate a natural (authentic) learning environment by allowing for individualized learning, question-driven teaching, and context-based instruction. It should be noted that authentic learning experiences often do not lend themselves to objective assessments. Studying and practice are useful, but the traditional grade-oriented system is believed to be of limited value. For the most part, today's schools have been designed around economic considerations and most reformers and policy makers focus their attention on standards and assessments. However, the significant improvements to be made may be related to developments in technology and cognitive science. The public education system as a whole, according to Schank, needs to be redesigned in order to develop experts rather than textbook-trained novices. He recommends that high-stakes testing be abandoned and that the assessment process be shifted from the schools to the "buyers" (the community) of the product (educated students). He also recommends that fixed curricula be eliminated and that the teacher's role be transformed from disseminating knowledge to motivating, challenging, and criticizing.

A SOCIAL LEARNING THEORY PERSPECTIVE

Albert Bandura (1997) constructed his theory of social learning in the 1960s to explain human behavior differently than previously described by others.

Bandura was very critical of the S–R models of behavior postulated by the behaviorists. He believed that these viewpoints are very limited. Bandura constructed his theory emphasizing the active influence and power of individuals to learn as they continuously and reciprocally interact with their environments. Behavior is thought to be determined by way of the observations of modeled behaviors and their consequences (Bandura, 1974).

Bandura (1977b) first employed the term "social learning theory" as he outlined his notions of the social influences that are involved in human thought and behavior. Nearly a decade later, he modified the language of the term to "social cognitive theory," reflecting his desire to highlight the cognitive processes that are thought to provide the mechanism for human actions (Bandura, 1986). Bandura envisions a learner's information processing capacity as a critical mediator of behavior. He also considers other intervening factors related to learning, including an individual's physical structure, sensory and neural systems, and level of maturation (Tudge & Winterhoff, 1993). Bandura has devoted a program of research to another crucial determinant of behavior (personal self-efficacy). This area of focus indicates that Bandura has continued to emphasize the cognitive factors that play a crucial role in learning.

Within the context of the social learning theory model, learning is thought to occur through the observation of models, and there is an emphasis on the capacity of learners to control their own behavior and act as principal agents with respect to their own behavioral changes. Individuals construct ideas of how new behaviors are performed as they observe modeled behavior, and later they use that coded information in memory as a guide for performance of the behavior. Bandura postulated that there are three ways in which human behavior is affected following exposure to a model: (1) entirely new behavior can be learned, (2) already learned behavior can be facilitated, and (3) already learned behavior can be inhibited or disinhibited.

From a social learning theoretical point of view, behavior is not governed by trial and error learning, and the individual does not have to overtly respond to the modeled behavior in order to have learned the behavior. In this theory, rewards and punishments for behavior are thought to influence the performance of the behavior by acting as a motivator, but they do not influence the actual acquisition of the behavior. In this theory, self-reactive and self-directive influences play a major role in human behavior.

As a theory of learning, Bandura's social learning model can provide an explanation for the components of the learning curve. The history of exposure to models provides a baseline for the curve. The pairing of observed modeled behavior and the representation of the behavior in memory allows for the acquisition of learning, which is maintained by an environment that supports the modeled behavior. Extinction of the learning can occur if there is a lack of model pairing.

Albert Bandura has engaged in a rigorous research program for the past four decades, with a strong desire to employ strict experimental controls in his examination of real-life situations. In his investigations of modeling and observational learning, he has documented effects on both the observer and the modeler of the behavior.

Components of Social Learning Theory

According to the social learning theorists, a great deal of learning occurs during commonplace situations as individuals engage in the causal or directed observations of modeled behaviors. Within the context of this theory, it is believed that the process of observational learning is identical across situations (i.e., if the modeling is in the form of live action, television, or a written communication). In addition to its effect on subsequent imitation of behavior, modeling can also be used to create novel thoughts and actions. Modeling is also capable of both inhibiting or disinhibiting already learned behaviors. In assisting individuals with attempting to change attitudes related to behaviors, an observation of the consequences experienced by the models can be very effective.

According to the social learning theorists, observational learning is governed by four processes (Bandura, 1977b, 1986). The first process involved in the modeling process is attention. Here the learner pays attention to the features of the object being modeled. A number of important variables are believed to affect the perceptions of the learner. These include the attitude of the learner toward the model, the way the model is treated in the environment, and the personal attributes of the model. Models perceived by the observer as higher in status, competency, and/or experience are more likely to be paid attention to by the observer. Observer variables also impact the attentional processes. The level of the observers' dependency needs, self-esteem, and/or the history of rewards given for imitative behavior are believed to be related to the attention directed to the modeled behavior. The number and types of models to which the observer is exposed are also believed to have some impact on the types of behaviors observed.

The second component of social learning is the retentional process, in which the learner cognitively encodes and organizes the modeled behavior in memory. Cognitive factors are believed to influence the observations and perceptions of modeled behavior, and determine the subsequent acquisition, retention, and expression of the behavior. Observed experiences are believed to be represented in symbolic form in the mind. Learners are thought to use verbal and/or visual imagery codes to assist them in retrieving the information as they attempt to reproduce the behavior. Mental rehearsal or overt perform-ance of the behavior impacts subsequent recall of the behavior from memory.

The third component of social learning is the reproduction process compo-nent. Here the learner converts the cognitive representations of the behavior into actions and performs the newly acquired behaviors. In order to success-fully reproduce the behavior, the learner must have acquired the skills neces-sary for its performance. Self-corrective feedback and information feedback from others regarding the performance can help the learner refine his or her behavior.

The fourth component of social learning is believed to be a set of motiva-tional processes that differentially increase or decrease a learner's likelihood of overtly displaying a modeled behavior. Although reinforcement as a moti-vational process is not considered to be a necessary condition for the modeled behavior to occur, it is believed to be capable of facilitating or hindering the overt expression of the modeled behaviors. Typically, when modeled behav-ior results in unrewarding or punishing effects, the behavior is discarded. When modeled behavior results in rewarding effects, the behavior is more likely to be retained.

Bandura (1977b) postulated that individuals anticipate the consequences of their modeled behavior, which influences the likelihood of their overt ex-pression of a particular behavior. Response consequences can take the form of immediately occurring external reinforcements, vicariously observed con-sequences, and/or personal self-reinforcement types of consequences. Exter-nal reinforcements influence nearly every kind of behavior, as the use of in-centives encourages human action. Vicariously observed consequences occur as individuals observe the outcomes of other people's experiences. Behavior can be both enhanced and inhibited by vicarious observations, providing a standard for judging whether the reinforcements one customarily receives are equitable, beneficent, and/or unfair. Self-reinforcement consequences occur as individuals set certain standards of behavior for themselves and respond to their own actions in self-rewarding or self-punishing ways. The develop-ment of self-reactive functions provides individuals with a capacity for self-direction.

Reciprocal Determinism and the Self-System of Human Agency

In explicating his theory of social learning, Bandura highlighted the continu-ous reciprocal interaction of mediating factors that influence human behavior. The three fundamental factors that are thought to interconnect as humans act include behavioral components, cognitive components, and environmental components. These factors comprise what Bandura calls triadic reciprocal determinism in the explanation of human behavior (Bandura, 1978). He claimed that reciprocal determinism is a critical principle related to the understanding of psychosocial functioning. In connection with this principle, he noted the continuous bidirectional effect of human behavior, human cognition, and the environment on intrapersonal development, interpersonal transactions, and organizational and social systems.

The Concept of Self-Efficacy

According to Bandura, one specific mechanism of the self-system that underlies behavior and plays a central role in the exercise of personal agency is the internal process of self-efficacy. Bandura emphasized the role of self-efficacy as a significant determinant of human thought, emotion, motivation, and behavior (Bandura, 1977a, 1991). Self-efficacy involves the individual's judgment of his or her own capabilities, as well as the resultant effect on motivation and behavior. "Perceived self-efficacy is defined as people's judgments of their capabilities to organize and execute courses of action required to attain designated types of performances. It is concerned not with the skills one has but with judgments of what one can do with whatever skills one possesses" (Bandura, 1986).

Perceived self-efficacy is thought to exert its impact on human functioning in four major ways: cognitively, motivationally, affectively, and by way of a set of selection processes (Bandura, 1992). Bandura has also discussed the effect of perceived self-efficacy on memory functioning by way of these four processes (Bandura, 1989).

Self-efficacy is thought to influence a number of variables involved in human action, including whether individuals initiate coping behaviors, how much effort will be expended, and how the effort that will be sustained in the face of obstacles and aversive experiences (Bandura, 1977a). When individuals persist with their efforts and subsequently experience mastery with activities that are threatening but relatively safe to initiate, enhancement of self-efficacy occurs. Four principal sources of information have been found to influence an individual's expectation of self-efficacy: performance accomplishments, vicarious experiences, verbal persuasion, and physiological states (Bandura, 1977a).

Bandura (1984) noted that individuals who regard themselves as highly efficacious act, think, and feel significantly different from those who perceive themselves as inefficacious. The results of empirically based studies have indicated that people who perceive themselves as inefficacious in wielding control over potentially aversive events view such events anxiously, conjure up possible injurious consequences, and display phobic avoidance of them (Bandura, 1983). In contrast, the higher the level of induced self-efficacy, the higher the efforts and performance accomplishments of the learner (Bandura, 1982). The relationship between the judgment of self-efficacy and behavior is seen as individuals tend to avoid circumstances that they consider beyond their own capabilities but willingly undertake and perform activities that they judge themselves to be capable of managing (Bandura, 1977a). An accurate appraisal of one's own capabilities is believed to have a significant impact on behaviors, thought patterns, and emotions, including levels of psychological coping and physiological stress reactions, levels of resignation and despondency to failure experiences, types of achievement strivings, growth of intrinsic interests, and career pursuits (Bandura, 1982).

Social Learning Theory and Education

There is great utility associated with Bandura's social learning theory with respect to its ability to induce a tutoring revolution. Much of school learning occurs in a social context, as students observe and imitate models as they attend to lectures, work cooperatively in groups, read, and use audiovisual aids for learning.

Teachers can employ the four processes (attention, retention, reproduction, and motivational processes) highlighted in social learning theory in their instructional practices within tutoring and other school settings. It is important to verify that students are paying attention as they learn. Teachers who are perceived by students as competent and experienced may command more attention from students than those perceived to be lower in status. In order to enhance retentional processes, learners can be assisted to effectively encode and organize their learning into memory. Verbal and visual imagery codes aid students in subsequent memory retrieval attempts. Students can be encouraged to mentally and overtly rehearse learning to enhance retention of the learning. In the behavioral specification of learning activities, teachers can provide consistent corrective feedback regarding student performance. Because motivational processes are necessary for the learner to adopt the modeled behavior, response consequences can be provided in the form of external rewards, vicariously observed consequences, and the encouragement of personal self-reinforcement.

Bandura's discussion of the self-regulatory processes of behavior within the social learning framework is also applicable to educational settings (Bandura, 1978). Students can observe their own performance by keeping records of their academic progress and conducting continuous self-evaluations related to multiple outcome measures. Students can judge their performance

according to educational standards and then determine appropriate consequences of their learning behaviors. Teachers can assist learners in the
process of self-regulation. They can verify that students are accurately monitoring their progress and establish contingencies in the classroom for behavioral changes. The control of these contingencies can be transferred to
the students with the gradual withdrawal of the extrinsic contingencies used
to initially shape behavior.

The concept of self-efficacy in social learning theory is believed to be
highly useful in educational settings. Bandura (1993) postulated that there are
three different levels at which perceived self-efficacy contributes to academic
development. First, students' beliefs in their ability to regulate their own learning and master academic activities determines their level of motivation and academic accomplishments. Second, teachers' beliefs in their ability to motivate
and promote learning affects their creation of academic learning environments,
impacting the students' level of academic progress. Third, the schools' level of
achievement is influenced by the faculty's belief in their collective instructional ability. Zimmerman, Bandura, and Martinez-Pons (1992) studied the effect of self-efficacy beliefs and academic goals on academic attainment. Subjects' beliefs in their ability to regulate their own learning affected their
perceived self-efficacy for academic achievement, which influenced the academic goals set for themselves and their final academic achievement.

MENTORSHIP

History of the Concept of Mentorship

The concept of mentorship has attracted considerable interest in a number of
disciplines, particularly in the past decade. This concept has historical roots in
the Greek myth of Odysseus, credited to Homer. In the *Odyssey,* Ulysses en-
trusts his valued friend and adviser, Mentor, to care for his son while he travels
the world for ten years. From this tale, qualities of a mentor have come to include that of a guide, protector, tutor, adviser, teacher, and friend (Fields, 1991).
The protégé or mentee is the person under the mentor's care and protection.

Although the empirical study of mentorship has been conducted since the
1970s in various disciplines, wide variety exists regarding its conceptualization. There is no widely accepted definition of the concept, nor is there a
widely accepted theoretical basis for it. One comprehensive definition presented in the literature by Yoder (1990) states that "mentoring occurs when a
senior person (the mentor) in terms of age and experience undertakes to pro-

vide information, advice, and emotional support for a junior person (the protege) in a relationship lasting over an extended period of time and marked by substantial emotional commitments by both parties. If the opportunity presents itself, the mentor also uses both formal and informal forms of influence to further the career of the protege."

Jacobi (1991) reviewed the literature from three different disciplines and highlighted fifteen definitions of mentorship, noting that many of these definitions revolve around the functions and roles of the mentor. Fifteen mentoring functions are consistently reported in the literature. Three primary components of mentorship extrapolated from those functions include (1) sponsorship of academic development, (2) psychosocial support, and (3) role modeling.

Issues Related to Mentorship

Madison, Watson, and Knight (1994) noted a number of key criteria necessary for an individual involved in a mentoring relationship, including a generosity of time, a willingness to learn, a sensitivity and ability to trust, an uncompromising intellectual rigor, a spirit of praise and encouragement, and an openness to another's limitations and imperfections. The mentor must believe in the mentee, recognize the potential of the mentee, and encourage the mentee's academic development and aspirations for the future.

Donovan (1990) cited other components of mentorship, stating that the mentor must feel a sense of responsibility for the mentee and provide assistance in both the cognitive and affective domains of the mentee's development. He cited three requirements of the mentorship relationship (attraction, affect, and action). The mentee should be attracted to the mentor with admiration, respect, and a desire to emulate the mentor. The mentor should be attracted to qualities in the mentees that are capable of being developed. The mentor and mentee should have positive feelings toward each other, as a significant amount of time and energy is invested by both the mentor and mentee in the relationship.

There are many issues regarding the concept of mentoring that have not been resolved since the systematic study of mentoring was initiated over two decades ago (Jacobi, 1991). One of these is the typical or recommended age difference between the mentor and mentee, with some suggesting that on average, the mentor is ten years older than the mentee. Another issue is the typical or recommended duration of time required for the mentoring relationship to solidify, with some suggesting that the average relationship endures from as little as one to as long as ten years. The typical or recommended quality of the mentoring relationship is also not as yet determined, although some suggest that the relationship is voluntary, serious, mutual, and nonsexual in nature. The question of the role and/or importance of gender or ethnic similarity between the mentor and mentee also remain unresolved. Additionally, the need and effectiveness of formal mentoring programs for those involved in mentorships has yet to be determined. Finally, estimates of the prevalence of mentoring and the availability of mentors are not yet available in the literature.

Many issues involved in the concept of mentoring have, however, been accepted and documented by empirical study (Jacobi, 1991). There is little disagreement in the literature that mentoring relationships typically focus on the achievements of the mentee, with the mentor providing assistance and support for the mentee to attain goals over an extended period of time. Also undisputed is that the mentoring relationship is typically reciprocal, carrying both positive effects and benefits for both the mentor and mentee. It is also widely accepted that psychosocial aspects of mentoring relationships involve direct interactions between the mentor and mentee. There is little doubt as well that mentors possess more experience and influence, and have greater achievements in the discipline than the mentee.

Methodological Issues

The study of mentorship is a relatively new area of scientific investigation. A review of its empirical study to date reveals a wide variety of methodological approaches and research designs. Many investigators have relied on retrospective correlational research designs in which data are collected at single points in time with limited, nonrepresentative samples (Jacobi, 1991). Self-report methods using questionnaires and interviews have been the major data collection techniques used to study mentorship. In many studies, inadequate controls for confounding factors are evident, and reliability and validity are not always firmly established in the measurement instruments, many of which are researcher developed. The descriptive nature of the studies has greatly limited the generalizability of the findings of many studies. The complex interactional, psychosocial, and longitudinal aspects of mentoring appear to have contributed to difficulties encountered with empirical measurements of the mentorship process.

Although researchers have systematically investigated the concept of mentorship for nearly three decades, much of the current literature related to mentoring focuses on a general discussion of the nature, benefits, and potential outcomes of mentoring without offering much empirical support for its use. Vance and Olson (1991) noted that researchers have employed exploratory and/or survey approaches to the study of mentorship, which is thought to be appropriate considering the relative infancy of the topic. These authors acknowledge that although there appears to be a popular consensus of what mentoring is, formal and/or operational definitions supported by empirically grounded data do not currently exist. Notably, there has not been a systematic, formalized study of the impact of gender, race, ethnicity, and/or culture on the mentoring process.

Theoretical Models

The literature regarding mentorship includes three theoretical frameworks that support the concept—Erik Erikson's (1963, 1968) developmental theory of the stages of man, Albert Bandura's (1977b) social learning theory, and L. S. Vygotsky's (1978) theory involving the ZPD.

Erikson's (1963, 1968) theory is often employed to support the concept of mentorship, since in this stage-dependent theory, the stage of generativity versus stagnation is postulated to provide an opportunity for mature adults to generate contributions to society with a concern for establishing and guiding future generations. It is thought that a significant contribution by adults to individuals within society can be in the form of mentoring a younger person. Around the age of forty, many persons cease to require a mentor and will themselves begin mentoring.

Bandura's (1977b) social learning theory is also invoked in support of the concept of mentorship. As noted previously, Bandura highlighted the significance of imitation learning. Role modeling is center stage. Role modeling is considered to be critical in mentoring situations in which the mentee incorporates the values and behaviors of the mentor through identification (Bidwell & Braser, 1989). However, Yoder (1990) noted a significant difference between role modeling and mentoring. In contrast to mentorship, a personal relationship between the model and imitator need not be present with role modeling. Additionally, although both role modeling and mentoring involve identification with another person, role model learning can occur by a more passive process, while mentoring is thought to be a more active process with engagement of both the mentor and mentee in the overall process of learning.

L. S. Vygotsky's (1978) theory appears to be particularly applicable to the concept of mentorship. This theory is described in greater detail in the paragraphs that follow.

L. S. Vygotsky's Theory of Cognitive Development

L. S. Vygotsky (1978) postulated that cognitive development progresses within a social context. He attempted to explain higher psychological processes including problem solving behaviors, and constructed his theory as a reaction to the preexisting explanations of behavior provided by proponents of behaviorism. In his theory, Vygotsky attempted to include both a natural science that explained sensory and reflex processes as well as a psychological science that explained higher mental processes. In his study of behavior, Vygotsky was interested in observing the relationship of the developing mind to society, rather than the attending simply to the performance and/or products of behavior. He wanted to identify components of psychological functioning, including the mechanisms of brain functions, the relationship between simple and complex forms of the same behavior, and the influence of societal contexts on behavior.

Vygotsky believed that human learners are active, vigorous participants in learning and that they act on and transform the environments in which they learn. He emphasized the impact of the background history and culture of individuals on their behavior. Vygotsky believed that the use of signs and tools (such as speech and language) within the cultural environment significantly influence the development of the mind. In his work, Vygotsky attempted to explore the science of the mind in a way that would apply to both education and practice. There is a great deal of research (Das & Gindis, 1995) that lends empirical support to Vygotsky's view of the overall learning process.

Vygotsky was very interested in the process of instruction and the related instructability of students in educational settings. He conceived of a ZPD defined as the distance between an individual's current cognitive developmental level, as determined by independent problem solving ability, and the individual's level of potential development, as determined by the individual's problem solving ability under the guidance of an adult or a more capable peer. Created in the course of a series of social interactions, the ZPD is defined as the difference between what a learner can accomplish independently and what he or she can achieve in conjunction with another, more competent person who possesses and can share the knowledge, skills, tools, artifacts, and technologies of the learning culture in which the learner participates. Vygotsky postulated that instruction is only useful when it moves ahead of the learner's current cognitive developmental level, focusing on the emerging functional capabilities of each individual. In this way, it is thought that instructional efforts will only be effective if geared to the level of potential development of the learner (i.e., that level just above what the individual can accomplish independently).

It is important to note that Vygotsky included the impact of maturational factors on development that set limits within which the social interaction of the ZPD can be effective. He made the following statements: "We say that in collaboration the child can always do more than he can independently. We must add the stipulation that he cannot do infinitely more. What collaboration contributes to the child's performance is restricted to limits which are determined by the state of his development and his intellectual potential" (Vygotsky, 1978, p. 209). As a mechanism for change, Vygotsky believed that instruction must (1) establish obstacles that will disrupt the learner's normal problem solving patterns, (2) provide many alternative forms of learning tools and data, and (3) provide tasks that are slightly too difficult than the learner's present level.

For Stremmel and Fu (1993), the notion of intersubjectivity, or mutual understanding, is critical to the teaching–learning process within the ZPD. Intersubjectivity refers to the construction and negotiation of shared meaning through conversational interactions among individuals. In order for teaching to be effective and learning to occur, the teacher must continually assess the learner's level of understanding in order to decide the most meaningful next step in the provision of learning assistance. An additional component of teaching within the ZPD as conceived by Vygotsky is the emphasis on the collaborative interaction that occurs within an activity setting—a learning experience in which there are opportunities for interactions and conversations among learners, and in which an emphasis is placed on the interactive processes that emerge within the context of teaching–learning process, as opposed to the independent contributions of teachers and/or learners. Activity settings also provide opportunities for collaborative interactions among learners and adults in the learning group. Within each activity setting, an equal partnership occurs as the result of joint efforts between teachers and learners.

According to Vygotsky (1978), the role of the teacher is to create opportunities for learners to perform at levels that they cannot achieve on their own. Additionally, teachers assist students in learning how to structure and manage their own learning. Clearly the ZPD exists in the process of the communications and interactions between the learning partners of teachers and students. Teaching within the ZPD involves assisting the performance of the learner, guiding the learner's participation in the learning task, providing a scaffolding for learners to build on, and participating in reciprocal teaching in which there are communicative interactions in meaningful learning activities. The teacher temporarily controls aspects of learning tasks and situations that are initially beyond the learner's abilities and gradually adjusts participation of the task, allowing for the learner to eventually assume full control of the task. Teaching within the ZPD is not restricted to the learning of task-specific skills. Rather, its purpose in a broad sense is to assist learners in problem solving through a collaborative instructional process. Because each teaching–learning situation is different and learners have different learning styles, teachers are encouraged to employ a repertoire of alternative teaching–learning strategies when teaching within the ZPD.

The teacher structures learning experiences just beyond the student's current level of independent functioning and provides assistance only at points within the ZPD at which the student's performance requires assistance. Stremmel and Fu (1993) stated that it is important for teachers to consider the personal history of the learner, which is believed to have a great influence on the learner's approach to the learning situation. In order to accurately and successfully assist in the overall learning process, the teacher must possess prior knowledge related to the student's current level of functioning and assess the learner's initial understandings and intentions in attempting a learning task and/or activity. As the learning process continues, the teacher must continue to assess the type and amount of assistance that are required to enable the student, through his or her own efforts, to assume increasing control of his or her performance. Eventually the learner is able to utilize strategies and/or skills on his or her own or with less adult (expert) assistance.

In the reciprocal model of teaching and learning presented by Vygotsky, Tudge and Winterhoff (1993) find it notable that both teacher and learner change in the course of their collaborative interactions. The learning process evolves over time as each person responds to the other's actions, and greater understanding is reached by way of the interactive processes of the collaborating participants.

Vygotsky clearly incorporated the essential elements of an individual's social interactions and experiences within family and community groups in his theory of cognitive development. He posited that the social systems in which individuals participate critically impact cognitive and affective development. He believed that the higher mental functioning of an individual originates in social, communicative processes. It was Vygotsky's position that the knowledge and skills necessary for learning and problem solving develop first in the context of social interactions, later becoming internalized and apparent in the independent activities of the individual learner.

According to Vygotsky, the multifaceted dynamic of the individual's historical and cultural background significantly influences cognitive development. He believed that the social and cultural institutions, technologies, and tools that are used to create learning environments influence the individual's interpersonal interactions, which in turn influence cognitive development. In this way, Vygotsky postulated that the social factors of history, culture, and interpersonal relationships act in conjunction with biological maturation to impel cognitive development.

According to Vygotsky, social role modeling, role playing, and the consistent use of symbol systems including speech are teaching methods that can be used to significantly impact learning. The teacher can use comments, questions, and actual demonstrations to enable learners to explore concepts and ideas in greater depth, reach new levels of understanding, and accomplish learning goals.

In activity settings discussed by Stremmel and Fu (1993), questioning is viewed as an important means of teacher assistance that can lead to meaningful and reciprocal interchanges and serve as a useful gauge of learning. Within the ZPD, mutual understanding between the teacher and learner is believed to be critical in order to determine appropriate and meaningful methods for learning. Teaching within the ZPD is not the same as formal instruction designed to teach narrowly defined academic skills. Nor is it the same as learner-centered instruction that encourages independent learning. In contrast, within the ZPD, teachers engage students in active learning activities while facilitating students' own pursuit of knowledge.

Ann Brown (1994) embraces Vygotsky's theory in her conception of the COL model of education. She envisions ideal learning environments as featuring a variety of activities promoting dialogue and facilitating interchange, reciprocity, and community among teachers and learners. Brown envisions appropriate learning opportunities operating within multiple ZPDs. Within these multiple overlapping zones, students learn by different methods and at different rates. She believes that individual differences among learners must be recognized and valued, as teachers continually encourage learners toward upper levels of competence. These levels continually change as learners become increasingly independent at successively more advanced levels. Four activities that Brown recommends to monitor current comprehension of the learners include asking questions, summarizing, clarifying, and predicting. In this way, Brown sees an essential role for teachers in the guidance of the overall discovery process involved in active learning. Her vision of ideal classrooms and learning situations are ones that foster interpretive communities in which there is active exchange and reciprocity of dialogue. Within these interpretive communities, both teaching and learning members are seen as critically dependent on each other, as there is a commitment to collaborative learning, joint responsibility, and mutual respect on the part of teachers and learners, as well as a sense of both personal and group identity.

Vygotsky's theory of cognitive development and his notion of the ZPD are considered to be a useful theoretical underpinning for the concept of mentorship. This theory involves the influence of people interacting with each other within a culture, employing the tools of the culture to assist each other in acquiring more complex and adaptive ways of thinking and problem solving. As individuals strive to gain mastery of the language and tools of a selected discipline, the personal interest of a caring and knowledgeable mentor allows for an engagement in the shared tasks of learning.

Vygotsky's theory provides us with a framework for those who act as guides and/or teachers in settings in which learners are able to actively participate in learning. These shared learning activities are believed to enhance both cognitive and affective processes among learners. The reciprocal nature of Vygotsky's theory, whereby both learners (novices) and teachers (experts) are viewed as participants in the overall process of development, is believed to be a critical component of the mentorship process. The mutual and guided learning that occurs within these mentorship experiences supports Vygotsky's belief that learning and cognitive development extend beyond the classroom into the broader COL.

A COGNITIVE SCIENCE–BASED EXPERT–NOVICE VIEW

Cognitive science–based expert–novice views (Ericsson & Charmes, 1994; Sternberg, 1998a, 1998b) of learning are not stage dependent. Considerable emphasis is placed on the importance of prior knowledge (the primacy of proactive interference). From this perspective, old learning greatly influences the acquisition of new information. New learning can be enhanced by using previous learning as an anchor, which can be remodeled and revised to incorporate (accommodate) new ideas and concepts. A mature expert learner is clearly not a blank slate. The cognitive scientist assumes that the learner has a set of perceptual and cognitive templates which permit the passive filtering of information and the active cognitive pigeonholing or classification of new information into existing schematic representations. Neo-Piagetians viewed the major constraint on learning to be attention that can be assumed to be more highly developed for an adult than for a child. The assumption is that mnemonic strategies, chunking strategies, and other metacognitive processes can be more easily learned by an adult who simply requires specific remediation in basic problem solving skills. This view is highly sensitive to the important role of experience in learning and the procedures by which a learner acquires expertise. Teaching the adult learner to build more advanced conceptual structures or schematic representations based on current or existing anchors would assist in the development of hierarchically arranged complex thinking and problem solving pattern recognition skills.

There are distinct differences between novice and expert learners, and these differences are reflected in the overall learning process. One very important difference is the volitional use of metacognition skills among the experts. In terms of a cognitive science model, an expert learner is likely to structure his or her learning environment so that information is more readily and efficiently taken in. The novice may not know how to do this or may not know how to create an effective learning environment in which to study and/or work.

Most learners can attend to 7 + 2 chunks of information (Miller, 1956). This number is believed to be determined early in life and is unalterable. An expert will have more content in each chunk compared to the novice learner. Expert learners know that there is a limit to what can be stored in short-term memory, and they have a good sense of what that capacity is. The novice, if he or she understands the concept, may misjudge the capacity limit. The expert learner finds a way to avoid memory overload through the use of performance supports, the use of capturing devices, and/or stopping the flow of information.

The expert learner knows to attend to and practice that which is to be learned. The external learning supports soon disappear. The novice learner is usually less alert and unable to attend to the complex details of a learning task. The expert learner may also be aware of performance support aids that can reduce the need for extensive memory encoding. The expert learner knows that these support tools must be practiced and automatized, or they will not be available for use. Novice learners may be aware of the need for performance support tools, but often do not recognize that they must be practiced and automatized to ensure their use.

Expert learners understand that information within short-term and working memories will disappear if not actively engaged and processed. The expert is likely to have a number of effective strategies for processing information (e.g., mnemonics, concept maps, recitation, and rehearsal strategies). Experts are aware that processing requires effort and active engagement of the information to be learned. Novices may expect information to passively flow into long-term memory.

The expert learner may explicitly or tacitly be aware of schema building, and that expertise is heightened by making connections between content modes in old and developing schematic representations. An expert learner's metacognitive search engine helps the learner find these open nodes and interconnects them. This process enhances retrieval, since there are more points to be recognized when new information is assimilated with old.

A novice learner may be willing to rely on a set of superficial anchors to develop new cognitive representations. His or her metacognition skills are not developed to the point that the learner recognizes holes in schematic structures, nor that the development of a richer set of schematic representations is possible. In designing instruction for expert performance, one can provide an "external" metacognitive brace of sorts by modeling the attributes of the expert performer. Experts are reported (Ericsson & Charmes, 1994; Sternberg, 1998a, 1998b) to perceive and represent problems in terms of patterns, while novices perceive problems in discrete, disjointed bits and pieces. The instructional designer can assist the novice learner by explicitly representing the "big picture" (but comprehensible) chunk of what is to be learned.

Expert performers know more and know it better. They have a fluent, well-organized knowledge base. Novice performers move to expertise by being exposed to a large amount of knowledge situated within digestible learning events. That which is learned is, therefore, not tacit but integrated into a series of authentically situated performance schematic representations.

Learning is designed to include many opportunities for practice and formative feedback in a range of situations that correlates with the range of options called for in expert performance. While this "for transfer" strategy is time-consuming, it does appear to be effective. The development of expertise requires considerable effort. Research (Ericsson & Charmes, 1994; Sternberg, 1998a, 1998b) indicates that it often takes ten years or more (the ten-year rule) to become an expert in a given domain-specific content area.

An aid to teaching for expertise is to reduce the initial memory load by making performance support tools (references, organizational materials, etc.) available to the learner. However, the novice learner must be taught to automatize the use of these support tools, or they will not be used to systematically solve problems.

Problem analysis is another transfer design device that is considered useful to teach, although weak. But experts have been reported (Ericsson & Charmes, 1994; Sternberg, 1998a, 1998b) to spend a great deal of time studying a problem before selecting an effective method to actually solve the problem. Novices tend to jump in quickly and often switch strategies, choosing multiple strategies apparently at random.

To teach expertise, it is recommended that you teach effective (domain-specific) problem solving solutions, problem analysis skills (what to look for, patterns of evidence), and propositional rules (provide opportunities for practice and continuous formative feedback, and don't allow practice without feedback, which can easily lead to mislearning which is difficult to dislodge). Also, team the novice with the expert mentor who is able to represent an expert model for solving problems. Unfortunately, many experts cannot overtly describe the problem solving activity and may not be the best teachers to the novice learner.

Experts are able to clearly frame a problem (generally in terms of recognized patterns of information), have a well-developed and automatized set of strategies from which to select, and have the metacognitive capacity to know when more information is needed to solve a problem. The novice tends to see the same problem as an overwhelming array of discrete information, and often does not recognize the true problem from the plethora of data, much less is able to select an effective solution. During the process of becoming an expert, the novice will learn a great deal of content, learn about the relationships within and among the content areas, learn a series of propositional solution rules, develop a set of metacognitive skills for monitoring what needs to be acquired or learned to solve the problem, and acquire the metacognitive skills to select effective learning events and environments. Finally, remember that it often takes ten or more years to become an expert in a given content area.

DO REWARDS UNDERMINE INTRINSIC INTERESTS?

Is the conventional view associated with the potential of rewards to undermine intrinsic interests in a task a reality or a myth? Abraham Maslow (1954, 1968) was a leading humanistic theorist who claimed that every human being has been created with a basic need for completeness and justice. We have the innate ability to successfully accomplish these goals even if we will be challenged by personal problems. Self-actualization can be achieved by allowing our natural, positive inclinations to lead the way. Similarly, Carl Rogers (1961) described self-actualization in the following fashion: "I would reaffirm . . . my belief that there is one central source of energy in the human organism; that it is a function of the whole organism rather than of some portion of it; and that it is perhaps best conceptualized as a tendency toward fulfillment, toward actualizing, toward maintenance, and enhancement of the organism."

The ongoing push to achieve self-actualization is the spirit which defines human learning and sets humans apart from other creatures. There is a remarkable power latent in every human being, a magnificent potential that is waiting to be utilized for outstanding accomplishments. If we recognize the gift that we have been vested with, we will have greater appreciation for our enormous talents and responsibilities. By harnessing our intrinsic characteristics, we can hope that we might realize "peak experiences," the "moments of ecstasy which cannot be bought, cannot be guaranteed, cannot even be sought" (Rogers, 1961).

Most of us would probably support the notion that our personalities are created by a delicate balance between nature and nurture. Part of a person's character is probably intrinsic and part is a result of training and environmental influences. Yet, regardless of one's character composition, a person has some capacity to determine his or her own behavior. The assumption is that freedom of choice exists in everyone. However, a person with certain character traits may be able to achieve something more easily than another. A person with certain other character traits may have a more difficult struggle with respect to

achieving goals. Our tendency toward self-actualization assists us in overcoming obstacles that block our paths. The positive nature of the human can
soar way beyond any impending attack of nurture.

In Western schools and workplace settings, the importance of individuality
is the message that most teachers and workplace trainers consistently emphasize (Cascio, 1995; Colarelli, 1998). There is even more urgency to place specific significance on this view in modern times. Mass production has spread
from industry to education and child rearing, with the result that individuality and creativity have been stifled to some degree by pressing the development of diverse personalities and talents into a single narrowly defined format. Mass education, particularly mass education efforts under the tutelage of
a single leader, is not considered to be conducive to the development of individualism. Every learner is considered to be unique with a set of special capabilities. From this point of view, society has the obligation to nurture the remarkable power in every human being toward individualized fulfillment and
personal satisfaction.

Schwartz (1990) reported that "reinforcement has two effects. First, pre-
dictably, it gains control of an activity, increasing its frequency. Second
. . . when reinforcement is later withdrawn, people engage in the activity
even less than they did before reinforcement was introduced." In a similar
vein, Condry (1977) maintained that individuals who have been offered rewards "seem to work harder and produce more activity, but the activity is of
lower quality, contains more errors, and is more stereotyped and less creative
than the work of comparable non-rewarded subjects working on the same
problems."

In contrast to the empirically based views of Schwartz (1990) and Condry
(1977), the most dominant layperson's view has been that rewards (reinforcements) create a sense of being controlled by others and reduce task interests and creativity. This view received considerable support from the work
of Deci (1975), Deci and Ryan (1985), and Lepper et al. (1973, 1975, 1985,
1989, 1996). That is to say that the use of extrinsic rewards is viewed as
smothering our potential for producing outstanding accomplishments. Our innate nature to achieve is trampled by the forces of nurture which are represented by enticing rewards. Being manipulated by others will decimate creativity and individualism. Clearly, if one is to fully accept the conclusions
associated with these conventional views, the impact on the field of education
would be enormous. Many teachers would desperately search for innovative
non-reward-based techniques to stimulate the educational process and to
maximize productivity.

Eisenberger and Cameron (1996) and Cameron and Pierce (1994) claim
that the "detrimental effects of reward" view stems from a basic flawed view

of human nature. Many (Skinner, 1973; Yankelovitch, 1972, 1981) believe that human happiness emanates primarily from the individual pursuit of self-discovery. Highlighting the primacy of the individual rather than the community made major inroads into Western civilization during the past century. Any structured system of rewards interferes with an individual's need for self-determination.

Eisenberger and Cameron (1996) and Cameron and Pierce (1994) reviewed the evidence related to the commonly held view that there are decremental effects related to decline in intrinsic task interests when extrinsic rewards are used to enhance learning. They reported that the results from one hundred studies which they examined revealed a "considerable diversity of results." The authors reported that the variability of findings was likely to result from one or more of the following conditions: the differences between rewarded and nonrewarded groups are small relative to individual differences within groups, the group differences are actually random variations from a true difference that falls close to zero, and/or the group differences are greatly influenced by the details of how the rewards are administered. Eisenberger and Cameron claimed that the decremental effects of reward occur under highly restricted, easily avoidable conditions; the mechanisms of instrumental and classical conditioning are basic for understanding incremental and decremental effects of reward on task motivation; and the positive effects of reward on generalized creativity are easily attainable using procedures derived from behavior theory.

Eisenberger and Cameron (1996) contended that the only reliable negative effects related to the negative effects of reinforcement on intrinsic interests and creativity are very limited. They claim that the negative effects occur only when the free time spent performing a task is assessed after an expected reward has been presented on a single occasion, without regard to the quality of performance or task completion. They concluded that any form of learning, including original thinking and creativity, can be effectively enhanced by the use of rewards. After a person receives a quality-dependent reward and then has the reward eliminated, he or she will generally continue to spend time on that activity. To some degree, Eisenberger's, Cameron's, and Pierce's views are congruent with Bandura's (1989) views. Bandura reported that a typical person who perceives that a reward is well deserved is likely to "maintain or enhance the perception of self-competence without undermining feelings of self-determination."

Lepper and colleagues (1973) offered young children the option to draw with felt tip markers. Most of the preschoolers gladly accepted the offer. At that point, the investigators randomly split the children into three separate groups. One group was notified that they would be rewarded for drawing a picture for a visitor. The second group became the surprise recipients of the same reward for their drawings. The third group was not rewarded for their artwork. Secretly, for several additional days, the investigators observed the preschoolers' free play activities. They reported that the first group spent about half as much time drawing with felt tip markers as the other two groups. Lepper claimed that the expectation of receiving an extrinsic reinforcer for a potentially enjoyable activity could significantly undermine intrinsic interest in the task. Slavin (1984) strongly objected to Lepper's generalization for several reasons: drawing with felt tip pens does not greatly resemble a common school task; children enjoy drawing at home but few (even those interested in regular school subjects) would independently study grammar, math, or science; and virtually all successful artists have been reinforced at some point for their efforts in artistic endeavors. Slavin reported that "the use of rewards more often increases intrinsic motivation, especially when rewards are contingent on the quality of performance rather than on mere participation in an activity." Our entire society, not just our educational system, is structured on a system of rewards and punishments. "We are constantly striving to elicit praise and encouragement from the people we respect. Few people work just for the fun of it; they expect to receive a definite reward for their efforts." An executive secretary's position depends on a high keystroke speed and a low error rate. A businessman who sells electronic components has a built-in commission that depends on his total sales.

Recent research indicates, according to Eisenberger and Cameron (1996), that offering rewards for successful creative performances can ultimately increase successful creativity in an entirely different activity. Success in one area breeds success in another realm. The self-confidence and reassurance that one gains from accomplishing a rewarded task will help facilitate the necessary development and personal growth to properly tackle other challenging settings.

It should be noted that Eisenberger and Cameron (1996), Cameron and Pierce (1994), and Slavin (1984) concur that it is desirable to rely on praise and other verbal reinforcements to influence children. A pat on the back and a smile, especially when given by an important individual, can be useful. A verbal boost in self-esteem and an inner feeling of satisfaction for a job well done is often more beneficial than a material reward. Of course, it is recommended that every instructor use verbal reinforcers to express clear expectations; provide clear feedback; offer immediate and frequent feedback; and praise in a contingent, specific, and credible fashion. Verbal reinforcers are considered to be a device used to enhance learning. Even when material rewards are used, they have been found to be most effective when they are administered intermittently; overrewarded learners lose their intrinsic desire. A basic goal of any teacher is to motivate students to be interested in the subject material. The teacher who has utilized material rewards to successfully inspire a student should gradually reduce material rewards and increase intrinsic rewards.

CONSTRUCTIVISM

Constructing a Room for Two

The constructivist perspective has a long history in education. Dating back to the French philosopher Jean-Jacques Rousseau, the progressive movement, humanistic education, the project method, the open classroom, and discovery learning, it has remained on the fringe. The mainstream, teacher-centered transmission of knowledge held court over the past century (1890–1980) (Cuban, 1990, 1998). The constructivist perspective includes a learner-centered, process-oriented, activist (both learner and environment transformations) viewpoint, with a focus on motivation, learning and remembering, and monitoring one's own comprehension (metacognition and self-regulation).

The outcome of the 1956 MIT symposium which gave birth to the cognitive movement in psychology and education did not refute the behaviorist perspective. It did, however, seem that the behaviorist's view was too simple to study language (Chomsky, 1972), and we now needed to enter the black box. The question about whether or not the methodologies are continuous across the behavioral and cognitive paradigms begs the question related to whether there was indeed a cognitive revolution (Rychlak, 1993, 1994, 2000).

From a cognitive constructivist's point of view, learners construct knowledge and remodel it; they do not just assimilate it. Learning is viewed as an active process. The social constructivists added the social situatedness and distributed cognition dimensions of learning to the cognitive constructivist's paradigm. In the 1980s, the cognitive science–based paradigm shifted to some degree from Piaget's boy on the beach counting pebbles to a social constructivists' view in which learning was believed to be socially situated. Knowledge was viewed as contextual. In the 1990s, the cultural constructivists added a postmodern cultural constructivist component that included valuing all cultures and their construction of knowledge, their multiple ways of knowing. Cognitive tools that are used to functionally extend the cognitive processing capacity limits of a learner include chunking (Miller, 1956), the use of mnemonic devices, concept maps, rehearsal strategies, and metacognition skills.

In the 1970s with the emergence of the computational view of learning (Newell & Simon's [1972] *Human Problem Solving*; De Groot's [1965] and then Chase's and Simon's [1973] work with chess players; and computer-assisted instruction advances), a shift did impact the cognitive constructivist direction of the cognitive revolution. In 1990, Jerome Bruner published *Acts of Meaning*. He questioned the role of the computational (or information processing) point of view and wondered if there was room for two ways of knowing (an information processing view taken in combination with a cognitive constructivist view).

Six years later, in his publication of essays, *The Culture of Education* (1996), Bruner stated that there was indeed room for two; this combined view including information processing and cognitive, social, and cultural constructivist components was a puzzle to be addressed and solved by students of epistemology. Those associated with the computational (or information processing) view made an effort to explain how knowledge is sorted, stored, and retrieved. Focus is given to the mechanical organization of knowledge and memory. Another way of knowing (culturalism) focuses on the human mind and its role in constructing meaning from symbols in a culture in which meaning inheres in symbols represented within that culture. Culture is superorganic but meaning resides in individual members of the culture. Meaning, communicating, and knowing are believed to be highly interdependent.

It is the different purposes inherent in two epistemologies (the computational and cultural) that Bruner (1996) sees as the puzzle. The computational view sees the purpose as one of explaining. Knowledge is organized, sorted, stored, and retrieved. Memory is likened to computer memory. In contrast, the culturalism (or meaning-making) view emphasizes the purpose as interpretation. It is fraught with ambiguity. Here hermeneutics, or text interpretation, comes into play. So we seek to find meaning (culturalism) in final outputs (computational). Bruner finds that there is room for two because one without the other is not enough.

A major influence on this current cognitive, social, and cultural constructivist view is the vast amount we have learned in the past decade about learning and knowing from the work done in the classroom. Bruner (1996) credits Ann L. Brown as a leading figure in much of the classroom-based research. Bruner visited the Oakland schools and witnessed fostering communities of learning in the classroom (Brown & Campione, 1994). There he saw the creation of exciting learning environments in which students constructed their knowledge. The students extended their knowledge capital with the use of technology, and they were self-monitoring their comprehension and progress in orderly and systematic ways.

Bruner (1996) identified four key elements within these learning communities: agency (students mindfully gauged their own knowledge acquisition), reflection (students reflected on their progress), collaboration (students used the resources of the mix of people available both in and out of school), and culture (students learned together and made meaning as members of a culture where communicating, meaning, and knowing were highly interdependent).

Brown and Campione's (1994) guided discovery programs in which COLs created and nurtured are firmly housed within the culturalism, or meaning-making, cultural psychology camp. When we look closely at these learning communities, we see that the information processing approach, along with the cognitive, social, and cultural constructivist components, are at the heart of what is taking place in these dynamic learning cultures.

Reciprocal teaching has become a commonly used cognitive science-based approach designed to enhance the comprehension of knowledge (Palincsar & Brown, 1984). This is a highly developed teaching and learning strategy that grew out of a desire to increase reading comprehension for low-achieving students. The guiding steps (components) of reciprocal teaching include summarizing, questioning, clarifying, and predicting. Teachers scaffold the strategy and eventually students take turns as instructoral leaders within small groups of learners.

The use of the RT method is a relatively small aspect of Brown and Campione's program of research in the Oakland schools. Other aspects of this research program include efforts to implement Dewey's (1972) pedagogic creed, Vygotsky's ZPD, Fish's (1980) interpretive communities, Aronson's (1978) jigsaw strategies, Slavin's (1990) cooperative learning approaches, and Bruner's (1996) spiral curriculum and intellectually honest curriculum.

Brown and Campione (1994) claim that their greatest strengths in these learning community programs are the distributed cognition components (Rogoff, 1990). They also cite a number of weaknesses. For example, limited knowledge capital appears to be present in many of these reciprocally taught classroom environments. Limited teacher competence is reported to be another weakness. Their complex and demanding role as a guide, facilitator, and coach is often challenging and new to many of them. Additionally, their training in the use of technology is often limited (for every $88 spent on computers, $6 is spent on teacher training; only one in five teachers is reported to be computer literate). Another weakness related to teachers is related to their position as critical thinking and problem solving models. Most teachers are not trained nor are they enculturated to view themselves as serious, disciplined learners.

In sum, the weaknesses seem to rest primarily with the teachers. Whether or not the cognitive revolution needs refreshing is addressed by Bruner in his 1996 book, *The Culture of Education*. He states that embracing both epistemologies is necessary for psychology's next chapter, "either-or won't do."

Both perspectives are necessary. The basic challenge is to move cognitive, so-cial, and cultural constructivist views from the fringe to center stage within the context of our efforts to reform schools and train our teachers in this con-structivist perspective.

Cognitive, Social, and Cultural Constructivism

As noted previously, from a constructivist point of view, learning is a process where the learner becomes an active constructor of his or her world, and in the process acquires knowledge. The learner is not a passive recipient of knowledge. The learner is active, strategic, self-motivated, and purposeful.

Social and cultural constructivists emphasize the important roles that social interactions and cultural contexts play in learning. Vygotsky (1962, 1978) talks of the learner within the cultural/social framework (a child learns by in-teracting with the people and things in his or her environment). As such, both play and language are believed to be critical in a child's development. Vygot-sky also stresses the importance of an expert/mentor guiding the child (a novice) from where he or she currently performs to the upper bounds with the assistance of people, materials, and artifacts (ZPD). Feuerstein, Hoffman, Jensen, & Rand (1985) agree that children learn through mediated learning experiences and that a child who is cognitively impaired is a child who is cul-turally deprived.

Hargreaves (1994) stresses the interactions and relationships in schooling and states that we don't need a restructuring but a reculturing of schools. He urges schools to develop more collaborations between teachers and principals and among other teachers. He also believes that schools should create sup-portive, encouraging environments to assist teachers to make positive changes. Emphasis is given to putting back the emotional content in our schools for both teachers and students (i.e., putting back the heart). Hargreaves has also urged educators to involve the communities in which they are housed.

Bruner (1996) sees culture as constantly being reshaped and renegotiated by its members. Reality is defined by a sharing of ideas—a communal shar-ing. Language is considered important for sorting thoughts and extending man's ideas across history.

Schools are part of a larger social framework within our communities. Brown's (1994) attempts to establish COLs within our schools which encul-turate multiple ZPDs is in direct response to learners being viewed as active, purposeful participants who strive to make sense out of their world. Students play the role of researcher while the teacher guides the discovery process. The teacher is always making an effort to help the students achieve the upper bounds of the ZPD. Cooperative learning, RT, and jigsaw procedures allow students to direct their own knowledge and meaning. And, as Slavin (1990) reports, cooperative learning allows students not only to build knowledge but also to gain understanding of individual differences, increase self-esteem, and add cooperative techniques to their repertoire of skills.

Cognitive constructivists emphasize the development of metacognitive skills which will assist a learner to derive meaning and hence knowledge. Most cognitive constructivists encourage students to dictate the topics of interest which will be studied knowing that motivation is key. Sternberg (1998a) emphasizes metacognitive skills for the processing of information yet also states that the meaningfulness of the material is critical if knowledge is to be gained. Banks (2000) urges teachers to teach students about how knowledge is constructed. They need to understand who determines what is studied in the classroom and they need to be able to differentiate personal knowledge, from popular knowledge and/or transformative knowledge. One way teachers can help students to understand this difference is by sharing their personal/cultural experiences and encouraging students to do the same. When Ogbu (1987) urges schools to concentrate on relationships among its students instead of a multicultural curriculum, he, like Banks (2000), is encouraging teachers and students to understand by sharing personal/cultural experiences. And when Takaki (1993) urges all schools to let the students see themselves within the curriculum, he appears to be encouraging knowledge and understanding through meaningfulness.

To discover and describe the meaning that human beings created out of their encounters with the world is to gain knowledge. Sternberg (1998b), Bruer (1993a, 1993b), Sizer (1997), and Bloom (1974, 1976) are simply suggesting ways to assist the process. After all, meaning is knowledge, knowledge is information. Teaching students a number of metacognitive techniques doesn't diminish the knowledge of the meaning. Trying to determine what teacher variables and home environment variables are alterable to bring about a 2 sigma effect among learners also doesn't diminish the focus given to the acquisition of domain-specific knowledge.

In *Engines for Education* (1995), Schank and Cleary stress the use of computer-assisted instruction in an attempt to make learning more creative and self-generating. Tailoring a program to an individual student's cognitive style doesn't detract from meaning or creativity.

Granted, current constructivist teaching methods/styles still need to be targeted for systematic study in an effort to determine their effectiveness. Many of us would probably rather see learning as a process of discovery with the learner considered to be an active, engaged partner with the teacher guiding the process rather than the perception of learning as a kind of passive, rote, repetitional drudgery many of us endured as primary and secondary school learners. We believe that cognitive, social, and cultural constructivist approaches to instruction can have a positive impact on schooling in the years to come. Meaning can be derived for the learner in all of its contexts. Isn't that the general organizing idea that was at center stage in a view of meaning and meaning making?

A Reaction to Bruner's Views of Constructivism

Cognitive constructivism refers to the mental processes that underlie observed behaviors. It does not reject the concept of behaviorism, but considers it to be too simplistic to handle the complex workings of consciousness. Within the concept of constructivism lies the belief that all knowledge is contextualized and all learning is socially and culturally situated. Knowledge and the mind that processes it cannot be separated from the social and cultural environment in which they have been created. Cognitive constructivists attempt to explain how meaning is made from our experiences in the outside world. Constructivism represents a major break from the behavioristic traditions of our past research traditions by focusing on the internalization process in which mental constructs are created.

Constructivism represents an active process in which the individual makes sense out of external stimuli. As noted earlier, Vygotsky (1962, 1978) is one of the most recognized theorists associated with the constructivist point of view. Vygotsky's theory is presented within the context of a socio-cultural-historical perspective in which the mind is viewed as being inherently social. He viewed education as the process by which individuals grow into the mental life of those around them. For Vygotsky, cognitive development occurs on two planes—intrapsychological and interpsychological. The intrapsychological demonstrates the emergence of new culturally valued skills acquired within the social interactions with others. A more highly skilled member of society (an expert) models the appropriate skills. The interactions are external at first. Then, in the interpsychological plane, cognitive development turns within. The mind is transformed as skills, problem solving abilities, and domain-specific knowledge are internalized. This process of internalization takes place in what Vygotsky refers to as the ZPD. The novice learner is led through the process of externalization to internalization by the expert guidance of a more skilled cultural member. The child's learning occurs within the ZPD as the child moves from his or her actual developmental level to the potential developmental level. Learning occurs within the ZPD The child's actual developmental level serves as a launching pad for the assimilation of new skills. The teacher or more skilled peer acts as the expert and is able to guide the child (a novice learner) to higher levels of mental functioning through questioning, designing appropriate activities, and modeling new skills. Language is believed to be the major cultural tool that influences the development of the mind. Thought and language have a reciprocal nature enabling ideas to be communicated, internalized, and remodeled. Language provides the link between external and internal cognitive development. Barbara Rogoff's (1990) theory rests on two main principles, guided participation and apprenticeships, both of which are closely related to and supportive of Vygotsky's basic constructs. The guided-participation component builds on Vygotsky's "more-skilled cultural other" principle. Guided participation is a process similar to the ZPD carried out within the context of dyads (e.g., mother–child, teacher–student, child–child dyads). One member of the dyad is a more highly skilled member taking the other through the process of a culturally valued activity. The gradual transference of responsibility occurs as the less skilled dyadic member progresses. Rogoff provides a carefully selected set of photographs in her book, *Apprenticeship in Thinking,* demonstrating the early entry point for the child within the cultural constructivist process. An apprenticeship is the construct that is used to demonstrate a special teacherlike quality in which novice learners continuously reevaluate their efforts. The mentor (expert) assesses in an ongoing fashion the needs of the learner and provides support for the learner's further development. Rogoff describes the personalized nature of the dyad interchange and the heightened awareness of the learner's developmental level and instructional needs. Rogoff's work is particularly important because it avoids two major pitfalls associated with popular views of child development. The first is to mistakenly view the child as a lone interpreter or discoverer, such as the one demonstrated by the little boy on the beach working on the skill of conservation (Piaget). The second is to view the child as a passive recipient of culture (as is sometimes the case of more simplistic interpretations of Vygotsky).

Bruner makes an effort to show how cognitive science can be the applied science of learning and teaching. Cognition is believed to be in a constant state of being remodeled. Jim Minstrell's (1982) benchmark lessons demonstrate this remodeling concept well. Minstrell applied cognitive development techniques to high school physics instruction. His students' preconceptions about the subject matter influenced their understandings about physics. He led them through the process of constructing, deconstructing, and then constructing once again. He helped them break down physics problems into facets. These facets or elements were then used for a series of physics experiments in which hypotheses could be tested and new meanings could be created. The teacher questioned, challenged, provided a set of activities designed to encourage the students to dissect and remodel their thought processes. Learning was active, students were engaged, and the environment was supportive.

Palincsar and Brown's (1984) concept of RT offers another example of how constructivism can be applied directly in the classroom to influence cognition. RT is based on the dynamic use of expert/novice relationships within small-group learning situations. Through a series of carefully planned group-based learning activities, all learners (experts and novices) advance their knowledge base and/or skills. The reciprocal nature of the instructional arrangement is seen as the less skilled members of the group become increasingly competent and develop a deeper understanding of the domain-specific content knowledge targeted for study. The most knowledgeable members of the group are given opportunities to take on the teaching or a more expert role to share their knowledge with those who are less knowledgeable.

McGilly's (1996) cognitive applications to classroom lessons demonstrate the highly specialized nature of domain-specific knowledge. She offers the right start example by Griffin, Case, and Sandieson (1992). A right start instructional situation involves something as simple as teaching the number line to first-grade students who come to school without the specific prior knowledge needed for success in the areas of mathematics. It recognizes the variety of entry point levels that children bring with them to school and demonstrates the highly effective intervention strategy of capitalizing on the specialized way students learn content in differing domains. McGilly's example shows how a student's prior knowledge can impede or enhance learning.

Linda Darling-Hammond (1997) discusses the special qualities of expert teachers as they attempt to enhance the cognitive abilities of their students. Teachers have been encouraged to use a number of cognitive science-based techniques such as the creation of two-way pedagogies; offering students more choices; designing instruction that can accommodate multiple entry points; making an effort to create learning environments in which there is a greater learner-centered/teacher-centered balance; establishing cooperative modes of learning and instruction; utilizing shared decision making activities; and creating schools in which teachers and students reflect on their learning activities. Information processing (IP) models of instruction are designed to focus on how humans acquire, store, and retrieve knowledge. The mind is viewed as being similar to a computer. IP models focus on the constructs of attention, perception, learning, and memory. Cognition is associated closely with memory. Input from the environment enters the sensory register. Short-term memory (STM) serves as a temporary storage place for information. The assimilation and accommodation processes associated with working memory

(WM) are considered crucial to the overall learning process. The concept of chunking (7+2/-2) shows the limited and important nature of information in the STM and WM. Long-term memory is often associated with the number and quality of connections. The greater the number and quality of connections, the greater the chance for retrieval. The importance of rehearsal in enhancing memory is seen in the demonstrations of the primacy and recency effects associated with memorization and exposure in recall. The use of schema-activating strategies such as advance organizers and mnemonics can greatly increase learning. Learning to learn is closely associated with an information processing view.

In conclusion, we agree with Bruner that the cognitive scientists have made numerous contributions to the field of learning theory and teaching. The cognitive, social, and cultural constructivists continue to demonstrate new cognitive applications for the classroom. A balance among all of these views appears to be essential for informing and supporting good instructional practices in years to come. We are not sure we would call it a cognitive revolution. To us what has taken place during the past three decades is more of an evolution, not a revolution, as an increasing number of cognitive, social, and cultural constructivist experts have guided us in our efforts to apply learning theory to teaching as well as tutoring.

A Postmodern–Neomodern Methodological Perspective

Modernists are characterized by their quest for representational truth, need for prediction, and belief in metanarratives. The hope for a knowledge that will advance science. Modernists' goal for science is to create order and understanding out of chaos. In contrast, postmodernists (PMs) deny a classical one-to-one correspondence between truth and reality. They view the world as an indeterminate place and attack positions of privilege. They question rationality and the use of metanarratives, favoring local knowledge over systemic understanding. PMs reject the concept of a grand theory and eschew large-scale studies. PMs challenge modernists on three assumptions: that knowledge is primarily the property of the individual, that science will eventually solve mind world problems, and that knowledge is the product of a foolproof inferential system.

Eisner (1997, 1998) offers a PM approach to conveying how we know what we know. Typically this is done through story, but of course meaning can be conveyed through diagrams, maps, art, poetry, films, and so on. The officers of the American Educational Research Association have recently sanctioned the exploration of alternative forms of data representation. Individuals who advocate alternative forms of data representation (AFDR) recognize the variety of ways in which our experiences can be coded and described. There is a need to transfer knowledge from private representations to public representations as demonstrated in, for example, the films *School Colors* and *Dead Poets Society*. These AFDR examples show us how research can depict rather than describe reality. From Eisner's point of view, research can echo the arts (i.e., arts-based research methodologies).

A number of positives can be associated with the use of postmodern (arts-based) research methodologies:

- Enhances empathy
- Enables people and events to take on their distinctive personalities
- Provides for productive ambiguity and multiple interpretations

Of course, PM research methodologies are not problem free. The Rorschach syndrome may be inevitable in which everyone attempts to convey his or her own highly personalized meanings to the data, especially since there is often no scholarly interpretation involved. Also, some risk exists and is expected (similar to the arts). Some forms of representation may be outlandish and/or bizarre. Finally, our publication system will be faced increasingly with the dilemma of how to disseminate alternative forms of data representation. They are simply not equipped to effectively manage this challenging task.

It is not our opinion that postmodernism is eroding the scientific methodological foundations of psychology. We believe that a mixed-methodological and balanced perspective is required to integrate the research traditions from our past with important PM directions for our future. Both perspectives are required to create a balance. In many respects, a PM perspective does not represent a break from the past but rather an evolution toward issues that were not effectively addressed by past traditions.

Gergen (1994) reported that the major distinction between modernism and postmodernism is our abandonment of traditional forms of data representation. He suggested a balanced methodological perspective that would place research in a broader, moral context. He stated that this can be accomplished through increased advocacy (psychology's ability to speak to moral issues) and broadened theoretical views (an ability to speak beyond our data). Smith (1994), who often bashes Gergen, is not far removed from the same point. Brewster-Smith calls for a balance in the field of psychology which can accommodate PM relativism and uphold high standards in research.

The ultimate goal of science is to increase learning. Consilience (Wilson, 1998) is an approach to be considered when facing this task. The dream of a unified learning theory and a greater understanding of the human can only be found by unifying our methodological approaches. This balanced perspective is expected to bring about greater cohesion in all branches of psychology.

Always Question Authority

In discrediting postmodernism as a separate movement from modernism (economic globalization), Callinicos (1997) defines aspects of postmodernism as denying truth as related to reality; denying metatheory; devaluing science; denying metanarratives; eschewing large studies; preferring a local scope (perspective); questioning any prevailing truth stemming from hegemony; fragmentation; ambiguity; depthlessness; pursuit of multiple and simultaneous perspectives (e.g., Warhol's soup cans or his multiple depictions of Marilyn Monroe).

E. O. Wilson (1998) describes postmodernism as the antithesis of the Enlightenment in which believers felt that we must know. PMs contend that we cannot know. As all movements tend to the extreme, Wilson describes postmodernism as extragent constructionism (i.e., each one constructs one's idea of reality). There is no truth, only the prevailing truth of the ruling social group. Power corrupts. Knowledge is power. Knowledge corrupts. And yet Wilson says (if he could talk to the dead) to Michel Foucault, "It's not so bad." Eisner (1997, 1998) and Constas (1998a, 1998b) concur.

In his 1997 *Educational Researcher* article, Eisner describes some alternative forms of data representation as having empathy, having a narrative focus, and being highly personalized. Additionally, in "Arts-Based Educational Research," Barone and Eisner (1997) add expressive language (i.e., the thick description of Geertz), aesthetic form, and the "local" use of language to the mix. Some of the weaknesses of alternative forms of data representation include the Rorschach effect, in which everyone sees his or her own conclusions (some forms may tend to be bizarre, and there are format limitations).

Constas (1998a, 1998b) sees postmodernism as having a decided impact on educational inquiry. He cites three areas that are affected, including methodological patterns tending to favor qualitative or narrative studies, summative content where conclusions are ambiguously drawn (if at all), and a disciplinary shift with a leaning to humanities-infused research base.

To the chagrin of the PMs, Constas (1998a, 1998b) sees a metanarrative developing. The political agenda of decentering and deconstructing and the constraints of rejecting metanarratives combine to form the postmodern dimensions of educational research. These dimensions include a concentration on developing methodological patterns, a political agenda, and a focus on a representational format.

An example of a postmodern alternative form of data representation taken from popular culture is Edmund Morris's (1998) authorized biography of Ronald Reagan. Morris conducted thirty-nine interviews with Reagan over fourteen years. He created eight yards of five-by-eight index cards full of factual documentation. During a writer's block in 1992, Morris visited Eureka College, Reagan's alma mater. As he stepped on an acorn he stated that he wished that he could have been there with Reagan in 1928. He decided then to write himself into the biography as a fictional character. He also gave himself a fictional son who was on campus in 1969, when Reagan called out the National Guard. For the final nail in his coffin (if you side with the modernists), he wrote the biography in the style of a movie script which Morris felt most accurately depicted the former movie star's life (i.e., he felt that Reagan lived his life like one long movie script).

Morris (1998) was nailed to the wall, mostly by Reagan's cronies, who were expecting a "factual" biography. *Dutch: A Memoir* is that, but Morris's blurring of genres and nonconclusions (Reagan remains a mystery to him) infuriates many of Reagan's contemporaries. *Newsweek, 60 Minutes, Larry King*—the full media catastrophe (to paraphrase Zorba)—took their shots at the controversy. We can only wait to see if the veracity of his extensive sources will prevail over time.

Another example of text that we can use to distinguish between the modernist and PM perspectives is this text. As a reader, do you consider what you are reading now as a representation of the authors' knowledge base or that of Derrida? "Is there nothing outside the text?" Here we side with the modernist view. Each perspective has a place in educational research.

Wilson's (1998) definition of postmodernism as a movement begs the question of its role in educational research. Wilson feels that there will always be a place for PMs, as for their counterparts, for how to strengthen organized knowledge and defend it from outside forces. Gergen (1994) discussed the importance of creating and maintaining a methodological balance. He stated that it would be a mistake to dismiss postmodernism's precursors; we must acknowledge PMs' impact on educational inquiry. In *The End of Education*, Postman (1995) quotes Nobel Prize–winning physicist Niels Bohr, "The opposite of a correct answer is an incorrect answer but the opposite of a profound truth is another profound truth." We need to educate our students to comfortably hold contradictory ideas in their minds and seek the truth therein. We do not believe that modernists are passive and/or transmissive, that Hirsch-esque core knowledge leads us on this passive and transmissive road. Likewise, we question if the Gardner-esque education for understanding adequately provides a firm foundation of domain-specific knowledge from which one can develop into an expert. Much more research is needed in the laboratory and especially in the classroom (Brown, 1994; Darling-Hammond, 1997) before anyone in the educational research community can feel comfortable with a single form of educational inquiry. Both empirical and narrative methods of inquiry occupy secure positions in the educational research community. As postmodernism evolves, gives way, becomes established and is deconstructed and constructed, the next chapter in educational psychology will be written. It will certainly include multiple perspectives. We need to train ourselves to hold contradictory ideas comfortably in our minds as we continue to infuse psychological perspectives into the classroom, as we passionately continue to improve all forms of education including tutoring.

5

Tutoring Research

A CRITICAL EXAMINATION OF
EVIDENCE-BASED EDUCATIONAL PRACTICES

Historic changes in education are currently under way. Schools are being subjected to extreme scrutiny and pressure to demonstrate to state and federal departments of education that they are indeed improving student achievement. Schools that fail to demonstrate student improvement may lose funding or, worse, be shut down completely. Much of this increased pressure is the result of the passage of the No Child Left Behind Act of 2001.

Education is also coming under a high level of scrutiny as a field of study. The No Child Left Behind Act contains repeated references to the promotion of evidence-based practices in terms of practices that have demonstrated, through intensive study, proof that they are effective. Included within the evidence-based doctrine is significant mention of science as it relates to what the federal government considers to be valid methodologies for studying problems in the field of education. Some researchers in the field have argued that what the federal government considers science focuses solely on quantitative methodologies while forsaking other qualitative and arts-based methods of inquiry.

Are the evidence-based practice policies now being pushed by the federal government a threat to the use of alternative forms of data representation and the insider (teacher) research movement? In this chapter, a critical evaluation of evidence-based practices will be presented. A general definition of science as delineated by federal policies will be used as a framework in which to present the argument that research methodologies in education and related fields should be considered along a quantitative-to-qualitative continuum with equal consideration given to all methods of disciplined inquiry. Detailed discussions of the characteristics of the insider (teacher) research movement, alternative forms of data representation, and the creation of functional learning environments with be included. Finally, an effort will be made to discuss what can be done to ensure that educational researchers, including doctoral students, acquire and maintain their identities as they join others to form communities of learners and researchers who advocate for evidence-based educational practices.

In this chapter, we present a broad, comprehensive, empirically derived perspective related to what we know and don't know about tutoring. We try to link theories, research, and practice together in a coherent, internally consistent manner, to form a basis for recommendations and/or strategies. We focus on integration of theories, research findings, and practices; a comprehensive and objective review of the extant literature related to tutoring; and a comprehensive review and critical analysis of the knowledge structures related to tutoring that have been documented using empirically based and more inclusive and broadly based qualitative disciplined methods of inquiry that might help support the tutoring revolution.

CONNECTIONS BETWEEN TUTORING AND THE NO CHILD LEFT BEHIND ACT: THEORIES; RESEARCH FINDINGS, AND PRACTICE POTENTIAL

Recent Developments in National Educational Policies

At the beginning of the twenty-first century, tutoring has emerged as a major public/private education phenomenon. Growing numbers of parents are looking for qualified tutors to help their children learn. A *Newsweek* poll (Kantrowitz, 2000) reported that 42 percent of Americans believed that there is a "great need" for children to receive tutoring. Bear Stearns marketing analysts (Nadel, 2000) estimated that the parents of students in the top 5 percent and the bottom 15 percent of their class are most likely to seek tutoring services for their children. Annual expenditures for tutoring programs are now (2002) estimated to exceed $5 billion.

With increasing frequency, the public has been barraged with headlines such as, "Does Your Child Need a Tutor?" a *Newsweek* cover story. In an article entitled "Going One on One" published in the *Washington Post Magazine*, it was stated that "as parents worry about their children's ability to compete, tutoring is becoming a high-profile business. But will tutoring help transform the education system?"

We may soon find out. On January 8, 2002, President George W. Bush signed his new education plan, the No Child Left Behind Act, into law. This is part of the reauthorization of the Elementary and Secondary Education Act. Known as Title I, it is the largest federal funding program for the education of the disadvantaged. No Child Left Behind makes significant changes in the Twenty-First Century Community Learning Centers Program. Originally funded as a $1 million demonstration program, it will now receive $1 billion for after-school tutoring or academic enrichment services for school-age youths. The No Child Left Behind program is structured to encourage partnerships between schools and a wide variety of community tutoring/educational service organizations. This program will have an impact on virtually every school district in America. The passage of the No Child Left Behind Act, taken in combination with the recent U.S. Supreme Court decision (June 27, 2002) related to the constitutionality of educational choice, is probably the most significant educational decision made since *Brown v. Board of Education* ended school segregation in 1954. These two events are likely to boost both choices in schooling and the provision of tutoring services in the schools.

Tutoring programs that are research based offer obvious advantages for child and adult learners. No Child Left Behind calls for programs with "instructional strategies that are of high quality, based upon empirically anchored research findings, and designed to increase student achievement."

As the educational choice movement continues to gain momentum, it is important for public and private educators to offer carefully designed educational interventions based on empirically anchored research findings. There is no excuse for offering tutoring or other educational programs largely based on slick advertising and attractive but empty promises of success. We have only to look at the scandal-ridden U.S. proprietary postsecondary school marketplace of the 1970s and 1980s to find examples of blemished reputations that those associated with the design, implementation, and evaluation of professional tutoring programs need to avoid.

Literature Search

Three electronic searches (an ERIC search, a PsycINFO search, and a Dissertation Abstracts search) of the literature related to tutoring, mastery learning, and personalized systems of instruction (PSI) were conducted. The findings are summarized in tables 5.1, 5.2, and 5.3. The tables are categorized across time periods (decades) (60–69, 70–79, 80–89, 90–99, 00–04), educational interventions (tutoring, mastery learning, and PSI), mentoring, and the 2 sigma effect. In some instances, the findings are categorized to indicate the

Table 5.1. Summary of Findings Related to the ERIC Search

Decade	Tutoring	Mastery Learning	Personalized Systems of Instruction	Mentoring	2 Sigma Effect
60–69	3	1	—	—	—
70–79	346	320	79	32	2
80–89	1,450	743	133	821	3
90–99	2,045	660	74	2,754	2
00–04 (03)	707	136	19	1,420	2
Total	4,551	1,860	305	5,027	7

source (a book, a journal article, a thesis or dissertation, or a speech or paper presented at a professional conference). The numbers reported in the tables refer to the number of citations found in each category. An examination of the number of citations reported in each category provides us with selective sets of historical and knowledge structure frameworks that we can use to describe the research contributions related to tutoring over time.

Table 5.1 contains findings related to the ERIC search. Across time periods, the scholarly contributions related to tutoring and mentorship are numerous. In each decade, there is a large increase in the number of citations over time for both areas of study. The time line trends related to the number of mastery learning and PSI citations appear to be similar. There was a beginning of research activity related to these two areas of study in the late 1960s and early 1970s. A considerable number of contributions in the 1970s, 1980s, and 1990s was followed by a large decline after the turn of the century. The decline in scholarly activity related to PSI is particularly noteworthy. We were surprised to find so few citations related to the 2 sigma effect. Taken together, the findings reported in table 5.1 indicate that the scholarship related to tutoring and mentoring is thriving. However, the same cannot be said for mastery learning and PSI. There has been and continues to be a reduced level of scholarly activity in these two areas of study. Overall, the scholarly contributions related to the 2 sigma effect appear to be very limited.

Table 5.2 summarizes information related to a reconfiguration of the findings reported in table 5.1 into source of scholarly contribution categories (books, journal articles, theses or dissertations, or speeches or papers presented at professional conferences). Assuming that an area of scholarship is more mature if books are written and other scholarly products are created to describe and interpret what we know and don't know about it, tutoring and mentoring seem to be more mature areas of scholarship than mastery learning and PSI. Scholarly contributions related specifically to the 2 sigma effect are very limited at this time. The number of journal articles, theses and dissertations, and

Table 5.2. Summary of Findings Related to Source of Scholarly Contribution Categories

Decade	Tutoring				Mastery Learning				PSI				Mentoring				2 Sigma Effect			
	B	J	D	P	B	J	D	P	B	J	D	P	B	J	D	P	B	J	D	P
60	2	—	—	1	—	—	—	1	—	—	—	—	—	—	—	—	—	—	—	2
70	26	106	30	184	34	90	27	169	9	31	2	37	2	15	—	15	—	2	—	1
80	32	947	37	434	16	415	17	295	—	85	2	46	13	499	9	300	—	—	—	2
90	141	1,266	91	547	47	364	31	218	2	43	2	27	180	1,705	76	793	—	—	—	2
00	49	490	12	156	10	77	7	42	4	10	—	5	125	950	16	329	—	—	—	—
Total	250	2,809	170	1,322	107	946	82	725	15	169	6	115	320	3,169	101	1,437	—	2	—	7

Note: PSI = Personalized Systems of Instruction; B = Books; J = Journal Articles; D = Dissertations/Theses; P = Speeches/Meeting Papers.

Table 5.3. Summary of Findings Related to the PsycINFO Search

Decade	Tutoring	Mastery Learning	Personalized Systems of Instruction	Mentoring	2 Sigma Effect
60–69	—	—	—	—	—
70–79	328	—	96	4	—
80–89	508	97	53	150	—
90–99	675	125	25	676	1
00–04	277	61	13	670	—
Total	1,787	283	187	1,499	1

speeches and paper presentations follow similar trends across time periods and educational intervention categories.

In table 5.3, the findings related to the PsycINFO search are presented. There are no surprises here. These findings are congruent with those reported in tables 5.1 and 5.2. Perhaps the most important set of numbers contained in table 5.3 are the ones that appear in the bottom (total) row. Once again, based on the scholarly activity documented across time periods and areas of study, tutoring and mentoring are very active areas of scholarship compared to the other categories.

In an effort to further document the degree to which research is being conducted in each of the areas of study, the findings related to theses and dissertations were parsed out of the total data set. These findings are reported in table 5.4. Once again, the numbers reported in the bottom row (total) are the most compelling. Tutoring and mentoring appear to be very active areas of research productivity.

Table 5.4. Summary of Findings Related to the Dissertation (Dissertations/Theses) Abstracts Search

Decade	Tutoring	Mastery Learning	PSI	Mentoring	2 Sigma Effect
60–69	15	—	—	—	—
70–79	147	69	25	2	—
80–89	439	177	54	299	—
90–99	675	104	14	1,189	1
00–04	298	10	7	943	—
Total	1,574	360	100	2,433	1

Note: U.S. and Canadian search. PSI = Personalized Systems of Instruction.

Given the large number of citations found in the existing literature, it may appear as though we already know a great deal about tutoring. However, a close examination of the contents of these books and/or other sources of scholarship indicates that most of the information reported and described in these sources is not grounded on empirically based research findings. For the most part, the information contained in these works consists of a number of case studies, testimonials, and conceptually-based and/or policy-based descriptions.

A review of commonly used educational psychology textbooks yielded an average of only seven citations related to tutoring. The Berliner and Calfee 1997 edition of the *Handbook of Educational Psychology* (a highly regarded, comprehensive, 1,000-page volume of existing knowledge structures in educational psychology and educational research) contains descriptive information related to tutoring on twenty pages, but only four empirically based index citations. Most of the citations in these sources (the educational psychology texts in print and the *Handbook of Educational Psychology*) were related to Bloom's 2 sigma tutoring effect findings and descriptions of the research efforts to find group-based methods of instruction (e.g., mastery learning, PSI, and the use of technology) that appear to have potential to yield a 2 sigma effect.

Summary and Interpretation of Findings

What do we know about tutoring? In this section, we will focus our discussion on a selected set of scholarly contributions that we believe represent a representative and balanced view of what we know and don't know about tutoring. Does tutoring work? Under what circumstances does it work?

Educational researchers have focused most of their attention on the cognitive aspects of tutoring (time on task, attention, and level of difficulty) rather than the social aspects of tutoring (needs for affiliation, approval, and social status). Numerous studies have been conducted related to peer tutoring. The enhancement of positive interpersonal relationships among the participants has been clearly documented (Shanahan, 1998). Shanahan (1998) states "that tutoring works best when students have a clear feeling that the tutors are trying to help." Tutor empathy (Colligan, 1974), same-sex tutoring (Galen & Mavrogenes, 1979), and perceptions of caring (Kaiden, 1994) have been linked to tutoring effectiveness. In sum, there is evidence supporting the importance of the social aspects associated with tutoring. But a more fine-grained examination of the dynamics of the tutoring process is needed to describe the process.

As noted in table 5.5 and the historical context section of this book, tutoring has been associated with remedial instruction educational reform initiatives.

For the past few decades, an emphasis has been given to one-to-one tutoring for remedial purposes. This instruction is typically delivered by one teacher to one student. But as Shanahan (1998) points out, the teacher is seldom the student's classroom teacher. There are a few exceptions. For example, in some Reading Recovery programs and summer and after-school programs linked to Title I, the classroom teacher is the tutor but the instruction does not take place in the regular classroom.

From 1970 to 1985, emphasis was given to peer and cross-age tutoring. Researchers focused much of their attention on the tutor rather than the achievement outcomes of the tutee. In the 1980s research attention shifted to remedial instruction educational reform initiatives. Emphasis was given to evaluating these large-scale initiatives. Many of these remedial programs included a tutoring component, but tutoring was only a small part of the overall effort. Tutoring was assumed to work, and studies focused on the systematic evaluation of large-scale education reform programs, not the outcome measures associated with tutoring.

Table 5.5. Overall Analytic Paradigm

		Treatment Conditions						
Hours		Xa1 Individual Tutoring Groups		Xa2 Peer Tutoring Groups		Xa3 Computer-Assisted Groups		Xa4 Class-room Control Groups
	Xb1							
10 to 19	Academic Xc1							
	Social–emotional Xc2	Yb	Ya	Yb	Ya	Yb	Ya	Yb	Ya
	Job-related Xc3							
	Xb2							
20 to 29	Academic Xc1							
	Social–emotional Xc2	Yb	Ya	Yb	Ya	Yb	Ya	Yb	Ya
	Job-related Xc3							
	Xb3							
30 to 45	Academic Xc1							
	Social–emotional Xc2	Yb	Ya	Yb	Ya	Yb	Ya	Yb	Ya
	Job-related Xc3							

Where: Independent variables:
- Treatment conditions Xa1, Xa2, Xa3, Xa4
- Time blocks Xb1, Xb2, Xb3
- Type of intervention

Dependent variables:
- Academic, social–emotional, and job-related pre- and posttest outcome measures
- Triangulation of quantitative and qualitative tutee, tutor, employer, and peer evaluations of tutoring outcomes

Historical Context

1960–1970	Efforts were made to document the effects of tutoring (Carroll, 1963) and other instructional procedures (e.g., mastery learning [Bloom, 1984] and personalized systems of instruction [Keller, 1968]).
	Educational researchers focused their attention on the use of effect size yields to make comparisons among instructional interventions.
1970–1980	Emphasis was given to peer and cross-age tutoring.
	Attention was focused on the effects of tutoring on the tutor rather than the achievement outcomes of the tutee.
1980–2000	Attention shifted to remedial instruction educational reform initiatives.
	Emphasis was given to the evaluation of large-scale educational reform initiatives.
	Many remedial programs included a tutoring component, but tutoring was only a small part of the overall intervention effort.
	It was assumed that tutoring worked, but the focus of study was on the systematic evaluation of the large-scale educational reform programs, not the specific outcome measures associated with tutoring.
	Studies related to tutoring were conducted in many academic content areas. However, the major focus of attention among the educational policy makers was and continues to be related to reading instruction.
2000–2005	The No Child Left Behind Act contained mandates related to evidence-based educational practices.
	Focus was given to high-stakes testing and outcome-based educational reform initiatives.
	The provision of tutoring instruction continued to be included within the context of these educational reform initiatives. The tutoring component was a larger part compared to the previous decade but remained a small part of the overall reform plans.
	Researchers continued to focus their efforts on documenting positive outcomes associated with tutoring interventions.
	Reading instruction remains the focus of the educational policy makers.
	Research efforts continue to be directed at the cognitive aspects of tutoring (time on task, attention, level of

difficulty, etc.) compared to the social aspects of tutoring (individual difference characteristics of the tutees
and tutors and the complex dynamics of the instructional environment).

Studies related to tutoring have been conducted in many academic content
areas. However, the major focus of attention among the educational policy
makers has been related to reading instruction.

Given the very large number of citations we found in our electronic
searches of the existing literature related to tutoring described in the previous
section, a decision was made to select a manageable number of citations to
create this section of our book. We have relied heavily on existing research
syntheses of the tutoring literature. We found the Shanahan (1998), Cohen,
Kulik, and Kulik (1982), Wasik and Slavin (1993), and Mathes and Fuchs
(1994) reviews to be very useful. Should readers desire a more fine-grained
description and interpretation of the research findings related to tutoring, we
strongly recommend that they read these comprehensive reviews of the literature.

Four comprehensive reviews of the educational research literature related to
tutoring (Devin-Sheehan, Feldman, & Allen, 1976; Ellison, 1976; Fitz-Gibbon,
1977; Rosenshine & Furst, 1969) were published between 1969 and 1982.
There was consensus among the reviewers that there were significant learning
gains in reading, math, and other content areas. In 1982, Cohen, Kulik, and Kulik reported an average academic achievement effect size of .40. Cook, Scruggs,
Mastropieri, and Casto (1985–1986) reported an average effect size of .53.
Wasik and Slavin (1993) reported an average effect size of .51. Mathes and
Fuchs (1994) reported an average effect size of .36. Shanahan and Barr (1995)
also reported positive academic achievement effect outcomes.

Taken together, these comprehensive reviews (meta-analyses) of the educational research literature indicate that tutoring works. But as Shanahan
(1998) points out in his review, "Tutoring does not always work . . . but in
some circumstances it works better than other methods of instruction. Tutoring is not a panacea." An effort is made to summarize the tutoring research
findings below.

Summary Description Related to Tutoring Research Findings

Tutoring interventions work for most students (Cohen et al., 1982; Cook et
al., 1985–1986; Mathes & Fuchs, 1994; and Wasik & Slavin, 1993).
But "tutoring does not always work . . . [it] is not a panacea" (Shanahan,
1998).

There are a wide range of documented effect sizes associated with tutoring (.07–.75).

In a few studies (see Cohen et al., 1982) students who were tutored displayed lower levels of achievement.

Regression to the mean effects may be responsible for some of the reported gains.

Tutoring is reported (Mathes & Fuchs, 1994) to be more effective with disabled students who are maintained in regular classrooms (effect size = .42) compared to those assigned to special education classes (effect size = .27).

Early tutoring is useful for many students having reading difficulties (Vellutino et al., 1996).

Tutoring has diagnostic value related to identifying poor readers with a cognitive limitation (in contrast to experiential limitations) who will likely require a great deal of support (Vellutino et al., 1996).

Most successful tutors engage in scaffolded interactions with their students (Juel, 1996).

In sum, there is considerable evidence to support the conclusion that tutoring works for most students. However, we don't know whether the outcome differences are attributable to the individual difference characteristics of the students, the quality of tutoring instruction, or the interactions of these two sources of variability.

Compared to other methods of instruction (reciprocal teaching, computer-aided instruction, and direct instruction) the findings related to tutoring interventions are mixed (Marston, Deno, Kim, Diment, & Rogers, 1995; Matthes & Fuchs, 1994).

There are positive findings related to combining tutoring with methods of direct instruction (Simmons, Fuchs, Fuchs, Mathes, & Hodge, 1995) and large-scale programmatic educational (curricular) reform efforts (Ross, Smith, Casey, & Slavin, 1995).

There are positive findings related to the use of tutoring in early educational intervention programs (Wasik & Slavin, 1993). However, it is important to point out that tutoring has been found to be effective across grade levels (Shanahan, 1998).

Most of the tutoring intervention efforts have been associated with reading. But tutoring interventions have been reported (Cohen et al., 1982; Greenwood, Terry, Utley, Montagna, & Walker, 1993) to be more effective in math (effect size = .57–.75) compared to reading (effect size = .28–.39).

At this time, we do not know whether tutoring interventions are more effective for the development of lower-level skills versus higher-level skills.

There are achievement gains associated with the tutoring interventions in which experienced teachers were used as tutors (Cohen et al., 1982;

Mathes & Fuchs, 1994; Shanahan & Barr, 1995; Wasik & Slavin, 1993).

There is some evidence (Duvall, Delquadri, Elliott, & Hall, 1992; Morris, Shaw, & Perney, 1990) to indicate that if tutors "are carefully supervised and instructional decisions are actually made by knowledgeable professional teachers," tutor training and/or teaching experience may not be necessary.

In contrast to the Carroll (1963) model of instruction in which greater amounts of instruction are typically associated with higher achievement scores, a "less is more effect" has been clearly documented with tutoring interventions (Cohen et al., 1982; Greenwood et al., 1993; Ross et al., 1995; Shanahan & Barr, 1995).

The "less is more effect" remains a force to be reckoned with.

Mathes and Fuchs (1994) and Cohen et al. (1982) reported a wide range (.07–.75) of effect sizes associated with tutoring. It should be noted that significant gains in achievement were found in only sixteen of the forty-five studies reviewed by Cohen and his colleagues. Wasik and Slavin (1993) reported that some tutorials taught by experienced teachers (e.g., Direct Instruction Skills Plan) did not result in significant short- or long-term achievement gains. There were a few studies cited by Cohen and colleagues in which the students who were tutored displayed lower levels of achievement compared to a group of similar students who were not tutored. How can these negative findings be explained? According to Cunningham and Allington (1994), valuable instructional time is often lost as students move from classroom instruction to compensatory instruction. Another possibility is that the tutoring instruction may not complement the regular classroom instruction. There may be a weak and/or nonexistent alignment of the tutoring curriculum and the regular classroom curriculum. According to Mantzicopoulos, Morrison, Stone, & Setrakian (1992), "One-to-one tutoring is not likely to result in comprehensive achievement gains if its focus is on narrow and isolated instructional activities." Shanahan (1998) stated that "tutoring can be undermined by poor teaching . . . Tutoring is usually effective, but the availability of tutoring does not guarantee learning."

Taken together, it is probably fair to say that the findings related to tutoring interventions are positive. The achievement gains documented in the tutoring groups are usually found to be higher than the achievement gains in the control groups. However, there is a wide range of effect sizes associated with tutoring. It is possible that "regression to the mean" effects may be responsible for some of these gains. Given that many students who are tutored have more than their fair share of academic difficulties, their achievement scores may increase during the course of tutoring because of the unreliability of the repeated achievement measures (the regression effect). In addition, it should be noted that pullout educational programs such as those associated with Title I do not increase instructional time. Many of these programs include tutoring components. Cohen and colleagues (1982) reported the slight superiority of replacement tutoring over supplementary tutoring. However, at this time, we are unable to clearly determine whether tutoring interventions replace or supplement classroom teaching.

The findings reported above indicate that it does appear to be important to design tutoring instructional environments in which students spend an adequate amount of time on task, that efforts are made to ensure that high-quality instruction is provided, and that there is underlying continuity between the tutoring curriculum and the regular classroom curriculum.

As noted above, tutoring instruction is often directed at low-achieving and/or at-risk students. According to Mathes and Fuchs (1994), tutoring interventions are not always effective with poor readers. They reported that tutoring is "more effective with disabled students who are mainstreamed in the regular classrooms (effect size = .42) than with those assigned to special education classes (effect size = .27)." An extensive amount of training is provided to tutors (the classroom teachers) in one of the most ambitious and best-designed tutoring programs (the Reading Recovery program). But as Shanahan (1998) states, "The Reading Recovery program fails to help a large number of students. . . . Many students are dropped from the program because of poor attendance or mobility problems that prevent their full participation." Hiebert (1994) and Lyons and Beaver (1995) reported that many Reading Recovery participants are referred to special education for their failure to make adequate progress.

In a comprehensive, well-documented analysis of a selected set of tutoring research, Vellutino and his colleagues (1996) reported that early tutoring is useful with respect to enhancing reading achievement scores for many students having reading difficulties. Tutoring has considerable diagnostic value related to identifying poor readers with some kind of cognitive limitation (in contrast to experiential limitations) who will likely require a great deal of support. In contrast to Vellutino and colleagues, Juel (1996) focused on the differences in tutoring instruction rather than the individual difference characteristics of the students. She found that the most successful tutors engaged in scaffolded interactions with their students. In sum, there is considerable evidence to support the conclusion that tutoring works better for some students. However, we don't know whether achievement outcome differences are attributable to the individual difference characteristics of the students, the quality of tutoring instruction, or the interactions of these two sources of variability.

In studies that compare tutoring to other teaching strategies (reciprocal teaching, computer-aided instruction, enriched classroom teaching, and direct instruction), the results are mixed. These findings were summarized by Marston and colleagues (1995) and Mathes and Fuchs (1994), who concluded that "tutoring works well, but not necessarily any better than other inventions." According to Shanahan (1998), "These findings indicate that tutoring can have great value but that the quality of classroom instruction needs to receive adequate attention in educational reform as well." Given that positive results have been documented in studies in which tutoring was combined with direct instruction (Simmons et al., 1995) and large-scale programmatic curricular reform efforts (Ross et al., 1995), there is evidence that can be used to support the use of tutoring instruction within the context of instructional design improvements and large-scale educational reform efforts.

Many early educational intervention programs have included a tutoring component. In a review of America Reads and other early intervention programs, Wasik and Slavin (1993) documented evidence to support the use of tutors in the primary grades. But as Shanahan (1998) points out, "Tutoring has been found to be effective for students at a variety of grade levels. . . . Policymakers might want to emphasize particular grade levels over others because of unbalanced achievement patterns or political expediency, but there appears to be no pedagogical justification for such an emphasis with regard to the use of tutors." Shanahan uses the findings reported by Cohen et al. (1982), Mathes and Fuches (1994), Mantzicopoulous et al. (1992), and Morris, Ervin, & Conrad (1995) to support these statements.

As described previously, most tutoring intervention efforts have been associated with reading. But Cohen et al. (1982) and Greenwood et al. (1993) reported that tutoring has been found to be more effective in math (effect size = .57–.60) compared to reading (effect size = .29–.39). Why there are differences in these achievement outcomes measures across content areas is unknown at this time. Perhaps these differences are related to a greater focus on the development of lower-level skills (simple computational skills) in the math programs compared to a focus on the development of higher-level skills in the reading comprehension programs. Are tutoring interventions more effective for the development of lower-level skills versus higher-level skills? At this time, we simply don't know.

Cohen and colleagues (1982), Mathes and Fuchs (1994), Shanahan and Barr (1995), and Wasik and Slavin (1993) have documented achievement gains associated with tutoring interventions that used experienced teachers as tutors. But there is some evidence (Duvall et al., 1992; Morris et al., 1990) to indicate that if tutors "are carefully supervised and instructional decisions are actually made by knowledgeable professional teachers," tutor training and/or teaching experience may not be necessary.

As described in chapter 4, Carroll (1963) reported that greater amounts of instruction are typically associated with higher achievement scores. However, in the most frequently cited review of tutoring research (Cohen et al., 1982), a "less is more" effect was documented. In tutoring programs that lasted up to four weeks, an average effect size estimate of .95 was found. In tutoring programs that lasted between five and eighteen weeks, an average effect size estimate of .42 was found. In programs that lasted between nineteen and thirty-six weeks, a .16 average effect size estimate was found. What is going on here? Shanahan (1998) stated that this "claim that amount of tutoring is negatively correlated with educational gains is especially troubling given that many studies have shown that gains from tutoring are not well maintained after the tutors are withdrawn." The less is more effect has been documented by many investigators. Ross et al. (1995) reported a very large effect size (.80–.90) for Reading Recovery students in the first grade. However, by the third grade the effect size had declined to .29. Greenwood and colleagues (1993) and Shanahan and Barr (1995) also documented declines in the outcome measures across time periods. How can these findings be explained? A set of explanatory possibilities could be related to variability in the quality of tutoring instruction over time and the establishment and maintenance of the underlying continuity between the tutoring curriculum and the regular classroom curriculum. Perhaps the positive early effects of tutoring become embedded within the context of the gains that are made in regular classroom instruction over time. The regular classroom instruction gains are likely to be stronger.

It should be noted that Juel (1996) and Jason and colleagues (1995) designed learning environments in which tutoring gains were documented along extended time periods. Shanahan (1998) stated that the "amount of tutoring matters, but the actual benefits are likely to be conditional with regard to amount of knowledge of tutors and the supervision and management structures that are in place."

Given what is presented here, there is considerable evidence to support the view that tutoring can be used to improve student achievement in many content domains. Do we know why tutoring works? There are many hypotheses but very limited evidence-based findings. Below is a list of explanatory possibilities and suggestions for future research. In addition to the three possible explanations discussed earlier in this chapter (increased time on tasks, quality instruction, and alignment of the tutoring curriculum with the regular classroom curriculum), there are some other possible explanations: greater social (personal) involvements between the tutor and tutee, the provision of immediate and relevant feedback, and a better alignment between what the student knows and the instructional task. Another relevant source of variability may be related to the tutors' training. These are possibilities, not clearly documented findings. Many reviewers (Cohen et al., 1982; Ellison, 1976; Rosenshine & Furst, 1969; Wasik & Slavin, 1993) have reported that well-structured tutoring programs work best. But the details related to why structuring yields positive findings remain unknown at this time. Taken together, the findings related to why tutoring works are limited. To clearly document possible sources of explanatory evidence, we will have to reconfigure the research efforts that are currently under way. A different type of research agenda will have to be designed to focus on the provision of explanations related to why tutoring works in contrast to the current prevailing focus given to merely documenting positive outcomes associated with tutoring interventions. If a decision is made to pursue this neglected line of scholarly inquiry, investigators will likely focus on descriptions of the social aspects of tutoring associated with Vygotsky, social learning, mentoring, and constructivist perspectives described in chapter 3. Until this happens, we have compiled a short list of recommended evidence-based practices related to the design of tutoring instructional environments.

Explanatory Possibilities and Suggestions for Future Research

Why does tutoring work? The explanatory possibilities include:

Increased time on task
Provision of quality instruction
Alignment of the tutoring curriculum with the regular education curriculum
Greater social (personal) involvement between the tutor and tutee
The provision of immediate and relevant feedback
Positive alignment between what the student knows and the instructional tasks
Positive outcomes associated with the use of structure

Suggestions for future research include a set of reconfigured research efforts:

A shift away from the current prevailing focus given to documenting that there are positive outcomes associated with tutoring interventions to a research agenda designed to yield information related to why tutoring works
A concentration of our research efforts on the systematic study of the social aspects of tutoring associated with Vygotsky, social learning, mentoring, and constructivist teaching and learning perspectives

Recommended Practices Related to
Designing Tutoring Instructional Environments

Align the tutoring curriculum with the regular classroom curriculum
Don't focus on narrow, isolated instructional activities
Spend an adequate amount of time on task
Provide high-quality instruction
Use scaffolded instruction
Maintain a high quality of classroom instruction
Combine tutoring with direct instruction and large-scale educational (curricular) reform initiatives
Use experienced teachers as tutors
Carefully monitor incremental changes in the outcome measures to guard against a less is more effect
Design and implement highly structured programs

BRIEF DESCRIPTION OF OUR TUTORING INTERVENTION RESEARCH PROGRAM

The information described above, combined with the prevailing theoretical and practical views of educational practitioners and educational researchers (e.g., cognitive, social, and cultural constructivist views and inclusive, disciplined methods of inquiry) as a context in which to situate what we know and don't know about tutoring, led us to use the following general organizing knowledge structures to anchor the content of our tutoring intervention research program: rethinking the relationship between psychology and the schools in the context of recent developments in national educational policies; a cognitive, social, and cultural constructivist theoretical perspective; systematic research for finding group-based methods of instruction that will yield a 2 sigma effect; viewing abilities as the development of forms of expertise (i.e., emphasizing differences between expert and novice learners); giving emphasis to disciplined methods of inquiry and the teacher (insider) research movement; creating a constructivist framework in which to develop an understanding for the use of technology in education; the role of assessment in a constructivist learning culture; and the need to build strong associations between teaching and learning.

The content domains listed above are being combined and are emerging as growing areas of research and interest. We have carried out a series of studies in which an embellished model of mastery learning, PSI, and tutoring instruction has been applied in the schools and the workplace. In these studies, teachers, workplace trainers, and administrator teams provided sequentially arranged, systematic tutoring with individuals and/or small groups. A number of specially crafted curriculum scripts were designed to teach learners a set of competencies at the introductory, maintenance, and/or expert levels of performance. Over 300 learning descriptors have been systematically developed and are being used to document academic achievement gains, improved social–emotional outcomes, and the acquisition of selected job-related skills.

Large data sets ($n = 7,000$) have been collected and examined in several content-specific domain areas. Performance differences across time blocks have been examined in samples of students and workers receiving individual tutoring instruction (see table 5.5). In addition, differences in performance are also being examined in relation to differences in instructional modes (i.e., individualized tutoring groups, peer tutoring groups, computer-assisted groups, and whole classroom instructional groups).

Findings

Comparisons of pre- and posttutoring outcomes have been made across treatment conditions (i.e., individualized tutoring groups, peer tutoring groups, computer assisted groups, and whole classroom instructional groups); across time blocks (10–19 hours, 20–29 hours, 30–45 hours); and across types of tutoring interventions (e.g., academic, job-related, social–emotional). Presently both quantitative and qualitative analyses of numerous data sets are under way. Results indicate that there are consistent performance differences across the time blocks. A six-month to one-year gain in skills improvement appears to occur around the thirtieth hour of instruction.

In addition, qualitative evaluations by tutees, tutors, and in some cases employers indicate growth in academic skills, thinking skills, problem solving skills, and motivation related to the value of learning in general, academic learning in particular, and work performance. Three important motivational factors appear to be (1) proximity and congruence of the instructional intervention program to the regular school or workplace environment, (2) a supportive learning community, and (3) individual perseverance. Emerging data from long-term follow-up reports of students and workers indicate that they retained what they learned. In addition, their attitudes toward learning, their personal motivational levels, and their individual performance showed consistent improvement.

6

Has Tutoring Worked?

A key element of the No Child Left Behind (NCLB) is the use of tutoring to enable the slowest learners to catch up to their peers. School districts across America are just beginning to produce evaluations on the results of these tutoring programs. The Chicago Public Schools (2005) issued such a report on the second year of Supplemental Education Services tutoring programs. A *Chicago Tribune* editorial (2005) asked the key question on the minds of most parents and educators, "Has Tutoring Worked?" The answer was, "That depends. "A mixed picture, it seems. And that might have much to do with *how* tutoring was provided and *who* provided it.

We could not agree more with this general conclusion. From the tutoring research we have reviewed there appears to be a wide variety of tutoring program results. We have found from our investigation a number of specific tutoring procedures that appear to hold considerable promise if used by tutors. Let us now review the individual tutoring best practices areas and discuss some of their ramifications for improving student classroom achievement.

DESIGN AND IMPLEMENT HIGHLY STRUCTURED PROGRAMS (COHEN, KULIK, & KULIK, 1982; ELLISON, 1976; ROSENSHINE & FURST, 1969; WASIK & SLAVIN, 1993)

To facilitate precise individualized tutoring covering a broad range of student achievement issues, tutors employ specifically crafted curriculum scripts designed to tutor skill competencies at the introductory, maintenance, and mastery levels.

The Morgan, Ponticell, and Gordon (1998) Individualized Instructional Program (IIP) systematically designed into its curricula more than 300 learning descriptions that documented academic skill achievement, specific learning-how-to-learn skills, and personal motivational outcomes. Separate IIP programs were designed and used with child, adolescent, and adult learners.

The tutor assessed these learning descriptions throughout the twenty-five hours of one-to-one instruction or forty hours of one-to-five instruction, using observations, diagnostic and developmental criterion-referenced tests, and normal achievement testing. The IIP was specifically designed to bring about rapid, verifiable skill tutoring. It facilitated the tutoring by allowing the tutor to follow a thoughtful, sequentially arranged, systematic presentation based on written methods and reporting materials. The IIP emphasized administrative quality control, student learning awareness, and ongoing feedback to parents and classroom teachers during the tutoring sessions.

TUTORING CAN BE EFFECTIVE AT
MULTIPLE GRADE LEVELS (SHANAHAN, 1998)

As part of our research we developed over fifty-six tutoring curriculum scripts covering a wide range of age groups: preschool, elementary, secondary, college, adult workplace, and adult basic skills. Specific subject areas included reading, math, identification of specific learning disabilities, basic to advanced math and science, over twenty foreign languages, writing skills, and other subject skill areas (Gordon, Ponticell, and Morgan, 1991).

DON'T FOCUS ON NARROW,
ISOLATED INSTRUCTIONAL ACTIVITIES

Using a tutoring curriculum script can help avoid many of the pitfalls of traditional classroom teaching. In the classroom too many students fail to learn one or more basic steps in the process of developing reading, writing, and math skills. Their lack of success becomes a self-perpetuating pattern of behaviors that may reinforce underachievement, slower learning, and lack of personal self-esteem, and lead students to become classroom mental dropouts at a young age. Tutoring can fail to alleviate these issues when it is relegated to the narrow role of homework helper, drill and practice, or test preparation.

The most promising tutoring results seem to be centered on efforts that help a student "learn how to learn." One-to-one tutorials are best at helping tutors use a curriculum script to adapt the tutoring to individual learning differences. By using a curriculum script with a checklist recording the tutor's observations of skill attainments and deficiencies, the tutor can update results after each class. This allows the better use of specific diagnostic tests to pinpoint skill weaknesses. As a student gradually achieves mastery over grade-related skills, the tutor can developmentally track each skill, class by class.

A well-prepared curriculum script that lays out individual state skill standard requirements grade by grade can save tutors a great amount of class time. Instead of informally guessing what the student has mastered, tutors are better prepared to concentrate on diagnosing individual student learning issues, analyzing the related skill areas, and selecting the tutoring instructional methods that will work best for each learner (Gordon, Ponticell, & Morgan, 1989, 1991).

USE DIAGNOSTIC TUTORING TO IDENTIFY POOR LEARNERS WITH COGNITIVE LIMITATIONS

Promising results have been shown by embedding individual diagnoses in a tutoring session (Vellutino et al., 1996). The tutor closely observes and records student learning skills on a class-by-class basis. This will aid in a more accurate diagnosis of specific learning disabilities by watching for particular learner behavior in cognitive processing areas such as vision, auditory skills, speech, and achievement issues. A well-written curriculum script can identify learner characteristics in these areas so that a tutor may observe and document learning responses from class to class.

If the number of errors establishes a definite learning pattern, the tutor may use simple diagnostic tests that will help pinpoint specific cognitive processing errors. Using this information, the tutor can more readily adjust tutoring instructions to improve a student's auditory memory or perhaps strengthen visual tracking skills. Promising research has found that using a curriculum script can accurately pinpoint specific cognitive limitations. This uses a test-tutor-test approach rather than the administration of lengthy diagnostic tests. Results may also be more accurate, since many academically challenged students tend to exhibit test-phobic behaviors.

A tutoring curriculum script itself can be a diagnostic test that may increase class instructional time and reduce time invested in testing. The curriculum scripts can also minimize the risk of an individual tutor overlooking significant cognitive limitations. Diagnosis becomes an ongoing process throughout the tutoring classes, rather than being concentrated only in a pretesting phase (Gordon et al., 1991).

TUTORING SUCCEEDS BECAUSE OF A BETTER ALIGNMENT BETWEEN WHAT THE STUDENT KNOWS AND THE INSTRUCTIONAL TASK (MANTZICOPOULOS, MORRISON, STONE, & SETRAKIAN, 1992)

How does a tutor discern when a student has learned a particular skill or learning concept and is ready to move on? In this regard, a tutoring curriculum script is a loosely ordered but well-defined set of skills and applied learning concepts that are tied to state grade-level standards. The tutoring process is driven by the skills the student brings to the learning task. A tutoring curriculum script can facilitate the gathering of this information from student performance cues and student learning strengths and rapidly identify learning difficulties or skill gaps.

The content areas that can be used to tutor these new skills can come directly from state skill standards related to the student's classroom instruction. Thus the tutoring curriculum script—not a tutor's preconceived lesson plan—can become the major determination of the content as the tutoring sessions evolve.

USE EXPERIENCED TEACHERS AS TUTORS (COHEN ET AL., 1982; MATHES & FUCHS, 1994; SHANAHAN & BARR, 1995; WASIK & SLAVIN, 1993)

Author (Gordon, 2002a, 2002b) interviews with hundreds of master tutors over several decades have revealed that the majority do not see themselves as homework helpers or test preparers but short-term "learning detectives," therapists, and mentors. The ideal tutor is a diagnostician who discovers the causes of a student's inability to learn in the classroom. The tutor must also be an expert therapist who uses the student's learning and motivational strengths to overcome his or her weaknesses. This tutor/mentor must encourage, motivate, and lead the student to the gradual recognition that learning is not about tests, grades, or school; it is about succeeding in life.

The best tutors are often frustrated classroom teachers. They are frustrated because they long to reach out to the student who seems lost in the classroom, but they don't have the time to do so during group instruction. Master tutors have an infectious love of learning and an overwhelming desire to pass it on to every student within reach.

Partnering with the child's local school is an important element of a successful tutor's program. Tutoring needs to translate into improved day-to-day classroom learning for the student. To reach this goal, successful tutors seek to collaborate in a diplomatic, nonconfrontational manner with the classroom teacher.

A qualified diagnostic/developmental tutor has a luxury denied to most classroom teachers: to individualize the tutoring to the exact instructional needs of the student. A competent tutor can offer a perspective regarding the student's learning style that the classroom teacher simply does not have time to observe. Although some parents may object to the tutor contacting their child's school, in most cases classroom teachers are open to such collaboration.

The level of experience and education the tutor brings to the tutoring process will have a major effect on student learning outcomes. Nondegreed student or adult tutors have achieved significant results tutoring students when:

- They follow an expertly designed tutoring curriculum for each tutoring session
- They receive extensive training and retraining on appropriate tutoring behaviors and instructional strategies
- They are closely supervised by experienced master teachers who have specific subject/instructional expertise to coach tutors regarding effective remedial tutoring strategies

Subject-degreed and credentialed teachers with extensive classroom experience are the best tutors for students with complex learning issues. This includes students who have significant reading and math skill deficiencies or need specific subject instruction in such areas as algebra, chemistry, Spanish, or French, and other complex academic skill areas.

THE LOCATION OF THE TUTORING SESSIONS MAY MAXIMIZE LONG-TERM STUDENT RESULTS

The authors (Morgan et al., 1998) have made comparisons of pre- and post-tutoring across tutor–student ratios (i.e., one-to-one tutoring, one-to-five tutoring group); across time blocks (10–19 hours, 20–29 hours, 30–34 hours); across types of tutoring interventions (e.g., academic, job-related) and across locations (e.g., student's home, community center, student's school, local library, adult's worksite).

The location of the tutoring sessions seems to play a major role in learners dropping out of a tutoring program due to poor attendance or family mobility problems (Shanahan, 1998). Though most NCLB tutoring programs are now school based, other alternatives that may lead to more effective tutoring results need consideration.

The authors (Gordon, Morgan, Ponticell, & O'Malley, 2004) conducted longitudinal research on the effect of location on tutoring outcome. They studied a tutorial school accredited by the North Central Association of Colleges and Schools (1982). For thirty-three years (1968–2001) it brought subject-certified teachers retrained as tutors into the homes of more than 12,000 children (K–12) and adults. These students represented every socioeconomic group and were tutored in their own homes across the six-county Chicago metropolitan area. Some of the students were dependent children living in foster homes as wards of the state. Others were being home tutored for their school districts. The majority of students were tutored in basic reading and math areas, though high school and even college subjects were also tutored (Gordon, 1983).

These tutoring programs were usually the parents' first experience of a teacher regularly visiting their home. Involving the parents in an ongoing education conversation over a typical ten- to thirteen-week tutoring program brought many families to a better understanding of their child's learning needs and learning abilities. For the first time many parents came to see that becoming literate takes time. Successful learning is an everyday activity involving both parent and child.

A provocative poll by Public Agenda (Farkas, Johnson, and Duffett, 1999) confirmed that many parents have a difficult time dealing with these home learning issues. They found that seven in ten families said they were more involved in their child's education than were their own parents, but most believed they were not doing enough. The same poll reported that only one in ten teachers found that parents regularly check to make sure that their child's homework was completed and done correctly.

In this tutoring program we found that these learning support issues could be more effectively addressed by tutoring a child in his or her own home rather than at school or in a library or community center. The tutor met with the parent after every tutoring class to review results, give homework assignments, and establish a dialogue on progress. Tutors coached parents on how to provide a quiet, comfortable, well-lighted place equipped with the necessary learning supplies for the child. Parents needed to become learning role models. The tutor's day-to-day coaching showed parents how to become more personally involved through reviewing the student's work and engaging in personal drill and practice or reading activities.

They found that the first principle of successful personal learning was "learning how to learn" at home coached by a supportive family environment before learning every day in a school classroom. This home tutoring program often overcame learning blocks, but of equal importance was the tutor acting as a learning coach to establish a supportive learning environment, improve study habits, and motivate the child to learn by enhancing self-discipline.

However, parents remained the primary motivators of their children. Only they can set the right example by personally demonstrating that they value learning and education as the key element in children's preparation for life (Gordon & Gordon, 2003).

Contemporary research supports parents becoming involved in these literacy activities, from establishing daily homework routines, to teaching for understanding, to developing basic student learning strategies. Even though younger children have shorter attention spans, the link between homework each night and student achievement grows progressively stronger as they age (Gordon, Morgan, Ponticell, and O'Malley, 2004).

We and other educational researchers believe that home background and parental support are more powerful influences than schooling in determining personal literacy achievement. We call this process "family cognition." Schools remain a developer and reinforcer of personal learning. But as the above research indicates, the family occupies center stage in originating and supporting vital behavioral and cognitive learning attitudes and processes throughout the stages of a student's maturational process. Home tutoring can serve as an important lever in actuating these activities.

Strommen and Mates (2004) studied the underpinning attitudes of the love of reading among older children and teens. Their survey results indicated that family cognition was a major determining factor. Students surely benefit when teachers recognize the need to motivate them to read. But they concluded that it is the child's immediate culture, the family, which must invest itself in the process of reading for pleasure. The family must consistently demonstrate to children as they grow up the pleasure that reading affords by providing a daily model for children to emulate. Tutoring can help many families learn these behaviors that in turn stimulate cognition and learning.

There are many other recent examples of family cognition supported by home tutorial interventions:

- Even Start and Early Head Start are federally funded early education programs that send teachers and other educators into the homes of parents with infants and young children. They coach parents on how to provide reading and other cultural activities as their child grows up (Armor, 2002; Geissler, 2002).
- In Mecca, California, teachers from Saúl Martinez Elementary School visit their students' homes to coach parents in areas they need to work on with their children. The home visit program also gets parents involved in out-of-school activities (Donaldson, 2002).
- In Santa Fe County, New Mexico, Healthy Families First provides parents with trained home coaches to promote positive parenting practices

that can enhance child health and educational development. This is one of 441 programs across the United States and Canada designed to strengthen family/child development (Davis, 2004).

- Practical Parenting Partnerships (PPP) provides a system of training and home visits to build strong home/school relationships. PPP operates through 530 Missouri schools and more than 200 schools in eleven other states and Canada. Parent development workshops have been provided to many additional schools (PPP, 2005).
- Kennedy Middle School in El Centro, California, established a Parents Academy, an eight-week course offered in both Spanish and English. It provides tips for helping with homework and communicating with adolescents. The program gives parents detailed outlines of student coursework. It explains the skills students need for success in high school and postsecondary education (Manzo, 2005b).
- The Literacy Connection in Elgin, Illinois, offers night classes for parents as part of the Family Literacy Program. These classes include parenting education and family art projects that encourage parents to read and communicate with their children. "I turn off the TV and read to them or just talk to them about their day," Olga Yaste says of her new nightly ritual (Fergus, 2005).
- Bakermans-Kranenburg, Van Ijzendoorn, and Bradley (2005) found that the most effective early childhood interventions were home based. Adolescent mothers often lack basic educational skills. Tutoring at home helps introduce a smaller number of clear, highly integrated objectives that can be individualized to increase student and parent comprehension.
- The Guilford County, North Carolina, school system began a nontraditional high school tutoring program that has helped cut the high school dropout rate from nearly 6 percent of students to just over 3 percent (2003–2004). Guilford Technical Community College teachers conduct home visits, and students can also take advantage of daily tutoring (Manzo, 2005a).
- In 1998 the Sacramento City Unified District began a Parent/Teacher Home Visitation Project as a way for teachers to communicate better with parents and understand students' diverse learning needs. The program trains and supports teachers in efforts to increase parental knowledge, understanding, and involvement. Teachers coach parents on three critical educational activities: organizing their children's daily learning time at home and monitoring them; helping with homework; and talking with their children about school, learning, and the importance of education. These coaching activities aim at developing parents as tutors for their children (EMT Associates, 2004).

The authors believe that home tutoring programs enhance family cognition. Offering a mixture of school-based and home-based programs may be the most realistic alternative for a local school district. Parents could be offered a choice between these two alternatives. Our research results show that many families willingly invite teachers into their homes as tutors for their children and coaches for the parents.

TUTORING NEEDS TO BECOME EMBEDDED IN THE CONTEXT OF THE GAINS MADE IN REGULAR CLASSROOM INSTRUCTION DAY TO DAY

One of the chief goals of a tutoring program is enabling a problematic student to "learn how to learn." In contrast to drill and practice, homework helper, or test preparation tutorial programs, appropriate diagnostic/developmental tutoring is designed to help ensure that the student has developed a personal repertoire of both behavioral and cognitive learning skills that underpin all classroom achievement (Gordon et al., 2004). The aim is to enable more students to become successful learners in their regular classroom.

Peer tutoring is another learning strategy that can reinforce or amplify classroom instruction. Peer tutors can reinforce concepts, help tutees practice skills, assist with individual projects, support problem solving, or challenge tutees' thinking or approaches to learning. Peer tutoring also strengthens tutors' understanding of concepts and skills, engages them in creative thinking and problem solving as they test alternative strategies for helping tutees, and enhances the tutors' self-image. This can become a promising component in building students' critical thinking skills (Gordon, 2005a, 2005b).

The use of peer tutors in classrooms opens opportunities for teachers to observe students more closely and gain a more detailed understanding of individual students' learning profiles and mastery of concepts and skills. Peer tutoring makes it possible to embed assessments of knowledge and skill in learning activities, thus giving teachers multiple ways to monitor and check student progress. Finally, peer tutoring can provide valuable time for teachers to work more closely with individual students needing reteaching or greater support in practicing less-developed skills.

Peer tutoring requires careful planning and is grounded in appropriate training of tutors. Effective peer tutoring is not a haphazard volunteer program. Peer tutoring requires a purposeful program of specific learning objectives, activities, and assessments for developing and determining students' mastery of concepts and skills. To be effective tutors, students need to learn how to interact with peers as learning partners. Peer tutors are more successful if their role is highly structured, if they are made aware of basic learning principles, if they understand curricular goals, and if they are trained in appropriate use of tutoring activities and materials (Gordon, 2005a, 2005b).

We must not ignore or dismiss the potential hurdles that teachers will face as they consider the utility of peer tutoring in their classrooms. Peer tutoring will require parent and organizational support. Parents generally know very little about peer tutoring; they need to be educated about the role of peer tutoring as a support and supplement to teacher instruction and the benefits of tutoring for both tutee and tutor.

Peer tutors can be organized in ways that optimize opportunities to learn in many meaningful ways. For example:

- Peer tutors can elicit their tutees' ideas and experiences in relation to key topics and then fashion learning situations that help them elaborate on or restructure their current knowledge.
- Tutors and tutees can be assigned complex, meaningful problem-based activities.
- Tutors and tutees can be encouraged to work collaboratively and be given support to engage in task-oriented dialogue with one another.
- Tutors can make their thinking processes explicit to tutees in their own language and encourage tutees to do the same through dialogue, writing, drawings, or other representations.
- Tutors and tutees can be routinely asked to apply knowledge in diverse and authentic contexts, to explain ideas, interpret texts, predict phenomena, and construct arguments based on evidence, rather than focus exclusively on the acquisition of predetermined "right answers." This encourages the growth of critical thinking skills.
- Tutors can encourage tutees' reflective and autonomous thinking in conjunction with the conditions listed above.
- Tutors can employ a variety of assessment strategies to understand how their tutees' ideas are evolving and to give feedback on the processes as well as the products of their thinking (Windschitl, 2002).

Peer tutoring can also help teachers reduce some of the negative impact of high-stakes testing on classroom instruction. Teaching and learning approaches are often discontinued to focus on high-stakes testing (e.g., Abrams, Pedulla, & Madaus, 2003; Barksdale-Ladd & Thomas, 2000; Herman & Golan, 1991; Johnston, 1998; McNeil, 2000; M. L. Smith, 1991). Teachers report spending more time on test preparation and less time on learning activities that provide reinforcement of skills, promote in-depth understanding of content, involve collaboration as well as independence, and invoke higher-order thinking skills (Barksdale-Ladd & Thomas, 2000).

Gordon (2005a, 2005b) provides compelling evidence from forty years of research on peer tutoring that it may not only help increase student mastery of subject knowledge and general learning skills, but also improve student motivation and sense of empowerment as learners. Peer tutoring can have extremely positive effects on student classroom achievement and has been shown to significantly improve reading comprehension (Gordon, 2005a, 2005b).

USE SCAFFOLDED INSTRUCTION (JUEL, 1996)

Testing is often a difficult hurdle for students who are academically challenged in school. They begin to believe that tests will only confirm how much they do not understand. A tutoring curriculum script helps eliminate the need for many tests. Instead, the tutor consistently observes and records student skills from each tutoring session. This allows the tutor to scaffold the instruction strategy using a test-tutor-test format based on continuous observation and shorter quizzes and diagnostic reviews that help establish meaningful learning goals and objectives for the student. Attainment of specific grade-related skill goals is reported in great detail back to the student throughout the tutoring classes. The use of realistic skills and learning goals and objectives motivates a student to persist to a higher level of educational attainment. The IIP gives a concrete picture of the student's progress and establishes a positive self-motivational process (Gordon, Morgan, and Ponticell, 1995).

SPEND AN ADEQUATE AMOUNT OF TIME ON TASKS (JASON ET AL., 1995; JUEL, 1996)

In our research, we assumed that the differences in tutoring outcomes over time blocks occurred because time was needed:

- To assess how a learner approached the learning situation
- To discover what specific sequential subject-matter skills the student lacked
- To reorganize learner achievement and study habits

The IIP small-group tutoring module is composed of forty hours of two-hour classes held twice a week for ten weeks or one-to-one tutoring with one-hour classes held twice a week for thirteen weeks, totaling twenty-five hours. This structure recognizes the importance of extending tutoring over time. It takes time to assess how a learner approaches the learning task, to discover what specific subject matter skills are missing, to reorganize the student's achievement and study habits, and to assess and improve personal motivation that supports learning related to the classroom. The hallmark of promising tutoring programs is precise, individualized diagnosis and applied tutoring, which allows each student to learn at his or her own pace.

Students who had complex learning issues and/or functioned far below their grade placement were sometimes enrolled in several tutorial cycles described previously. However, the objective of most of the tutoring programs we have reviewed was to keep tutoring as a short-term learning aid. The goal of most effective tutoring is to help students learn how to learn at their optimum achievement level in a daily classroom environment.

CAREFULLY MONITOR INCREMENTAL CHANGES IN OUTCOME MEASURES TO GUARD AGAINST A LESS IS MORE EFFECT (COHEN ET AL., 1992; ROSS, SMITH, CASEY, & SLAVIN, 1995; GREENWOOD, TERRY, UTLEY, MONTAGNA, & WALKER, 1993; SHANAHAN & BARR, 1995)

For each of the written learning objectives that a tutor records using a curriculum script, task analysis can describe the incremental skill changes the student must learn to achieve mastery. The authors see taking this a step further by using a curriculum script that includes both educational skill requirements and recording student cognitive strengths and weaknesses. Therefore, the tutoring curriculum script not only lays out for the tutor the specific skill components of an academic area (i.e., reading, math, science), but also serves as a diagnostic tool for uncovering potential learning-how-to-learn cognitive skill roadblocks.

A tutoring curriculum script monitors the progress of incremental changes during each tutoring session. These scripts can be developed into curriculum-based measures (CBMs). Our research shows how a test-tutor-test regime often can become a CBM that produces accurate, meaningful information about student academic levels and growth (Fuchs & Fuchs, 1998).

TUTORING SUCCEEDS BECAUSE OF GREATER PERSONAL INVOLVEMENT BETWEEN THE TUTOR AND TUTEE AND PROVISION OF IMMEDIATE AND RELEVANT FEEDBACK

Research suggests that at every step of tutoring session activities, the student has a need to know, How am I doing? Immediate feedback is critical for improving personal motivation (Shanahan, 1998). At the beginning of a tutorial program it is crucial to overcome a student's fear that the learning task is impossible and that he or she will again experience failure. Promising tutoring practices break down a student's long-term learning goals into small skill objectives a student can recognize, understand, and master at his or her own pace.

Promising research (Gordon et al., 1995) shows that to increase student motivation, initial tutoring sessions best focus on academic material at the student's independent skill level. This will help the tutor give the student the positive reinforcement of immediate success. The student will begin to believe he or she has the ability to achieve. Tutoring can then be gradually adjusted to the student's capacity and instructional levels while still reinforcing a positive self-image as a learner.

Tutors can also coach students on their formal study skills and habits. The closer interpersonal nature of individualized tutoring gives the opportunity to embed study skills in informal exercises and homework, rather than present them out of context. Tutors can teach more difficult study skill concepts as the learning progresses.

As these skills improve, independent homework activities are designed to help students see their own small but recognizable steps in the learning process. As a result students may begin to see learning new skills as an attainable personal challenge they can ultimately master rather than a punishment to be feared or avoided.

In summary, our research (Morgan et al., 1998) on cognitive tutoring strategies may provide us with teachable cognitive process variables that could supplement and perhaps replace traditional intelligence tests in the successful matching of students' individual differences and educational treatment approaches. Detailed cognitive task analyses of tutoring sequences have been done. The identification of individual differences in cognitive information processing capacities could be utilized to design tutoring that compensates for a particular deficiency by providing for learners what they cannot provide for themselves. Such information could be used to capitalize on the learners' strengths and could be particularly valuable for diagnosing reasons for current learning difficulties and in suggesting tutoring instructional procedures (prescriptions) for overcoming them.

What we are proposing here is a general information processing approach to tutorial instruction. Tutoring should be directed at modifying student attention, cognitive expectances, and memory. Cognitive information processing is enhanced when students actively engage in the learning tasks, discuss, rehearse, analyze, problem solve, use graphs to represent experience, and share observations, understandings, and knowledge.

Teachers who are called on to design tutoring environments should attempt to include instructional procedures having potential for the modification of cognitive learning components (i.e., attention, knowledge and language templates, cognitive strategies, attitudes, expectancies, and mood). We know that mastery learning, personalized systems of instruction, and tutoring instructional systems work. The three instruction systems have been carefully tested in highly controlled laboratory, field experimental, and applied settings. What is now needed is a greater focus and appreciation for attempts to relate recent findings reported in the cognitive science literature to these behaviorally anchored tutorial modes.

TEN KEY TUTORING COMPONENTS

What are the key factors that can potentially make a tutoring program more effective? Based on what researchers (Gordon et al., 2004) now know, we can identify at least ten components that show considerable promise for high-quality tutoring:

1. Tutors can be effective regardless of their training and education by just giving students more personal attention. However, teacher education, prior professional experience, and specialized training as a tutor can make a major difference. Professionally prepared tutors consistently produce significantly higher levels of student achievement than tutors with little or no special preparation.
2. Tutors need to use a diagnostic/developmental template to organize and implement each student's tutoring program.
3. Tutors must be able to track the session-to-session progress of each student in order to modify tutoring content and use student academic strengths to overcome weaknesses.
4. Principles of learning drawn from both cognitive and constructivist thinking seem to offer the strongest contemporary tutoring methods.
5. Tutors need to use continuous feedback to help students develop positive self-images as learners.
6. Formal/informal assessment needs to be used throughout the tutoring process.
7. Mentoring/coaching students on learning how to learn through providing guidance on study habits, test taking, attention to school, and learning in general is a significant informal part of effective tutoring.
8. Mentoring/coaching each student's parents on sustaining the day-to-day learning process in the home after the tutoring ceases is an important role for effective tutors.

9. To facilitate the coaching of parents, it is desirable to conduct the tutoring in the student's home outside of school hours. If this is not possible, a community center, school, or library can be used, but the tutors should still try to provide coaching to the parents.

10. Tutors must collaborate closely with each student's classroom teacher. The final measure of the effectiveness of the tutoring is the short-term and long-term improvement of the student's daily classroom achievement.

7

The Ethics of Tutoring

In this chapter we will review professional tutoring ethical standards and trade practices that have been developed for regulatory purpose from three different perspectives: (1) the Better Business Bureau (BBB), (2) the Education Industry Association (EIA), and (3) model rules and regulation of tutoring standards for state education agencies (SEAs) prepared by the authors. Please see chapter 2 for a complete discussion on the regulation of tutoring.

BBB TRADE PRACTICE STANDARDS

In 2001 the Council of Better Business Bureaus developed, in collaboration with the BBB of Chicago and Northern Illinois, the first national consumer protection standards for tutoring. A national committee of tutoring experts met in Chicago to help the council prepare these standards.

These standards have been published in *The Do's and Don'ts in Advertising Copy* to provide an important benchmark for the advertising industry. The over 110 local BBBs across the United States and Canada are now using these standards to resolve consumer tutoring program complaints.

The authors believe that a joint collaboration between the SEA, local education agency, and the BBB will offer the most effective pathway in resolving most of these consumer tutoring issues.

NATIONAL BBB TRADE PRACTICE STANDARDS AND PROFESSIONAL GUIDELINES FOR EDUCATIONAL TUTORING

Introduction

The trade practices set forth below are basic principles in the purchasing and offering of educational tutoring programs. The foundation of these trade practices is the Better Business Bureau's "Code of Advertising." Adherence to this Code's provisions by the tutoring industry will make a significant contribution toward effective self-regulation. These guides outline the requested professional conduct of individuals responsible for educational tutoring.

Sellers, advertising agencies and the media should be sure they are complying with federal, state and local laws and regulations as they relate to advertising and selling practices including licensing requirements, when applicable.

I. Purpose

These guidelines are intended to assist parents, students and their tutoring providers, advertising media and the Better Business Bureau in their efforts to understand and implement fair, accurate and truthful advertising and selling practices. Adherence to this code will be a significant contribution to self-regulation in the public interest. The Better Business Bureau will assist in the standards' uniform application through conciliation, mediation and arbitration, when needed.

The following are general standards for the tutoring industry. Additionally, we recommend that consumers and tutors develop practices and/or guidelines to fit the particular needs of their professional relationship.

The exact nature of the services provided by a tutor are in many ways unique in education. Much of what is asked of the tutor by the student is the basic reorganization of their ability to learn something. This idea of "learning how to learn" is at the heart of the concept of tutoring.

University researchers have long considered tutoring as part of understanding the overall psychology of learning. Tutoring then is a psycho-educational service that can have a major positive or negative impact on the child or adult's overall self-concept. This means that the scope of a student's tutoring experience, which usually is rather short-term, could have major potential long-term effects on personal self-esteem, motivation, study habits and knowledge of a subject (ex. reading, math, a foreign language, etc.).

For these reasons it is important to make available fair tutoring trade practices and advertising standards. Consumer standards are very important for this industry as for any other that seek self-regulating improvements. However, parents aren't shopping here for a new vacuum cleaner or a car. The consumer expects to receive a professional educational serve that has the potential to improve a student's ability to learn over a lifetime.

II. Behaviors

These trade practices outline current standards, practices and guidelines of ethical concepts that have evolved from the tutoring industry's professional activities. Additional changes are anticipated in the future. The practices promote the concept of business self-regulation.

III. Definitions

Standards are defined as very specific rules (requirements and criteria) that are widely accepted by educational experts. *Practices* include the everyday behaviors of operational methods (application and execution) that are followed consistently throughout the contemporary tutoring industry. *Guidelines* are generally accepted concepts, opinions or theories that are often usually followed by different members of the tutoring community.

Buyers include parents, institutions, schools and others. *Sellers* are tutors, teachers, administrators, owners and those responsible for developing and delivery of tutoring programs.

Conciliation is the involvement of a neutral third party to help disputants communicate by letter and/or phone and work out a resolution to a problem. *Mediation* is a structured process guided by a neutral third party with specific steps that are followed to clarify the issues, to discuss options and solutions. *Arbitration* is a process in which two or more persons agree to let an impartial person or panel decide their dispute with the award being enforceable through the appropriate local legal jurisdiction.

IV. Development

This document was developed (2001) by the Better Business Bureau of Chicago and Northern Illinois in conjunction with industry representatives and subject matter experts including:

Edward E. Gordon-Committee Chair
President
Imperial Tutoring & Educational Services
Chicago, Illinois

Jim Giovannini
Founder and Owner
Academic Tutoring Centers
Park Ridge, Illinois

Yvonne Jones, Project Manager
Chicago Public Schools
Chicago, Illinois

Jerry Loyett, Illinois State Director
North Central Association of
Colleges and Schools
Champaign, Illinois

John McLaughlin, Editor-in-Chief
The Educational Industry Report
Sioux Falls, South Dakota

Ronald R. Morgan, Professor
Loyola University
Chicago, Illinois

Chris Yelich, Administrative Director
Education Industry Association
Watertown, Wisconsin

Dan Bassill, President
Cabrini Connections
Tutor/Mentor Connection
Chicago, Illinois

Mike Zenanko, Coordinator
Teaching/Learning Center
Jacksonville State University
Jacksonville, Alabama

James Baumhart, BBB Staff Liason
President/CEO
Better Business Bureau of Chicago and
Northern Illinois
Chicago, Illinois

V. Professional Guidelines

Throughout the United States few states attempt to license or regulate educational tutoring services whether provided by a single practitioner or a corporation. Therefore, the tutoring standards review committee has developed the following basic guidelines in an effort to professionalize the tutoring industry.

Consumers reviewing trade practice standards need a general "tutoring yardstick" to help them successfully use the services of this industry. As part of their selection process we recommend that a consumer receive the following information that will help them compare the quality of each individual tutoring program.

1. Program Information
   a. Firm's location and phone number.
   b. Date firm began operation.
   c. Educational qualifications and professional experience of tutors and administrators.
   d. Licensing/accreditation.
   e. Exact description of professional services offered. Program objectives shall be clearly stated regarding the content of any professional service. The use of tests, remedial work, therapy formats, etc. shall be clearly explained to the layperson.

f. The availability of a competent referral program to other professionals (i.e., speech and hearing, vision, counseling, etc.) if and when needed.

g. Anticipated duration of each program.

h. The availability of confidential written educational outcome reports to parents, school, other professionals or others.

2. Preliminary Evaluation—Eligibility & Ineligibility: Every tutoring program shall contain a definitive preliminary evaluation phase so that decisions shall be reached to determine the student's eligibility for a tutoring program—that the professional service in the specific program is actually needed by the client and that the client shall indeed improve his/her educational skills as a *direct* result of the specific program, or his/her ineligibility and an immediate referral made to another qualified educational program. The parent, guardian or adult shall be informed if at any time during a program the student does not respond positively to the tutoring help given, or no longer needs additional tutorial help.

3. Final Program Evaluations shall be made and conducted by qualified tutoring or other professionals germane to the service(s) offered.

4. Time Frame of Program: All tutoring programs shall have a definite calendar beginning, middle and end. All modifications in the program time frame shall be agreed to by the client before they are made. Modifications in the program time frame shall be based upon re-evaluation of the client's progress.

5. Fees: When a fee is quoted for services, the tutoring service shall be available at such a fee. If more than one fee is quoted, the differences in each related tutoring service shall be stated. Finance charges shall be fully explained in writing to the consumer. If the professional does not have a published fee list, then fees shall be clearly explained verbally to the client before professional service is rendered.

6. Use of Insurance, State or Federal Aid: If insurance, or State or Federal Aid is to be used by the client to pay the professional fees, the consumer shall be fully briefed as to its applicability in each specific case *before* he/she agrees to begin any tutoring program.

VI. Advertising/Selling

1. The primary responsibility for truthful and non-deceptive advertising rests with the advertiser. Advertisers should be prepared to substantiate any claims or offers made before publication or broadcast and, upon request, present such substantiation promptly to the advertising medium or Better Business Bureau.

2. Advertisements which are untrue, misleading, deceptive, fraudulent, falsely disparaging of competitors, or insincere offers to sell, shall not be used.

3. An advertisement as a whole may be misleading although every sentence separately considered is literally true. Misrepresentation may result not only from direct statements but by omitting or obscuring a material fact such as: description of services, nature of children's learning

problems, exact fees, qualifications of tutors, time duration of program, availability of written final summary reports to other professionals, availability of a clear and accurate final report to the parents, schools or other professionals.

4. Advertising Layout: The layout of an advertisement including the heading, text matter, illustrations and prices, shall not permit an erroneous impression as to exactly what type of professional service is offered at any quoted fee.

5. Illustrations: The illustrations of any activity performed by the tutoring service will state if this is an integral part of the program. It shall not exaggerate the services performed and shall not be used to knowingly or unknowingly mislead the client as to the positive results that have normally resulted from this educational program.

6. Trial Offers: If a "trial offer" or any special offer is made, an expiration date shall be stated. "Free trial" means no obligation. The client shall be given the offered tutoring service without any obligation.

7. Lowest price, underselling claims: Despite an advertiser's best efforts to ascertain competitive prices, the rapidity with which prices fluctuate and the difficulty of determining prices of all sellers at all times preclude an absolute knowledge of the truth of generalized underselling/lowest price claims. Advertisers should have proper substantiation for all claims prior to dissemination; unverifiable underselling claims should be avoided.

8. Testimonials and Endorsements: In general, advertising which uses testimonials or endorsements is likely to mislead or confuse it:
   • it would provide a misleading anticipation of results to most people;
   • it contains representations or statements which would be misleading if otherwise used in advertising;
   • while literally true, it creates deceptive implications;
   • the endorser is not competent or sufficiently qualified to express an opinion concerning the quality of the service being advertised or the results likely to be achieved by its use;
   • it is not clearly stated that the endorser, associated with some well-known and highly-regarded institution, is speaking only in a personal capacity, and not on behalf of such an institution, if such be the fact;
   • broad claims are made as to endorsements or approval by indefinitely large or vague groups, e.g., "the homeowners of America," " the doctors of America;"
   • an endorser has a pecuniary interest in the company whose product or service is endorsed and this is not made known in the advertisement.

   Advertisers should consult Federal Trade Commission Guides on Testimonials and Endorsements for detailed guidance.

9. Claimed Results: Claims as to educational performance, test results, etc., which will be obtained by or realized from a particular service should be based on recent and recognized psychological, educational, or other objective published professional data.

10. Superlative Sales Claims-Puffery: Superlative statements, like other advertising claims, are objective (factual) or subjective (puffery):
    - *objective claims* relate to tangible qualities and performance values of a service which can be measured against accepted standards or tests. As statements of fact, such claims can be proved or disproved and the advertiser should possess substantiation.
    - *subjective claims* are expressions of opinion or personal evaluation of the intangible qualities of a service. Individual opinions, statements or corporate pride and promises may sometimes be used, but they should not promise educational results that are unrealistic and without professional substantiation.

11. Guarantees: If a guarantee should be offered, a guarantee or warranty should be specific, clearly and conspicuously disclose its nature, time or other limitation, the manner in which the guarantor will perform and the identity of the guarantor. Unless otherwise stated, the responsibility for adjustment rests with the advertiser. An advertiser offering a guarantee or warranty should read and adhere to the "Guide Against Deceptive Advertising of Guarantees" issued by the Federal Trade Commission.

    Money Back Guarantee: "Money Back Guarantee," or phrases of similar import, mean a cash refund in full without any deduction.

EIA STANDARDS FOR BEST PRACTICE

In 2005 the EIA issued best practice standards to help establish ethical guidelines for over 1,200 member tutoring services. The EIA also issued tutor qualification standards (March 2005) in order to establish for the public three different levels of expertise by individuals who are employed as tutors.

In November 2004 the EIA provided a code of conduct and ethics for supplemental service (SES) providers offering services for the No Child Left Behind (NCLB). Additional EIA professional conduct standards were issued (January 2006) for other EIA members providing educational programs other than tutoring or NCLB services.

Education Industry Association
Standards for Best Practice
for Education Service Providers
Approved by the Board of Directors, January 27, 2005

Introduction

The Education Industry Association (EIA) and its education service provider members are committed to upholding standards of professional practice that set high benchmarks for quality, innovation, and accountability. The standards outlined below are guiding principles for the education service industry, which includes individual tutors, and companies that operate learning centers, test prep services, schools (including charter schools), education management services, and alternative and special education programs.

As a statement of best practices, they are appropriate for professionals and companies of all experience levels, business sizes, and instructional delivery models. The EIA believes that service providers become stronger and more effective with practice, training, and experience.

The creation of industry standards also provides the general public and, more specifically, consumers, with confidence that the service provider with whom they work ascribes to national quality standards. Informed consumers of private education services should make better decisions about the selection and performance of service providers in their community.

These standards are initially envisioned to be self-regulating with each member of member organization implementing its own system of oversight and compliance. Additional review and monitoring of their implementation may be forthcoming based on guidance from the industry.

Standards for education service providers are described by three core competencies including <u>Knowledge of the Practice</u>, <u>Business Processes</u> and <u>Ethical Practices</u>. Each of these core competencies are further defined by a series of *value statements* that EIA members shall internalize in their respective organizations. More descriptive guidance of each of these value statements is provided to assist members in their interpretation and implementation of the Standards. However, each member may adopt other practices that are more appropriate to their philosophy and practice.

1. <u>Knowledge of the Practice Competency</u>—the EIA believes the main objective of education service providers, including individual instructors, supervisors and the organization is to enhance and improve student learning. The ESP:
   - *Shall demonstrate knowledge of how a student learns.*
     1. Understands that students learn through developmental levels, cognition, self-esteem, motivation and overall learning theory.
     2. Understands and plans for student differences regarding abilities, strengths, weaknesses and interests.
   - *Shall demonstrate knowledge of tutoring outcomes.*
     1. Understands that independent learners are created by teaching learning strategies and self-advocacy techniques.
   - *Shall demonstrate knowledge of commitment to consumer.*
     1. Utilizes academic goals and objectives critical to developing appropriate instruction.
     2. Utilizes continuous evaluation using multiple forms of evaluations and documents results to all appropriate stakeholders.
2. <u>Business Processes Competency</u>—the EIA believes education service providers carry the obligation to operate a business which will protect con-

sumers, offer fair trade opportunities for the provider, and provide a professional work environment for employees/contractors. The ESP:

- *Shall demonstrate commitment to consumer.*
  1. Accurately and completely describes services to consumers in easy to understand terms.
  2. Educates consumers regarding the need for services.
  3. Creates and uses promotional materials and advertisements which are free from deception.
  4. Maintains a system of addressing consumer grievances and concerns, such as maintaining an up to date file with the local Better Business Bureau, a third-party organization that already has significant experience with mediation.
- *Shall demonstrate a commitment to the organization.*
  1. Creates and adheres to, without bias, company policies and procedures.
  2. Provides training opportunities to staff to strengthen professional skills and expand knowledge base of tutoring theory and practices.
  3. Requires employees and contractors to subject to rigorous pre-employment background checks.
  4. Maintains a financially sound business.

3. Ethical Practice Competency—the EIA believes in principles constituting highly ethical behavior which provides a guide for decision making at all levels of an organization. The EIA also believes that conducting business in a sound ethical manner results in benefits to the consumer and to the financial health of the member organization. The ESP:

- *Shall obey all applicable laws, statutes, regulations and ordinances.*
  1. Conduct business honestly, fairly and with integrity.
  2. Comply with the confidentiality and non-disclosure provisions of all applicable federal, state and local laws, including those relating to student identity, records, reports, data, scores and other sensitive information.
  3. Apply these guidelines and standards throughout the company by insuring all employees understand them and act accordingly.
- *Shall support the continued education of oneself and your employees.*
  1. Actively participate in professional organization's seminars, training programs and other methods of life-long learning.

Guidelines for Qualifications of the Tutor/Education Service Provider (ESP)
Approved 3-2-05

The EIA believes in the importance in promoting a broad continuum of educational options for students and their families. Students learn in different ways and instruction must reflect this diversity. Our members embody the many different instructional strategies that advance good instruction and student learning. Student achievement should be the primary measure of the tutor's and ESP's effectiveness.

Each EIA member must establish their own internal standard for who they employ as tutors. We provide the following guidelines to assist our members in establishing their own procedures.

1. A **Master Tutor** may acquire the requisite knowledge to help students achieve learning gains through:
   * demonstrated knowledge of the ESP's education program/model,
   * possess at least a Bachelor's degree and/or teaching certificate, <u>and</u>
   * completion of a research supported tutor training program if degree is not in education.

2. A **Tutor** may acquire the requisite knowledge to help students achieve learning gains through:
   * demonstrated knowledge of the ESP's education program/model,
   * may be an undergraduate college student with at least 60 credit hours,
   * completion of a research supported tutor training program, <u>and</u>
   * supervised by ESP.

3. An **Education Assistant** may acquire the requisite knowledge to help students achieve learning gains through:
   * demonstrated knowledge of the ESP's education program/model,
   * possess at least a High School diploma
   * completion of a research supported tutor training program, <u>and</u>
   * supervised by ESP.

We strongly urge the use of pre-employment background screening to verify education, work history, and potential criminal records that may disqualify the individual.

EIA
Education Industry Association
Code of Professional Conduct and Business Ethics
For
Supplemental Educational Services Providers
Amended November 15, 2005

This <u>revised</u> code of ethics, as adopted by the EIA Board of Directors on November 15, 2005, shall become effective November 15, 2005.

SES Providers (and other education service providers) operate in an environment that touches communities, school officials, parents, students and other providers. The importance of the activities and complexity of the interactions make it paramount that EIA member organizations adhere to the highest standards of professional conduct and business ethics. In its role of providing critical leadership to the education industry, both public and private, EIA has adopted this voluntary code to describe key organizational behaviors and policies that will guide its member companies.

High quality educational programs delivered by trained professionals represent the core value that is to be reflected throughout all of our partnerships with schools, parents and students. The following structure represents the collective judgment of what constitutes ethical behavior. EIA members are committed to using it to guide to decision-making and performance at all levels of their organizations—from the CEO to the employee in the classroom. Accountability for achieving desired results consistent with these guidelines and standards is the ultimate benchmark upon which EIA member service providers will be judged.

We encourage States and Local School Districts to adopt these guidelines into their governance, contractual and oversight systems and apply all appropriate sanctions when the guidelines have been breached.

General Guidelines
In the conduct of business and discharge of responsibilities, Providers commit to:

1. Conduct business honestly, openly, fairly, and with integrity.
2. Comply with applicable laws, statues, regulations and ordinances.
3. Avoid known conflict of interest situations.
4. Never offer or accept illegal payments for services rendered.
5. Apply these guidelines and standards throughout the company by insuring all employees understand them and act accordingly.
6. Refrain from publicly criticizing or disparaging other providers.
7. In the case of a conflict, first attempt resolution directly with each other. However, the parties involved may ask EIA to help mediate potential disputes.
8. Comply with the confidentiality and non-disclosure provisions of all applicable federal, state and local laws, including those relating to student identity, records, reports, data scores and other sensitive information.
9. Be factual and forthright in reporting and documenting attendance rates, effectiveness of their programs, and in explaining the theoretical/empirical rationale behind major elements of its program, as well as the link between research and program design.
10. Take appropriate corrective action against provider employees, consultants or contractors who act in a manner detrimental to the letter or spirit of this code.
11. Take immediate steps to correct any actions on its part that will fully or inadvertently violate of the letter or spirit of this code.

Standards Specific to SES
EIA Members will consistently implement the NCLB Supplemental Services provisions and promote full access to SES services. To that end, Providers will NOT:

1. Compensate school district employees personally in exchange for access to facilities, to obtain student lists, to assist with marketing or student recruitment, to promote enrollment in a provider's program at the exclusion of other providers, to obtain other similar benefits for their SES program, or for any illegal purpose.

2. Employ any district employees who currently serve the districts in the capacity of Principal, Assistant Principal, or school or district SES Coordinator.

3. Employ any individuals, including teachers, parents or community leaders, who have any governing authority over a school district or school site.

4. Hire school-employed personnel for any purpose other than instruction-related services or program coordination, as described in item #3 in the next section below.

5. Make payments or in-kind contributions to schools or school personnel, exclusive of customary fees for facility utilization in exchange for access to facilities, to obtain student lists, to increase student enrollment, to obtain other similar benefits for their SES program or for any illegal purpose.

6. Misrepresent to anyone, including parents (during student recruitment), the location of a provider's program, principal/district or state's approval of a provider, or the likelihood of becoming so approved.

7. Offer a student any form of incentive for signing-up with a provider

8. Employ any District-enrolled student.

9. Use a district enrollment form that has the selected provider's name pre-printed as part of the form.

10. Encourage students/parents to switch providers once enrolled. A student is considered enrolled once the District has issued the formal student / Provider selection list.

Providers MAY:

1. Provide simple door prizes of a nominal value (approximately $5 per prize) and refreshments to potential students and their families, while attending informational sessions.

2. Offer enrolled students performance rewards with a maximum value of 5% of the district's PPA that are directly linked to documented meaningful attendance benchmarks and/or the completion of assessment and program objectives.

3. Employ school district employees (subject to items #2, #3, and #4 in the previous section above) for instruction-related services or program coordination purposes as long as the person does not restrict the marketing or enrollment opportunities of other providers, subject to District policies governing conflict of interests and other District-imposed requirements.

4. Include in tutor compensation, incentives for student achievement consistent with a company's written policy.

Industry Guidance for the Professional Conduct Of Members of the Education Industry Association Draft February 23, 2006

Education business, regardless of their service or product, operate in an environment that touches communities, school officials, parents, students and competitors. The importance of the activities and complexity of the interactions make it paramount that Education Industry Association (EIA) member organizations adhere to the highest standards of professional conduct and business ethics. In its role of providing leadership to the education industry, EIA has adopted this code for its members, who affirm their acceptance of these standards when they join and renew their annual membership in the organization.

High quality educational programs and products provided by professionals represent the core value that is to be reflected throughout all of our partnerships with schools, parents and students. The following structure represents out collective judgment of what constitutes ethical behavior. EIA members are committed to using it to guide to decision-making and performance <u>at all levels</u> of their organizations—from the boardroom to the employee in the classroom. Accountability for achieving desired results consistent with these guidelines and standards is the ultimate benchmark upon which EIA member service providers will be judged.

Violations of Code provisions are best adjudicated by government regulatory and licensing authorities or the Better Business Bureau. A member who is found to have violated the Code shall be afforded the opportunity to explain the issue to an ad hoc committee of their EIA-member peers.

EIA Member Guidelines
In the conduct of business and discharge of responsibilities, EIA members shall:

1. Conduct business honestly openly, fairly, and with integrity.
2. Comply with applicable laws, statutes, regulations and ordinances.
3. Avoid known conflict of interest situations.
4. Never offer or accept illegal payments for services rendered.
5. Apply these guidelines and standards throughout the company by insuring all employees understand them and act accordingly.
6. Refrain from publicly criticizing or disparaging other member-companies.
7. In the case of any conflict, first attempt resolution directly with each other. However, the parties involved may ask EIA to help mediate potential disputes.
8. Comply with the confidentiality and non-disclosure provisions of all applicable federal, state and local laws, including those resulting to student identity, records, reports, data, scores and other sensitive information. While members understand that unintentional disclosure of student identity, records, data, scores and other sensitive information could be damaging to the students, all efforts will be made to put in place systems to avoid such, and information to this effect will only be discussed between interested parties and documentation will be kept in a secure location.
9. Be factual and forthright in reporting and documenting effectiveness of their programs, services or products.
10. Take appropriate corrective action against employees, consultants or contractors who act in a manner detrimental to the letter or spirit of this code.
11. Take immediate steps to correct any actions on its part that willfully or inadvertently violate of the letter or spirit of this code.

MODEL RULES AND REGULATIONS OF TUTORING BY AN SEA

We are including the model rules and regulations for use by SEAs as a balanced and practical evaluation process of the qualifications for individuals, whether solo practitioners or major corporations, who wish to provide quality tutoring services for students. We wish to encourage more tutors to qualify for NCLB approval as supplemental service providers in their local communities.

We believe that many of these providers will expand their services beyond NCLB (if they have not already done so). It is clearly in the public interest for SEAs to develop meaningful industry regulations of these services as well. Tutoring services can be expected to continue expanding across the United States. Each state needs to broaden its ability to better regulate these services for use by parents and local schools.

MODEL RULES AND REGULATIONS IN RELATION TO NONPUBLIC EDUCATION TUTORING SERVICES

TABLE OF CONTENTS

Introduction

This document contains law and rules and regulations pertaining to the governance of non-public educational tutoring services doing business in the State of _____. A tutoring service is defined as an educational program privately owned and operated by an owner, partnership, or for-profit or not-for-profit corporation tutoring subjects for which tuition is charged for such tutorial instruction or other methods to prepare students to improve, enhance, or add to the skills and abilities of the individual relative to their general educational needs. Not included are volunteer-based educational tutoring services.

A tutoring service is considered to be doing business in _____ when it maintains an office, sells courses, mails instructional materials, grades lessons, holds classes, solicits enrollment by advertisement originating in _____ or performs a combination of any of these within the state.

1.0   CERTIFICATE OF APPROVAL—JURISDICTION.

    1.01   Certificate of Approval—Person Voluntarily Eligible—Nontransferability—Display—Approved Lists.

        A person, partnership or for-profit/not-for-profit corporation that conducts a non-public educational tutoring service in this State may voluntarily apply to be a certificate of approval by the State Education Agency (SEA). A person, partnership or corporation is qualified to receive a certificate of approval who complies with every standard, rule and regulation of the SEA pertaining to this Act, who pays the fee for a certificate of approval, and whose tutoring service, after an examination conducted under the direction of the SEA, is approved by the SEA. Such certificates of approval are not transferable. The SEA shall maintain, open to public inspection, a list of non-public educational tutoring services approved under this Act and may annually publish such list.

    1.02   Exemptions.

        1. Non-public educational tutoring programs offering a vocational or recreational courses shall be exempted if the main objective of instruction is not the development of educational skills but is instead entertainment, recreation, individual edification, hobby interest or cultural self-improvement.

2.0   CERTIFICATE OF APPROVAL—CONDITIONS.

    2.01   Application for Certificate—Contents.

        Every person, partnership or corporation doing business in _____ desiring to obtain a certificate of approval shall make a verified application to the SEA upon forms prepared and furnished by the SEA, setting forth the following information:

        1. The title or name of the tutoring service together with ownership and controlling officers, members, managing employees and director.

        2. Firm's location and phone number.

        3. Date firm began operation.

        4. Educational qualifications and professional experience of tutors and administrators.

        5. Professional licensing/accreditation.

        6. Exact description of professional tutoring services offered. Program objectives shall be clearly stated regarding the content of any professional service. The use of tests, remedial work, therapy formats, etc. shall be clearly explained.

        7. The availability of a competent referral program to other professionals (i.e. speech and hearing, vision, counseling, etc.) if and when needed.

        8. Anticipate duration of each program.

        9. The availability of confidential written educational outcome reports to parents, tutoring service, other professionals or others.

10. Evidence that it provides up-to-date educational materials to be used by the tutoring program.

11. Copies of student agreement to be used.

12. Method used to collect tuition and the procedure for collecting delinquent payments.

13. Copies of all brochures, films, and promotional material.

14. *Preliminary Evaluation-Eligibility & Ineligibility*: Every tutoring program shall describe and contain a definitive preliminary evaluation phase so that decisions shall be reached to determine the student's eligibility for a tutoring program— that the professional service in the specific program is actually needed by the client and that the client shall indeed improve his/her educational skills as a *direct* result of the specific program, or his/her ineligibility and an immediate referral made to another qualified educational program. The parent, guardian or adult shall be informed if at any time during a program the student does not respond positively to the tutoring help given, or no longer needs additional tutorial help.

15. *Final Program Evaluations* shall be described and conducted by qualified tutoring or other professionals germane to the service(s) offered.

16. *Time Frame of Program*: All tutoring programs shall have a definite calendar beginning, middle and end. All modifications in the program time frame shall be agreed to by the client before they are made. Modifications in the program time frame shall be based upon re-evaluation of the client's progress.

17. *Fees*: A fee list will be detailed. When a fee is quoted for services, the tutoring service shall be available at such a fee. If more than one fee is quoted, the differences in each related tutoring service shall be stated. Finance charges shall be fully explained in writing to the consumer. Fees shall be clearly explained verbally and in writing to the client before professional service is rendered.

18. *Use of Insurance, State or Federal Aid*: If insurance or State of Federal Aid is to be used by the client to pay the professional fees, the consumer shall be fully briefed as to its applicability in each specific case *before* he/she agrees to begin any tutoring program.

2.02 If the tutoring is performed in a "center," the non-public tutoring program shall provide information which shall include descriptions of:

1. Classrooms, laboratories, shops, libraries and other facilities for instruction and administration with detailed floor plans for

the places of instruction including dimensions, purpose and number of students to be accommodated.

2. Administrative/supervisory offices, conference rooms, restroom/toilet facilities, checkrooms, lockers or equivalent storage space.

3. The tutoring service shall maintain and make available upon request of the SEA copies of signed leases.

2.03   A non-public educational tutoring program shall provide evidence of financial resources sufficient to meet its operating demands for at least one (1) calendar year. If the tutoring service is owned by a corporation listed on a major national stock exchange, it will present a corporate financial statement accompanied by a notarized resolution signed by an officer of the corporation declaring that the corporation will guarantee any and all obligations of the tutoring service's operation.

2.04   The SEA may, with written reasons, require a financial audit of a publicly traded non-public educational tutoring program by a certified public accountant at the expense of the tutoring service and may request upon thirty (30) days' notice interim financial statements as circumstances warrant.

2.05   Tutors

All applications for approval to teach shall be made on forms provided by the SEA. They shall be accompanied by relevant transcripts and letters or documents supporting the statement of qualifications in the subjects for which the applicant seeks approval to tutor from individuals who can be reached for verification of the applicant's qualifications. Upon written petition to the SEA, the applicant may provide other evidence as reasonable proof of qualifications.

1. A current, valid state or post-secondary institution issued teacher's certificate in a relevant subject area issued by the SEA; or

2. A permanent, valid state or post secondary institution issued teacher's certificate in a relevant subject area issued by another state; or

3. Graduation from a state-approved, four-year college or university with a minimum of twenty-four (24) semester hours in the specific subject area of the instructional program in which the applicant intends to tutor. The non-public educational tutoring program shall establish and maintain policies which set forth qualifications and duties and procedures for supervision and evaluation of tutors.

2.06   Application Commitments.

Each application for a certificate of approval shall also contain the following commitments:

1. To conduct the non-public educational tutoring service in accordance with standards, rules and regulations from time to time established by the SEA;
2. To permit the SEA or his designee to inspect the tutoring classes thereof from time to time; and to make available to the SEA or his designee, at any time when required to do so, information pertaining to the activities of the tutoring service required for the administration of this Act;
3. That all advertising and solicitation will be free from misrepresentation, deception or fraud, or other misleading or unfair trade practices.

2.07 Signing of the application.

Each application for a certificate of approval shall be signed by the applicant. If the applicant is a partnership, it shall be signed by each member thereof. If the applicant is a corporation, it shall be signed by all the officers thereof.

Each application for a certificate of approval shall be signed and certified to under oath by all officers of the tutoring service.

1. All officers of the tutoring service for signing purposes for a tutoring service application shall be the president, secretary, treasurer and designated supervisor (director).

2.08 Restrictions of Certificate to Subjects Indicated in Application— Supplementary Applications.

Any certificate of approval issued shall be restricted to the subjects specifically indicated in the application for a certificate of approval. The holder of a certificate shall present a supplementary application as may be directed by the SEA for approval of additional subjects in which it is desired to offer tutoring during the effective period of the certificate of approval.

2.09 Annual Renewal of Certificate.

Each tutoring service that continues voluntarily to seek approval as such shall annually during the month of December renew its or his certificate of approval. The SEA shall have the authority to designate alternate renewal and expiration dates for all certificates of approval.

1. The certificate expiration date shall be December 31 of each year.

2.10 Grounds for refusal to issue, renew or to revoke certificates or permits.

In addition to any other cause herein set forth the SEA may refuse to issue, or to renew, or may revoke any certificate of approval or permit for any one or any combination of the following causes:

1. Violation of any provision of this Act or any rule or regulation made by the SEA that is unresolved through the complaint process.

2. Furnishing of false, misleading or incomplete information to the SEA or failure to furnish information requested by the SEA;

3. If any person who signed an application has entered a plea of nolo contendere or been found guilty of any crime involving moral turpitude;

4. If any person who signed an application is addicted to the use of any narcotic drug; has been found mentally incompetent, or has been convicted of any subversive activity;

5. Violation of any commitment made in an application for a certificate of approval;

6. Presenting to prospective students information relating to the tutoring service which is false, misleading or fraudulent;

7. If a tutoring center, failure to provide or maintain premises or equipment in a safe and sanitary condition as required by laws, regulations or ordinances applicable at the location of the tutoring service;

8. If a publicly traded corporation fails to maintain financial resources adequate for the satisfactory conduct of the courses of instruction offered;

9. Failure to retain a sufficient and qualified instructional and/or administrative staff;

10. Conduct of tutoring in a subject which has not been approved by the SEA for the particular tutoring service;

11. Refusal to admit applicants solely on account of race, color, creed, or sex;

12. Where the registrant has been convicted of any crime, an essential element of which is dishonesty, or has been convicted in this or another State of any crime which under the laws of any State or the United States is a felony, if the SEA determines, after investigation, that such person has not been sufficiently rehabilitated to warrant the public trust;

2.11 Issuance, revocation, renewal or restoration of certificates upon action and report of the SEA.

No certificate of approval shall be issued, revoked, renewed or restored except upon the action and report in writing of the SEA. The SEA shall preserve a written report of his findings and recommendations.

2.12 Periodic Review

The SEA shall review and investigate all approved non-public educational tutoring programs. Consideration should be given to complaints and information collected by the Federal Trade Commission, the Better Business Bureaus, and the _____ Attorney General's Office, Department of Consumer Protection, other State or official approval agencies, local school officials or interested programs. The SEA shall also conduct the following points of review:

1. Confer with the tutoring service against whom complaints have been lodged;
2. Investigate the involved tutoring service by visitation;
3. Initiate investigations upon receipt of complaints from interested persons.
4. Response to the individual submitting the complaint.

3.0 STUDENT AFFAIRS/ADMINISTRATION

   3.01 Enrollment Agreements

All contracts and agreements used by any non-public educational tutoring service approved by the SEA shall include the following disclosures:

1. The name and address of the tutoring service.
2. The name and description of the tutoring program subject including the number of hours of tutorial instruction.
3. The total cost of the course of instruction including any charges made by the tutoring service for tuition, books, materials, tests, and other expenses.
4. A clear and conspicuous statement that the agreement is a legally binding instrument when signed by the student or parent and accepted by the tutoring service.
5. An enrollment agreement is a contract, shall be separate and distinct from any other document, and be clearly labeled as a contract.
6. The enrollment agreement shall bear a date which indicates its current validity.

4.0 ADVERTISING

   4.01 In all advertising, tutor programs shall:

a. Indicate the complete and correct name and locations of the tutoring program as listed on its approval certificate.
b. If a tutoring center, indicate the exact locations where tutoring is to be given.
c. Convey true meanings, relationships and conditions when using any illustrations, diagrams, pictures or statements.
d. Use letters of approval, endorsement, commendation and recommendation, from any source, only with the written consent of the authors of such letters. Evidence of such consent shall be on file and subject to inspection. There shall be no payment for the use of such letters. Letters used shall include dates of authorship.
e. Indicate the exact extent or nature of the association with the tutoring program of any persons identified in the tutoring service's advertising whether:
  1. A bona fide working member of its faculty.
  2. A member of its governing or advisory board.

3. A consultant in any capacity.

4. An owner or investor in the tutoring program

4.02   The tutoring service shall not:

    a. Place its courses of instruction and programs in help-wanted columns in any publication.

    b. Represent that the tutoring service is "recommended" by the SEA.

4.03   A tutoring service shall be limited to the use of one of the following statements in advertising when referring to its _____ approval:

    a. "Approved by the _____ SEA";

    b. "Approved by the _____ SEA, non-public educational tutoring.

4.04   Advertisements/Content

1. The primary responsibility for truthful and non-deceptive advertising rests with the advertiser. Advertisers should be prepared to substantiate any claims or offers made before publication or broadcast and, upon request, present such substantiation promptly to the advertising medium or the SEA.

2. Advertisements which are untrue, misleading, deceptive, fraudulent, falsely disparaging of competitors, or insincere offers to sell, shall not be used.

3. An advertisement as a whole may be misleading although every sentence separately considered is literally true. Misrepresentation may result not only from direct statements but by omitting or obscuring a material fact such as: description of services, nature of children's learning problems, exact fees, qualifications of tutors, time duration of program, availability of written final summary reports to other professionals, availability of a clear and accurate final report to the parents, schools and other professionals.

4. Advertising Layout: The layout of an advertisement including the heading, text matter, illustrations and prices, shall not permit an erroneous impression as to exactly what type of professional service is offered at any quoted fee.

5. Illustrations: The illustrations of any activity performed by the tutoring service will state if this is an integral part of the program. It shall not exaggerate the services performed and shall not be used to knowingly or unknowingly mislead the client as to the positive results that have normally resulted from this educational program.

6. Trial Offers: If a "trial offer or any special offer is made, an expiration date shall be stated. "Free trial" means no obligation. The client shall be given the offered tutoring service without obligation.

7. Lowest price, underselling claims: Despite an advertiser's best efforts to ascertain competitive prices, the rapidity with which prices fluctuate and the difficulty of determining prices of all sellers at all times preclude an absolute knowledge of the truth of generalized underselling/lowest price claims. Advertisers should have proper substantiation for all claims prior to dissemination; unverifiable underselling claims should be avoided.

8. Testimonials and Endorsements: In general, advertising which uses testimonials or endorsements is likely to mislead or confuse if:

   a. It would provide a misleading anticipation of results to most people;

   b. It contains representation or statements which would be misleading if otherwise used in advertising;

   c. While literally true, it creates deceptive implications;

   d. The endorser is not competent or sufficiently qualified to express an opinion concerning the quality of the service being advertised or the results likely to be achieved by its use;

   e. It is not clearly stated that the endorser, associated with some well-known and highly-regarded institution, is speaking only in a personal capacity, and not on behalf of such an institution, if such be the fact;

   f. Broad claims are made as to endorsements or approval by indefinitely large or vague groups, e.g., "the homeowners of America," "the doctors of America."

   g. An endorser has a pecuniary interest in the company whose product or service is endorsed and this is not made known in the advertisement.

   Advertisers should consult Federal Trade Commission Guides on Testimonials and Endorsements for detailed guidance.

9. Claimed Results: Claims as to educational performance, test results, etc., which will be obtained by or realized from a particular service should be based on recent and recognized psychological, educational or other objective published professional data.

10. Superlative Sales Claims-Puffery: Superlative statements, like other advertising claims, are objective (factual) or subjective (puffery):

    a. *Objective claims* relate to tangible qualities and performance values of a service which can be measured against accepted standards or tests. As statements of fact, such claims can be proved or disproved and the advertiser should process substantiation.

b. *Subjective claims* are expressions of opinion or personal evaluation of the intangible qualities of a service. Individual opinions, statements of corporate pride and promises may sometimes be used, but they should not promise educational results that are unrealistic and without professional substantiation.

11. Guarantees: If a guarantee should be offered, a guarantee or warranty should be specific, clearly and conspicuously disclose its nature, time or other limitations, the manner in which the guarantor will perform and the identity of the guarantor. Unless otherwise stated, the responsibility for adjustment rests with the advertiser. An advertiser offering a guarantee or warranty should read and adhere to the "Guide Against Deceptive Advertising of Guarantees" issued by the Federal Trade Commission.

12. Money Back Guarantee: "Money Back Guarantee," or phrases of similar import, means a cash refund in full without any deduction.

5.0   PROGRAM INFORMATION/LITERATURE/CATALOG

5.01   The non-public educational tutoring program shall submit at the time of application or renewal three printed or duplicated copies of its program information with current supplements, if any.

5.02   The tutoring program shall provide all prospective students with a printed or duplicated copy of its program prior to any signing of the enrollment agreement or contract.

5.03   The tutoring program literature shall contain the following information:

a. The educational philosophy and itemized specific objectives of the tutoring service in complete, clear and simply stated language.

b. Month and year of publication.

c. Names, addresses, and telephone numbers of the principal tutor and/or administrative offices.

d. Names and titles of the administrative staff on the date of publication.

e. A description of the tutoring program offered including specific objectives, content, and length of course including clock hours. Such description shall be consistent with the course of instruction approved by the SEA.

f. Schedule of tutor fees and costs, books, supplies, equipment, or other services.

g. Minimum terms for payment, including the method used to collect tuition.

h. Policy and regulations pertaining to missed tutoring classes and student rules of conduct.

5.04   The tutoring program information shall reflect the tutoring service's current operations. Supplements shall be filed with the SEA at the time of implementation of operational changes.

6.0   <u>TUTORING PROGRAM</u>
The non-public educational tutorial program shall provide the SEA a description of the tutoring program which shall include a statement of the tutorial methods used, curriculum content, materials and equipment used by the tutorial program.

7.0   <u>RECORD KEEPING</u>

7.01   The tutoring program shall establish and maintain policies and procedures and have available for inspection a record-keeping system which shall include:
1. A safe, central repository for all records.
2. Length of time active and inactive files shall be maintained and provisions for their storage and disposal.
3. Administrative/supervisory and tutor records which verify the information required by the SEA.

7.02   The tutoring service shall establish, maintain and have available for inspection students' records which include:
1. A safe, central repository for all records.
2. Name, address, and date of birth.
3. Education/training given the student.
4. Records of all tests and other student data.
5. Name of tutored subject area.
6. Date of enrollment.
7. Payment record.
8. Schedule of classes or required hours of attendance.
9. Attendance and absences
10. Evidence that students or parents have been informed regularly about rate of progress in each tutoring program.
11. Final recommendations/results at the end of the tutoring program.

8.0   <u>COMPLAINT RESOLUTION</u>

8.01   Consumer complaints on tutoring services can be filed in writing through the local SEA, LEA and Better Business Bureaus located in the state or the national web site BBB.org.

8.02   The Better Business Bureau where the company is headquartered will process each complaint based on the inherent buyer-seller issues it includes using its usual complaint processing system and if appropriate:
1. The Better Business Bureau Advertising standards for tutoring services (included in State Tutoring Standards).
2. The Better Business Bureau tutoring business practice standards (included in State Tutoring Standards).

    3. The General Code of Advertising used by the Better Business Bureau.

8.03   Consumer complaints that are unresolved by the Better Business Bureau will be referred, to the SEA and LEA for further action.

9.0   HEARING PROCEDURES.

    9.01   Hearing of Charges—Notice—Opportunity to Present Evidence—Continuances.

The SEA or his designee shall before refusing to issue or renew, and before revocation of any certificate or permit, at least ten (10) days prior to the date set for the hearing, notify in writing the applicant for or holder of a certificate or permit, hereinafter called the respondent, that a hearing will be held on the date designed to determine whether the respondent is privileged to hold such certificate or permit, and shall afford the respondent an opportunity to be heard in person or by counsel in reference thereto. Such written notice may be served by delivery of the same personally to the respondent, or by mailing the same by registered mail to the place of business last theretofore specified by the respondent in the last notification to the SEA. At the time and place fixed in the notice, the SEA or his designated hearing officer shall proceed to hear the charges and both the respondent and the complainant shall be accorded ample opportunity to present in person or by counsel such statements, testimony, evidence and argument as may be pertinent to the charges or to any defense thereto. The SEA or his designated hearing officer may continue such hearing from time to time. If the SEA shall not be sitting at the time and place fixed in the notice or at the time and place to which the hearing shall have been continued, the SEA or his designated hearing officer shall continue such hearing for a period not to exceed thirty (30) days. Failure of the respondent to appear on the date set for hearing or failure to proceed as ordered by the SEA or his designated hearing officer shall constitute a default and automatic revocation.

    1. Notice of hearing shall be accompanied by a complaint containing a complete statement of charges and grounds for revocation or refusal to issue a certificate or solicitor permit. Any complaint filed with the SEA shall be attached to the notice given hereunder.

    9.02   Power to Subpoena and Administer Oaths.

The SEA is authorized to subpoena and bring before a hearing officer any person or persons in this State and to take testimony either orally or by deposition or by exhibit, with the same fees and mileage and in the same manner as prescribed by laws in judicial procedure in civil cases in Circuit Courts of this State.

9.03   Power of Circuit or Superior Courts.
        Any circuit court or any judge thereof, upon the application of the
        respondent or complainant, or of the SEA, may by order duly en-
        tered, require the attendance of witnesses and the production of
        relevant books and papers before any hearing the SEA is author-
        ized to conduct, and the court or judge may compel obedience to
        its or his order by proceedings for contempt.

9.04   SEA to Provide Stenographer—Record of Proceedings—
        Transcripts—Costs.
        The SEA shall provide a stenographer to take down the testimony
        and preserve a record of all proceedings at the hearing of any case
        involving the refusal to issue or renew, or the revocation of a cer-
        tificate or permit. The notice of hearing, complaint and all other
        documents in the nature of pleadings and written motions filed in
        the proceedings, the transcript of testimony, and the orders of the
        SEA shall be the records of such proceedings. The SEA shall fur-
        nish a transcript of such record to any person(s) interested in such
        hearing upon payment therefore, of $ ___ per page for each orig-
        inal transcript, and $____ per page for each copy thereof ordered
        with the original; provided, that the charge for any part of such
        transcript ordered and paid for previous to the writing of the orig-
        inal record thereof shall be $___ per page.

9.05   Service of SEA's Report upon Respondent—Motion for
        Rehearing –Time—Surrender of Certificate.
        The SEA or his designated hearing officer shall prepare written
        findings including: (a) a summary of the complaint; (b) findings
        of fact; and (c) reasons or basis for the order. In any case involv-
        ing the refusal to issue or renew or the revocation of a certificate
        or permit, a copy of the SEA's order shall be served upon the re-
        spondent, either personally or by certified mail as provided in this
        Act for the service of the notice of hearing. Within twenty (20)
        days after such service, the respondent may present to the SEA a
        motion in writing for a rehearing or a rescission of the order,
        which written motion shall specify the particular grounds there-
        fore. In the event no such motion for rehearing or rescission be
        filed, then upon the expiration of the time specified for filing a
        motion for rehearing, or in the event such motion be filed and de-
        nied, then the SEA shall order such denial. If such applicant or
        registrant shall order and pay for a transcript of the record as pro-
        vided in this Act, the time elapsing thereafter and before such tran-
        script is ready for delivery shall not be counted as part of such
        twenty (20) days. Upon the revocation of a certificate or permit,
        the holder shall be required to surrender such certificate or permit
        to the SEA, and upon failure or refusal so to do, the SEA shall
        have the right to seize the same.

9.06   Enforcement by the Attorney General—Office of Consumer Protection.
The SEA shall forward copies of all complaints of salesperson misrepresentations, deceptive advertising, or other unfair or misleading trade practices by tutoring services or their agents to the Office of Consumer Protection in the _____ Attorney General's Office. Questionable practices will be considered by that office to discover if any violation of the "Consumer Fraud and Deceptive Business Practices Act," as now or hereafter amended, has occurred.

9.07   Violations.
Any person or corporation violating the provisions of this Act shall, if a person, be guilty of a Class A misdemeanor. Any officer or agent of a corporation or member, or agent of a co-partnership, or association, shall be subject to the penalties herein prescribed for individuals; and the State's Attorney of the county where such offense is committed shall prosecute all persons violating the provisions of this Act upon proper complaint being made.

9.08   Injunction.
Upon application of the SEA through his attorneys, the Circuit Court of each county in which a violation of this Act or the Rules and Regulations has occurred, shall have jurisdiction to enjoin any violation thereto.

9.09   Private Action for Damages.
Any person who suffers damages as a result of a violation of this Act committed by any tutoring service or its representative may bring an action against such tutoring service. The court in its discretion may award actual damage or any other relief which the court deems proper.

1. Such action may be commenced in the county in which the tutoring service is located, has its principal place of business, or in the county where the transaction or any substantial portion thereof occurred.

2. In any action brought by a person under this Section, the court may award, in addition to the relief provided in this Section, reasonable attorney's fees and costs to the prevailing party.

APPENDIX—DEFINITIONS

Better Business Bureaus—non-profit business membership corporations located in almost 150 major U.S. cities which implement self-regulatory programs to assist the public in obtaining satisfaction in the marketplace.

Certificate of Approval—The document issued by the Superintendent after all the mandated conditions of the Non-Public Educational Tutoring Service Act and its rules and regulations in relation to the regulation of tutoring in _____ have been formally met by the applicant tutoring service. The certificate permits operation as a tutoring service.

course—a unit of subject matter, organized for both instructional and administrative purposes, given within a specified period of time, and covering a specified amount of subject matter.

curriculum—the entire set of tutoring instruction and learning experiences a service offers.

date of enrollment—the date of the latest signature affixed to the enrollment agreement as evidenced by signature by the student and the tutoring service.

LEA—Local Education Agency.

non-public educational tutoring programs or "tutoring service"—an educational institution privately owned and operated by an individual, partnership, or for-profit/not-for-profit corporation offering tutoring subjects, or programs for which tuition is charged, for such instruction to improve, enhance, or add to the learning abilities of the individual student. Not included are non-profit volunteer-based tutoring services.

refund policy—the course of action followed by a tutoring service to reimburse students canceling a contract and not completing a course of study.

renewal of approval—A "tutoring service" holding a current, valid certificate making application for uninterrupted continuation of its approved status.

SEA—State Education Agency

student—a person enrolled for study in a "tutoring service."

supervisor—a specific title designating an individual in a head administrative/ supervisory capacity, often referred to as a director in tutoring programs.

tuition—any payment or compensation for instruction and related costs whether paid by an individual, private organization or any agency of the United States, State of _____ or any political subdivision thereof.

tutor—a specific title designating an individual who provides tutorial instruction to students enrolled by the tutoring service.

tutoring program—a series of lessons having a unified purpose which lead to achievement of instructional objectives.

8

The Future of Tutoring

WHAT IS THE PURPOSE OF EDUCATION?

A 2006 Associated Press America Online Learning Service Poll (conducted by Knowledge Networks) surveyed parents and teachers of kindergarten through twelfth grade students (Feller, 2006). The results indicate that parents and teachers have widely varying views on the purposes of education and who has responsibility for student learning.

Jason Cleveland, a thirty-four-year-old teacher in East Troy, Wisconsin, asks the eternal question about students who show no interest in learning. "How do you motivate somebody like that? They are kids who, for whatever reasons, don't see a connection for themselves."

The poll found that 43 percent of parents say students' low expectations are a serious problem. Fifty-four percent of teachers agree, including almost two out of three high school teachers. But who drives this motivational process?

Parents think that teachers should both challenge and reward students to increase academic expectations. Teachers look to parents to instill respect, manners, and a basic motivation for learning. However, the poll reveals that what should be a shared learning partnership between parents and teachers in many cases has broken down.

Mike Randell, an Indiana health teacher, relates, "I hear these parents saying, 'Well, my children aren't doing very well, so you must not be a very good teacher.'"

Randell's response: "Wrong. Sorry. It's more like, 'If you child would follow the curriculum, open the book, and apply himself, you would see how good this could all be.'"

211

Real school reform is only possible if we have the courage to challenge the present cultural bias toward maintaining the status quo and attempt something new. The role that tutoring may serve was highlighted by the personal experience of Karin Klein (2006), an editorial writer for the *Los Angeles Times*. In 1968 while they were both attending Walt Whitman Junior High, Klein tutored a fellow student, Johnny Patrello, in algebra. Klein recently reflected on this peer-tutoring experience:

> I thought about Johnny again as I read *The Times'* series this week on L.A.'s dropout problem. Algebra, the reporters found, is an insurmountable stumbling block for many high school students.
>
> What struck me was that the reasons why Johnny can't do algebra in L.A. today are remarkably similar to why Johnny Patrello couldn't do algebra almost four decades ago in Yonkers, N.Y. . . .
>
> Things looked pretty hopeless to both of us those first couple of sessions. . . . Then, as we took it down to each step of each little calculation, the trouble became clear: Johnny somehow had reached ninth grade without learning the multiplication tables . . .
>
> As Johnny tried to work algebraic equations, his arithmetic kept bringing up weird results. But at least we knew where to start. We spent about half of those early sessions on multiplication drills. Seven times eight, eight times seven — Johnny could never remember. As an adult in memory of Johnny's struggles, I would rehearse my kids at an early age in that one math fact. Get that 56 down, I would tell them, and the rest of multiplication is a snap. . . . Today's failing high school students . . . bring the same scanty skills to algebra class, according to *The Times'* series . . .
>
> Who can focus on the step-by-step logic of peeling back an equation until "*x*" is bared when it involves arithmetic that comes slow and slippery, always giving a different answer to the same calculation?
>
> Yet in all these decades, the same school structure that failed Johnny goes on, dragging kids through the grades even if they don't master the material from the year before. . . .
>
> What I learned from Johnny . . . children's skills are all over the map, yet we corral them into second grade, third grade and so forth, where everyone moves at one pace in all subjects. . . .If they're not getting it, give them extra tutoring, but don't push them forward until they're ready. . . . It requires a sea change in thinking.

Before Klein used Johnny's name in her story she called him to get permission. She learned that he had died a year and a half earlier leaving behind his wife, Joann, and four children. The eldest is a doctor, the second a teacher. The teenage daughter wants to become a journalist.

Johnny became an auto mechanic. "He loved math, and you know auto repair involves a lot of math," Joann told her. One last thing his wife related about Johnny. He was "incredibly fast at multiplication."

Many of the same academic achievement problems that bedeviled Johnny in 1968 remain with U.S. education today. Yet the tutoring that helped him pass a New York State Regents Examination is still beset by serious professional issues. These problems continue to limit the future availability of high-quality tutoring services across American education. Gordon (2004a, 2004b) sees many of these issues are cultural; others strike at identifying the theoretical and empirical foundations of tutoring. They can be summarized under four major themes:

1. The need for tutoring services versus the perceived value of tutoring
2. The essential nature of tutoring
3. Changing the current cultural attitudes concerning tutors and tutoring
4. Tutoring at a crossroad

NEED VERSUS PERCEIVED VALUE

The American public spends between $8 billion and $10 billion on tutoring services annually (2004 estimate). Currently this seems to be driven by two major factors. First, the continuing national and international reports that find far too many U.S. students and adults are educationally deficient in some respect. Their literacy skills are low (Brown et al., 1994, Kutner et al., 2005), up to 50 percent of our urban youth fail to graduate from high school (Losen, et al., 2004), and Americans are reading less (National Endowment for the Arts, 2004).

The second factor may be the dramatic increase in high-stakes testing as part of the No Child Left Behind Act (NCLB). Many parents fear having their child retained.

Yet just as the demand for tutors is increasing, teacher shortages are growing across America. The demographic shift has begun that will see many baby boomers retiring from the classroom. By 2010 up to 2.6 million new teachers will be needed in the United States (Hecker, 2001). The supply of professional, expert tutors is diminishing, particularly in the areas of reading disabilities, learning disabilities, and higher math and science. (These areas have traditionally required the most tutors.) Therefore, the price for high-quality, expert tutoring is going up and will keep rising.

But ironically neither the general American public nor schooling professionals recognize the tutor as a professional educator with well-defined expertise.

From this viewpoint, almost anyone can tutor. Thus the majority of parents and educators look for the lowest-price tutoring available in their community or alternatively for free, volunteer-based tutoring.

Although Americans want more tutoring, they view it as a "one-size-fits-all" activity. If anyone can do it, why pay a higher price for an expert, professional tutor?

WHAT IS TUTORING?

The general public and schooling professionals do have differences in their views of tutoring. The general public's viewpoints commonly fall into three categories:

1. The most common perception is that tutors are paid or volunteer homework helpers. Many parents see tutoring as a short-term activity, such as getting homework done, preparing for a test, or helping boost a grade in a subject. The tutor is a helper "who puts out the fire."
2. Another popular view is that tutors are volunteers or paid helpers in elementary or high schools, college learning centers, community centers, or local churches. They act as tutors or in some cases mentors, usually focusing on the short-term, immediate learning emergency.
3. Less widely known, though gaining in popular use, are paid professional tutors who offer extensive help centering on diagnostic/developmental tutoring. They focus on helping a student learn how to learn as well as build skills. These tutors tend to be used for a longer duration, typically from three to six months.

Among schooling professionals, tutoring is generally viewed at best as well-intentioned help provided by volunteers and education amateurs. At worst, schooling professionals view tutoring as commercial hucksterism preying on parental fears to exploit the public for a quick profit. These views are supported by at least four basic cultural tensions between schooling professionals and professional tutors:

1. The schooling bias against tutoring has historic roots. The rise of the common school replaced tutoring in the home as the basis of American literacy. The use of a tutor is a step backward.
2. There is a bias against using peer tutoring in school classrooms. The predominant images of being students and teacher is summed up by the medieval monastery rule, "It belongeth to the master to speak and to

teach; it becometh the disciple to be silent and to listen." Students should be trained as passive observers rather than trained to become active participants as peer tutors in their own education.

3. Paid professional private tutors are only for the rich. Learning in school is the bedrock of the republic, while private home tutoring is elitist and almost un-American. Also, using a private tutor implies that the teacher has failed. Educators generally believe that parents do not have the expertise to make that judgment.

4. Tutoring is not "real education." No significant research has been published proving that it works. Tutoring methods and practices have not been the focus of college undergraduate or graduate courses, and therefore tutoring is not a degreed career specialty in the education profession.

The general public and most schooling professionals see tutoring as having relatively low value. Tutoring is not a profession universally recognized by American popular culture or by the education establishment. The bottom line is that the culture expects tutoring to be informal, quick, and cheap, or even free. The tutor as an "automaton." Almost anyone can be a tutor. This is the overall cultural environment in which tutoring has been struggling for the past 30-plus years and even before.

CHANGING THE CULTURE: ATTITUDES AND EXPECTATIONS ABOUT TUTORS AND TUTORING

When we were children many of us used to play, What do you want to be when you grow up? Remember the old childhood rhyme? "Rich man, poor man / Beggar man, thief / Doctor, lawyer, Indian chief."

How many children wanted to become a teacher? What about a tutor? The authors of this book believe that the professional tutor is an education expert, a specialist. The professional tutor is not a homework helper. The professional tutor is not a volunteer.

The Tutoring Revolution has begun the process of reviewing the body of research from the past thirty years that will help define for the general public and school systems two key elements of tutoring:

1. The components of an effective tutoring curriculum and what constitutes tutoring best practices.

2. The background of a professional tutor in terms of education and experience.

From the author's research we previously identified ten key components for more effective tutoring that merit repeating:

1. Tutors can be effective regardless of their training and education by just giving students more personal attention. However, teacher education, prior professional experience, and specialized training as a tutor can make a major difference. Professionally prepared tutors consistently produce significantly higher levels of student achievement than do tutors with little or no preparation.
2. Tutors need to use a diagnostic/developmental template to organize and implement each student's tutoring program.
3. Tutors must be able to track the session-to-session progress of each student in order to modify tutoring content and use student academic strengths to overcome weaknesses.
4. Principles of learning drawn from both cognitive and constructivist thinking seem to offer the strongest contemporary tutoring methods.
5. Tutors need to use continuous feedback to help students develop a positive self-image as learners.
6. Formal/informal assessment needs to be used throughout the tutoring process.
7. Mentoring/coaching students on learning how to learn through providing guidance on study habits, test taking, and attention to school and learning in general is a significant informal part of effective tutoring.
8. Mentoring/coaching each student's parents on sustaining the day-to-day learning process in the home after each tutoring session seems an important component of tutoring.
9. To facilitate the coaching of parents, it is desirable to conduct the tutoring in the student's own home outside of school hours. If this is not possible, a community center, school, or library can be used, but the tutor should still make an effort to provide mentoring to the parents.
10. Throughout the tutoring, tutors must collaborate closely with each student's classroom teacher. The final measure of the effectiveness of the tutoring is the short-term and long-term improvement of the student's day-to-day classroom achievement.

At its core identifying professional tutors and defining effective tutoring is a quality versus quantity issue. The most promising tutoring practices seem to be found among different types of well-educated, paid professional tutors and highly trained and closely supervised groups of volunteer tutors.

The end result is that changing cultural attitudes and expectations will mean better defining the who, what, why, when, where, and how of tutors and tutoring. If the general public and other professional educators are ever going to recognize that a tutoring profession exists and that quality tutoring is more effective in increasing student achievement, there needs to be more consensus on:

Who tutors are: What educational preparation should a professional tutor receive?

What tutors do: What curricula and methods work best?

Why tutoring works: How can tutoring best practices use principles from the psychology of learning?

When does tutoring become effective: How much time on a task is needed?

Where does tutoring happen best: Under what conditions do we get the best results?

How do we ensure high-quality tutoring programs?

TUTORING AT A CROSSROAD

Tutoring is now at an educational crossroad. Whatever the future course of NCLB, either professional tutoring will become recognized as an education discipline and defined as a professional career, or tutoring will remain essentially a nonprofessional activity using low-paid semiprofessionals or unpaid amateurs.

Professional tutoring offers important opportunities for significantly improving the achievement of students in the classroom. The establishment of a recognized tutoring profession requires two courses of action: Additional credible research on tutoring needs to be published by researchers and tutoring practitioners and needs to be used in the education of tutors.

Do we know why tutoring is effective? As previously noted, there are many hypotheses but very limited evidence-based findings. The details related to why certain tutoring structures yield positive results require additional investigation.

We believe that future tutoring research may result from pursuing two paths of inquiry:

1. A focus on the provision of detailed explanations indicating why specific tutoring practices and procedures yield better student learning outcomes. Merely continuing to document that there are positive outcomes associated with a particular tutoring intervention is of little value in helping to identify tutoring best practices.

2. A concentration of efforts is needed on a more systematic study of the social aspects of tutoring. This inquiry might begin with Vygotsky, social learning, mentoring, and constructionist teaching and learning perspective as outlined by the authors in chapter 3.

Colleges and universities across America need to use the research described here to create new undergraduate and graduate courses on tutoring that include instructional methods, curricula, and research methodology. The time has come for every prospective teacher to receive a required undergraduate course on tutoring. A graduate degree in tutoring will assist the education establishment in conducting research and recognizing this important area of educational practice and inquiry as a professional career area.

SOME CLOSING THOUGHTS

We believe that tutoring has made a significant contribution to education in the evolution of schooling. Today the schools are synonymous with education, but this was not always true. There is much evidence that a sizable amount of education took place in the home using one-to-one instruction by a variety of tutors, including parents. Through many centuries in aristocratic and later middle-class households children were commonly educated by tutors and governesses. At their best, these educators were able to discern the strengths and aptitudes of each child and design an individualized educational program. Some of the most important philosophers of the West developed educational theories based on their practical experience as tutors, rather than as schoolteachers. Their tutorial philosophy developed into many of our modern educational principles (Gordon & Gordon, 1990, 2003).

In the late nineteenth and early twentieth centuries, educational theorists incorporated concepts from the tutor-philosophers into the broader context of the American common school movement. Modern theorists, however, overlooked the fact that the original context of the tutor-philosopher was one-to-one instruction at home, not group instruction in a classroom. This remains a fundamental reason why many classroom teachers experience daily frustration as they attempt to carry out educational principles originally formulated in a tutorial environment.

Schooling has dominated the twentieth century, but tutoring still holds an important role. Peer-tutors, after-school remedial programs, home-bound instruction, home schooling, and NCLB are tutoring's modern expressions. Modern educators obscured this issue by describing one-to-one instruction using terms other than "tutoring." Through this exclusionary process tutoring has been almost eliminated from our modern notion of serious education in the United States.

The development of tutoring has largely been the study of individuals, not institutions. What has been lost is the evolution of tutoring best practices. However, schooling and tutoring did not develop as socio-educational phenomena isolated from each other. Instead, at many times they have supported each other in providing for the broader educational needs of society. As we have already seen, compelling evidence now exists that tutors have enhanced many children's educational foundations through one-to-one relationships.

Today the challenge of twenty-first-century schooling requires a broader study of tutoring practices and methods. We hope that *The Tutoring Revolution* helps begin a national reassessment of tutoring as a vital component of American education. The tutor and teacher are not in competition. Instead, we need additional research focusing on how a new alliance of tutoring and teaching will better serve America's students and future education reform.

Appendix

Consumer Tutoring Quality Rating Scale

1. What is the professional record of the program? (Years in operation, number of students served)

1	2	3	4	5
Very New	Moderate	Experienced	Very Experienced	Highly Experienced

2. How strong are the tutor's or program's references? (Community knowledge and reputation)

1	2	3	4	5
Unknown or Poor	Somewhat Questionable	Fair	Good	Highly Esteemed

3. What licensing has an individual tutor or program received? (Teacher certification, state approval, program accreditation)

1	2	3	4	5
None	Applying for licensing or Accreditation	Professional Licensing	State Licensing (if available)	Accreditation

4. What percentage of tutors are college degreed and only tutor in subjects they are certified to teach?

1	2	3	4	5
Not Required	20%	40%	60%	80% and above

5. To what degree are the tutors supervised by a qualified, degreed educational administrator?

1	2	3	4	5
No Supervision	Little Supervision, Few Qualifications	Some Supervision, Fairly Qualified	Well Supervised, Fairly Qualified	Fully Supervised Fully Qualified

6. Does the program offer the exact type of tutoring services you need? (Curriculum and convenience)

1	2	3	4	5
Program Unclear	Generic, One Size Fits All Program	Fairly Good Fit To Many Needs	Good, Close To My Needs	Precise Fit To My Needs

7. How clear are program fees and other contract charges?

1	2	3	4	5
Very Confusing	I Still have Questions	Complex but Understandable	Clear	Very Clear and Simple

8. Does the program feature student progress reports? (When, by whom, in what form)

1	2	3	4	5
Unclear	Final Verbal Report	Informal & Final Verbal Report	Informal & Final Written Report	Formal, Often, Both Verbal & Written Final Reports

9. What are the customer service capabilities of the program? (Inquiries, complaints, questions, responsiveness)

1	2	3	4	5
Little Ability to Respond to Problems	Usually Voice Mail Only Response Available	Some Effort to Respond	Tutor Can Usually Be Reached & is Responsive	Tutor & Program Administrator Usually Reachable & Reply Promptly

10. How safe is the tutoring program? (Tutoring site and staff background)

1	2	3	4	5
Security Questionable	Casual Attitude Toward These Issues	Fairly Safe	Good Environment	Extremely Safe Professional Environment

My overall rating of the tutoring program's quality:

1	2	3	4	5
Poor	Fair	Good	Very Good	Excellent

NOTE: All factors will not be applicable in all situations. For instance, supervision will not be an issue if an individual teacher is engaged as a tutor.

Bibliography

Abrams, L.M., Pedulla, J.J., & Madaus, G.F. (2003). Views from the classroom: Teachers' opinions of statewide testing programs. *Theory into Practice, 42*(1), 18–29.

American School Board Journal. (2005, May). National School Boards Association.

Ames, C., & Ames, R.E. (Eds.). (1985). *Research on motivation in education: Vol. 2. The classroom milieu.* Orlando, FL: Academic Press.

Ames, C., & Ames, R.E. (1989). *Research on motivation in education: Vol. 3. Goals and cognitions.* Orlando, FL: Academic Press.

Ames, R.E., & Ames, C. (Eds.). (1984). *Research on motivation in education: Vol. 1. Student motivation.* Orlando, FL: Academic Press.

Anderson, G.L., & Herr, K. (1998). The new paradigm wars: Is there room for rigorous practitioner knowledge in schools and universities? *Educational Researcher, 28*(5), 12–21.

Anderson, J., & Labiere, C. (1998). *The atomic components of thought.* Mahwah, NJ: Erlbaum.

Anderson, J.R. (1993). *Rules of the mind.* Hillsdale, NJ: Erlbaum.

Anderson, J.R., Corbett, A.T., Koedinger, K.R., & Pelletier, R. (1995). Cognitive tutors: Lessons learned. *The Journal of the Learning Sciences, 4*(2), 167–207.

Anderson, L.W., & Burns, R.B. (1987). Values, evidence, and mastery learning. *Review of Educational Research, 57*(2), 215–224.

Annis, L.F. (1983). The processes and effects of peer tutoring. *Human Learning, 2*, 39–47.

Armor, D.J. (2002, November 19). Environmental effects on IQ, from the family or from schools? *Education Week,* 32–33.

Aronson, E. (1978). *The jigsaw classroom.* Beverly Hills, CA: Sage.

Azevedo, R. (Ed.) (2005a). Special issue: Computers as metacognitive tools for enhancing learning. *Educational Psychologist, 40*(4), 193–271.

Azevedo, R. (2005b). Using hypermedia as a metacognitive tool for enhancing student learning? The role of self-regulated learning. *Educational Psychologist, 40*, 199–209.

Bakermans-Kranenburg, M.J., Van Ijzendoorn, M.H., & Bradley, R.H. (2005). Those who have, receive: The Matthew effect in early childhood intervention is the home environment. *Review of Educational Research, 75*, 1–26.

Banchero, S. (2005, September 1). U.S. will let city schools run tutoring. *Chicago Tribune, 2*, pp, 1, 6.

Bandura, A. (1974). Behavior theory and the models of man. *American Psychologist, 29*(12), 859–869.

Bandura, A. (1977a). Self-efficacy: Toward a unifying theory of behavioral change. *Psychological Review, 84*(2), 191–215.

Bandura, A. (1977b). *Social learning theory.* New Jersey: Prentice-Hall.

Bandura, A. (1978). The self system in reciprocal determinism. *American Psychologist, 33*(4), 344–358.

Bandura, A. (1982). Self-efficacy mechanism in human agency. *American Psychologist, 37*(2), 122–147.

Bandura, A. (1983). Self-efficacy determinants of anticipated fears and calamities. *Journal of Personality and Social Psychology, 45*(2), 464–468.

Bandura, A. (1984). Recycling misconceptions of perceived self-efficacy. *Cognitive Therapy and Research, 8*(3), 231–255.

Bandura, A. (1986). From thought to action: Mechanisms of personal agency. *New Zealand Journal of Psychology, 15*(1), 1–17.

Bandura, A. (1989). Regulation of cognitive processes through perceived self-efficacy. *Developmental Psychology, 25*(5), 729–735.

Bandura, A. (1991). Social cognitive theory of self-regulation. *Organizational Behavior and Human Decision Processes, 50*(2), 248–287.

Bandura, A. (1992). On rectifying the comparative anatomy of perceived control: Comments on "cognates of personal control." *Applied and Preventive Psychology, 1*(2), 121–126.

Bandura, A. (1993). Perceived self-efficacy in cognitive development and functioning. *Educational Psychologist, 28*(2), 117–148.

Bandura, A. (1997). *Self-efficacy: The exercise of control.* New York: Freeman.

Banks, J.A. (2000). The social construction of difference and the quest for educational quality. In R.S. Brandt (Ed.), *Education in a new era: 2000 ASCD yearbook* (pp. 21–46). Alexandria, VA: Association for Supervision and Curriculum Development.

Barksdale-Ladd, M.A., & Thomas, K.F. (2000). What's at stake in high-stakes testing: Teachers and parents speak out. *Journal of Teacher Education, 51*(5), 384–397.

Barone, T., & Eisner, E. (1997). Arts-based educational research (pp. 73–94). In R.M. Jaeger (Ed.), *Complementary methods for research in education.* Washington, DC: American Educational Research Association.

Baumeister, R.F., Campbell, J.D., Krueger, J.I., & Vohs, K.D. (2003). Does high self-esteem cause better performance, interpersonal success, happiness, or healthier lifestyles? *Psychological Science in the Public Interest, 4*(1), 1–44.

Berliner, D.C. (2002). The hardest science of all. *Educational Researcher, 31*(8), 18–20.

Berliner, D.C., & Calfee, R.C. (1997). *Handbook of educational psychology.* New York: Simon & Schuster/Macmillan.

Bidwell, A., & Braser, M. (1989). Role modeling versus mentoring in nursing education. *Image: Journal of Nursing Scholarship, 21*(1), 23–25.

Black's Law Dictionary (7th ed.). (1999). B.A. Garner and H.C. Black (Eds.). St. Paul, MN: West Publishing Co.

Block, J.H. (1971). *Mastery learning: Theory and practice.* New York: Holt, Rinehart & Winston.

Block, J.H., & Burns, R.B. (1976). Mastery learning. In L.S. Shulman (Ed.), *Review of research in education* (Vol. 4). Itasca, IL: Peacock.

Bloom, B.S. (1968). Learning for mastery. *Evaluation Comment, 1*(2), 460, 463–465.

Bloom, B.S. (1971). Mastery learning. In J.H. Block (Ed.), *Mastery learning: Theory and practice* (pp. 47–63). New York: Holt, Rinehart & Winston.

Bloom, B.S. (1974). Time and learning. *American Psychologist, 29*, 682–688.

Bloom, B.S. (1976). *Human characteristics and school learning.* New York: McGraw-Hill.

Bloom, B.S. (1984). The search for methods or group instruction as effective as one-to-one tutoring. *Educational Leadership, 41*(8), 4–18.

Bloom, B.S. (1995). The search for methods of instruction. In A.C. Ornstein & L.S. Behar (Eds.), *Contemporary issues in curriculum* (pp. 208–225). Boston: Allyn & Bacon.

Boneau, C.A. (1990). Psychological literacy: A first approximation. *American Psychologist, 45*(7), 891–900.

Borman, G.D., Hewes, G.M., Overman, L.T., & Brown, S. (2003). Comprehensive school reform and achievement: A meta-analysis. *Review of Educational Research, 73*(2), 125–230.

Bower, G.H., & Hilgard, E.R. (1981). *Theories of learning* (5th ed.). Englewood Cliffs, NJ: Prentice-Hall.

Bower, G.H., & Hilgard, E.R. (1998). *Theories of learning.* Englewood Cliffs, NJ: Prentice-Hall.

Brainin, S.S. (1985). Mediating learning: Pedagogic issues in the improvement of cognitive functioning. In E.W. Gordon (Ed.), *Review of research in education* (Vol. 12). Washington, DC: American Educational Research Association.

Bransford, J., Sherwood, R., Vye, N., & Rieser, J. (1986). Teaching, thinking, and problem solving. *American Psychologist, 41*(10), 1078–1089.

Brophy, J. (1981). Teacher praise: A functional analysis. *Review of Educational Research, 51*, 5–32.

Brophy, J. (1988). Research linking teacher behavior to student achievement: Potential implications for instruction of chapter 1 students. *Educational Psychologist, 23*(3), 235–286.

Brown, A.L. (1978). Knowing when, where, and how to remember: A problem of metacognition. In R. Glaser (Ed.), *Advances in instructional psychology.* Hillsdale, NJ: Erlbaum.

Brown, A.L. (1994). The advancement of learning. *Educational Researcher, 23*(8), 4–12.

Brown, A.L. (1997). Transforming schools into communities of thinking and learning about serious matters. *American Psychologist, 52*(4), 399–413.

Brown, A.L., & Campione, J.C. (1994). Guided discovery in a community of learners. In K. McGilly (Ed.), *Classroom lessons: Integrating cognitive theory* (pp. 229–270). Cambridge, MA: MIT Press.

Brown, H., Prisuta, R., Jacobs, B., & Campbell, A. (1996). *Literacy of older adults in America: Results from the National Adult Literacy Survey.* (NCES 97576). Washington, DC: U.S. Separtment of Education.

Bruer, J. (1993a). The mind's journey from novice to expert. *American Educator, 17*(2), 6–46.

Bruer, J.T. (1993b). *Schools for thought: A science of learning in the classroom.* Cambridge, MA: MIT Press.

Bruer, J.T. (1997). Education and the brain: A bridge too far. *Educational Researcher, 26*(8), 4–16.

Bruner, J.S. (1990). *Acts of meaning.* Cambridge, MA: Harvard University Press.

Bruner, J.S. (1996). *The culture of education.* Cambridge, MA: Harvard University Press.

Brunken, R., Plass, J.L., & Leutner, D. (2003). Direct measurement of cognitive load in multimedia learning. *Educational Psychologist, 38*(1), 53–62.

Burke, A.J. (1984). Student's potential for learning contrasted under tutorial and group approaches to instruction (Doctoral dissertation, University of Chicago, 1983). *Dissertation Abstracts International, 44,* 2025A.

Buss, A.R. (1976). The myth of vanishing individual differences in Bloom's mastery learning. *Instructional Psychology, 3,* 4–14.

Calhoun, J.F. (1973, August). *Elemental analysis of the Keller method of instruction.* Paper presented at the annual meeting of the American Psychological Association, Montreal, Canada.

Callinicos, A. (1997). Postmodernism: A critical diagnosis. In *The great ideas today* (pp. 206–255). Chicago: Encyclopaedia Brittanica.

Cambridge Dictionary of American English. (2004). Cambridge, MA: Cambridge University Press.

Cameron, J., & Pierce, W.D. (1994). Reinforcement, reward, and intrinsic motivation: A meta-analysis. *Review of Educational Researcher, 64,* 363–423.

Carroll, J.B. (1963). A model of school learning. *Teachers College Record, 64,* 723–733.

Cascio, W.F. (1995). Whither industrial and organizational psychology in a changing world of work? *American Psychologist, 50,* 928–939.

Case, R. (1985). A developmentally based approach to the problem of instructional design. In S.F. Chipman, J.W. Segal, & R. Glaser (Eds.), *Thinking and learning skills* (Vol. 2). Hillsdale, NJ: Erlbaum.

Ceci, S.J., & Papierno, P.B. (2005). The rhetoric and reality of gap closing: When the "have-nots" gain but the "haves" gain even more. *American Psychologist, 60*(2), 149–160.

Center on Education Policy. (2005). *From the capital to the classroom: Year 3 of the No Child Left Behind Act.* Retrieved April 20, 2005, from www.cep-dc.org/nclby3/press/cep-nclby3_21Mar2005.pdf.

Chase, W.G., & Simon, H.A. (1973). Perception in chess. *Cognitive Psychology, 1,* 33–81.

Chicago Public Schools, Office of Research, Evaluation, and Accountability, Department of Evaluation and Data Analysis. (2005). *SES tutoring programs: An evaluation of the second year: Part one of a two-part report.* Chicago: Chicago Public Schools.

Chomsky, N. (1972). *Language and mind.* New York: Harcourt Brace Jovanovich.

Cohen, J. (1988). *Statistical power analysis for the behavioral sciences* (2nd ed.). Hillsdale, NJ: Erlbaum. As a general guideline an effect size value of 0.20 is currently used benchmark for a small effect, 0.50 for a medium effect, and 0.80 for a large effect.

Cohen, P.A., Kulik, J.A., & Kulik, C.C. (1982). Educational outcomes of tutoring: A meta-analysis of findings. *American Educational Research Journal, 19*(2), 237–248.

Colarelli, S.M. (1998). Psychological interventions in organizations: An evolutionary perspective. *American Psychologist, 53*(9), 1044–1056.

Colligan, J.T. (1974). *Achievement and personality characteristics as predictors of observed tutor behavior.* Doctoral dissertation, Arizona State University.

Collins, C., Brown, J., & Newman, S. (1989). Cognitive apprenticeship: Teaching the crafts of reading, writing, and mathematics. In L. Resnick (Ed.), *Knowing, learning, and instruction: Essays in honor of Robert Glaser* (pp. 453–494). Hillsdale, NJ: Erlbaum.

Cognition and Technology Group at Vanderbilt. (1990). Anchored instruction and its relationship to situated cognition. *Educational Researcher, 19*(6), 2–10.

Condry, J. (1977). Enemies of exploration: Self-initiated versus other-initiated learning. *Journal of Personality and Social Psychology, 35,* 459–477.

Constas, M.A. (1998a). Deciphering postmodern educational research. *Educational Researcher, 27*(9), 36–42.

Constas, M.A. (1998b). The changing nature of educational research and a critique of postmodernism. *Educational Researcher, 27*(2), 26–33.

Cook, S.B., Scruggs, T.E., Mastropieri, M.A., & Casto, G.C. (1985–1986). Handicapped students as tutors. *Journal of Special Education, 19,* 155–164.

Council of Better Business Bureaus, Inc. (2000, September). *The Do's and Don'ts in Advertising Copy.* Supplement 607–25, Section 19, 863–65.

Council of Chief State School Officers. (2002). *State education agency toolkit on supplemental educational services.* Retrieved January 12, 2005, from www.ccsso.org/content/pdfs/SSPTToolkit.pdf.

Cuban, L. (1990). Reforming again, again, and again. *Educational Researcher, 19*(1), 3–13.

Cuban, L. (1998). *How teachers taught: Constancy and change in American classrooms, 1890–1990* (2nd ed.). New York: Teachers College Press.

Cunningham, P.M., & Allington, R.L. (1994). *Classrooms that work: They can all read and write.* New York: HarperCollins.

Darling-Hammond, L. (1997). *The right to learn: A blueprint for creating schools that work.* San Francisco, CA: Jossey-Bass.

Das, J.P., & Gindis, B. (Eds.). (1995). Special issue: Lev S. Vygotsky and contemporary educational psychology. *Educational Psychologist, 30*(2), 55–104.

Davis, D. (2004, May 9). Parenting 101. *The Santa Fe New Mexican,* A5.

De Groot, A.D. (1965). *Thought and choice in chess.* New York: Basic.

Deci, E.L. (1975). *Intrinsic motivation.* New York: Plenum.

Deci, E.L., & Ryan, R. (1985). *Intrinsic motivation and self-determination in human behavior.* New York: Plenum.

DeGrandpre, R.J. (2000). A science of meaning: Can behaviorism bring meaning to psychological science? *American Psychologist, 55*(7), 721–739.

Dell'Angela, T. (2005, August 11). Tutoring study shows promise in key group. *Chicago Tribune.*

Devin-Sheehan, L., Feldman, R.S., & Allen, V.L. (1976). Research on children tutoring children: A critical review. *Review of Educational Research, 46,* 355–385.

Dewey, J. (1963). *Experience and education.* New York: Collier.

Dewey, J. (1972). My pedagogic creed. In *The early works, 1828–1898. Volume 5: 1895–98* (pp. 84–95). Carbondale, IL: Southern Illinois University Press. (Original work published in 1897)

Donaldson, J. (2002, March 17). Teachers now make house calls. *The Desert Sun,* A8.

Donovan, J. (1990). The concept and role of mentor. *Nurse Education Today, 10,* 294–298.

Duvall, S.F., Delquadri, J.C., Elliott, M., & Hall, R.V. (1992). Parent-tutoring procedures: Experimental analysis and validation of generalization in oral reading across passages, settings, and time. *Journal of Behavioral Education, 2,* 281–303.

Education Industry Association. (2005, March 2). *Guidelines for qualifications of the tutor/education service provider (ESP).* Retrieved November 20, 2005, from www.educationindustry.org.

Eisenberger, R., & Cameron, J. (1996). Detrimental effects of reward: Reality or myth? *American Psychologist, 51,* 1153–1166.

Eisner, E.W. (1997). The promise and perils of alternative forms of data representation. *Educational Researcher, 26*(6), 4–11.

Eisner, E.W. (1998). *The kinds of schools we need: Personal essays.* Portsmouth, NH: Heinemann.

Ellison, D.G. (1976). Tutoring. In N. Gage (Ed.), *The psychology of teaching methods.* Chicago: University of Chicago Press.

EMT Associates. (2004). *Parent/Teacher Home Visitation Project evaluation report.* Sacramento, CA.

Erickson, F., & Gutierrez, K. (2002). Culture, rigor, and science in educational research. *Educational Researcher, 31*(8), 21–24.

Ericsson, K.A., & Charmes, N. (1994). Expert performance: Its structure and acquisition. *American Psychologist, 49*(8), 725–747.

Erikson, E. (1963). *Childhood and society.* New York: Norton.

Erikson, E. (1968). *Identity, youth, and crisis.* New York: Norton.

Farkas, S., Johnson, J., & Duffett, A. (1999). *Playing their parts: Parents and teachers talk about parental involvement in public schools*. New York: Public Agenda.

Feller, B. (2006, February 9). Teachers, parents of students see schools very differently. *The Desert Sun,* p. A2.

Fergus, M. A. (2005, November 27). Literacy lessons spell success. *Chicago Tribune, 4*, p. 3.

Feurer, M.J., Towne, L., & Shavelson, R.J. (2002). Scientific culture and educational research. *Educational Researcher, 31*(8), 4–14.

Feuerstein, R., Hoffman, M.B., Jensen, M.R., & Rand, Y. (1985). Instrumental enrichment, an intervention program for structural cognitive modifiability: Theory and practice. In J.W. Segal, S.F. Chipman, & R. Glaser (Eds.), *Thinking and learning skills: Vol. 1. Relating instruction to research.* Hillsdale, NJ: Erlbaum.

Fields, W. (1991). Mentoring in nursing: A historical approach. *Nursing Outlook, 39*(6), 257–261.

Fish, S. (1980). *Is there a text in this class: The authority of interpretive commentaries.* Cambridge, MA: Harvard University Press.

Fisher, C., Filby, N., Marliave, R., Cahen, L., Dishaw, M., Moore, J., et al. (1978). *Teaching behaviors, academic learning time, and student achievement. Final report of Phase III-B Beginning Teacher Evaluation Study.* San Francisco, CA: Far West Laboratory for Educational Research and Development.

Fitz-Gibbon, C.T. (1977). *An analysis of cross-age tutoring.* Washington, DC: National Institute of Education. (ERIC Document Reproduction Service No. ED 148 807).

Foster, S.F. (1986). Ten principles of learning revised in accordance with cognitive psychology: With implications for teaching. *Educational Psychologist, 21*(3), 235–243.

Fowler, F.C. (2003). School choice: Silver bullet, social threat, or sound policy? *Educational Researcher, 32*(2), 33–39.

Franklin, J. (2003, March). Tutoring's trials and triumphs. *Education Update, 45*, 4–5.

Freire, P. (1995). *Pedagogy of the oppressed.* New York: Continuum. (Original work published in 1970)

Fuchs, L. S. & Fuchs, D. (1998). Treatment validity: A unifying concept for reconceptualizing the identification of learning disabilities. *Learning Disabilities Research and Practice, 13*, 204–219.

Gage, N.L., & Berliner, D.C. (1992). *Educational psychology.* Boston, MA: Houghton Mifflin.

Galen, N.D., & Mavrogenes, N.A. (1979). Cross-age tutoring: Why and how. *Journal of Reading, 44*, 17–20.

Geissler, B. (2000). *Leading the way to family literacy: A study of Whiteside County Even Start.* Sterling, IL: Whiteside County Parenting Project.

Gergen, K.J. (1994). Exploring the postmodern: Perils or potentials? *American Psychologist, 49*, 412–416.

Gergen, K.J. (2001). Psychological science in a postmodern context. *American Psychologist, 56*(10), 803–813.

Gerjets, P., & Scheiter, K. (2003). Goal configurations and processing strategies as moderators between instructional design and cognitive load: Evidence from hypertext-based instruction. *Educational Psychologist, 38*(1), 33–42.

Gerwertz, C. (2005a, November 16). Ed. Dept. grants N.Y.C., Boston waivers on NCLB tutoring. *Education Week,* p. 13.

Gerwertz, C. (2005b, June 22). Guide seeks new clarity on tutoring. *Education Week,* pp. 1, 35.

Gerwertz, C. (2005c, May 4). Tutoring comes under review in Congress. *Education Week,* p. 32.

Glaser, R. (1978). *Advances in instructional psychology* (Vol. 1). Hillsdale, NJ: Erlbaum.

Glaser, R. (1982). *Advances in instructional psychology* (Vol. 2). Hillsdale, NJ: Erlbaum.

Glaser, R. (1984). Education and thinking: The role of knowledge. *American Psychologist, 39,* 93–104.

Glaser, R. (1986). *Advances in instructional psychology* (Vol. 3). Hillsdale, NJ: Erlbaum.

Glaser, R. (1990). The reemergence of learning theory within instructional research. *American Psychologist, 45*(1), 29–39.

Glaser, R., & Takanishi, R. (1986). Special issue: Psychological science and education. *American Psychologist, 41*(10), 1025–1168.

Going One on One. (1998, November 8). *Washington Post Magazine,* p. 19–35.

Good, T.L., & Brophy, J.E. (1987). *Looking in classrooms.* New York: Harper & Row.

Gordon, E.E. (1983). Home tutoring programs gain respectability. *Phi Delta Kappan, 64,* 398–399.

Gordon, E.E. (2002a). *Tutor quest: Finding effective education for children and adults.* Bloomington, IN: Phi Delta Kappa Educational Foundation.

Gordon, E.E. (2002b, Fall). Tutor quest: Finding effective education for children and adults. *Enterprising Educators, 11,* 8.

Gordon, E.E. (2003). Looking beyond the stereotypes: Ensuring the true potential of tutoring. *Phi Delta Kappan, 84,* 456–459.

Gordon, E.E. (2004a, August 6). *The state of tutoring in America.* (Keynote address). Northwestern University, Evanston, IL.

Gordon, E.E. (2004b, Spring). Tutoring, learning, and careers. *Tutor/Mentor Connection,* p. 4.

Gordon, E.E. (2005a). *Peer tutoring: A teacher's resource guide.* Lanham, MD: Scarecrow Education.

Gordon, E.E. (2005b). *The 2010 meltdown: Solving the impending jobs crisis.* Westport, CT: Praeger.

Gordon, E.E., & Gordon, E.H. (1990). *Centuries of tutoring: A history of alternative education in America and Western Europe.* Lanham, MD: University Press.

Gordon, E.E., & Gordon, E.H. (2003). *Literacy in America: Historic journey and contemporary solutions.* Westport, CT: Praeger.

Gordon, E.E., Morgan, R.R., & Ponticell, J.A. (1994). *FutureWork: The revolution reshaping American business.* Westport, CT: Praeger.

Gordon, E.E., Morgan, R.R., & Ponticell, J.A. (1995). The individualized training alternative. *Training & Development, 49,* 52–55.

Gordon, E.E., Morgan, R.R., Ponticell, J.A., & O'Malley, C.J. (2004). Tutoring solutions for No Child Left Behind: Research, practice, and policy implications. *National Association of Secondary School Principals Bulletin, 88,* 59–68.

Gordon, E.E., Ponticell, J., & Morgan, R.R. (1989). Back to basics. *Training and Development Journal, 43*(8), 73–75.

Gordon, E.E., Ponticell, J., & Morgan, R.R. (1991). *Closing the literacy gap in American business.* Westport, CT: Quorum.

Graesser, R.C., McNamara, D., & VanLehn, K. (2005). Scaffolding deep comprehension strategies through AutoTutor and iSTART. *Educational Psychologist, 40,* 225–234.

Greeno, J. (1998). The situativity of knowing, learning, and research. *American Psychologist, 53,* 5–26.

Greeno, J.G. (1978). Review of Bloom's human characteristics and school learning. *Journal of Educational Measurement,* 67–76.

Greeno, J.G. (1989). A perspective on thinking. *American Psychologist, 44*(2), 134–141.

Greenwood, C.R., Terry, B., Utley, C.A., Montagna, D., & Walker, D. (1993). Achievement, placement, and services: Middle school benefits of classwide peer tutoring used at the elementary school. *School Psychology Review, 22,* 497–516.

Griffin, S., Case, R., & Sandieson, R. (1992). Synchrony and asynchrony in the acquisition of everyday mathematical knowledge: Towards a representational theory of children's intellectual growth. In R. Case (Ed.), *The mind's staircase: Exploring the central conceptual underpinnings of children's theory and knowledge.* Hillsdale, NJ: Erlbaum.

Gruenewald, D.A. (2003). The best of both worlds: A critical pedagogy of place. *Educational Researcher, 32*(4), 3–12.

Guskey, T.R. (1987). Rethinking mastery learning reconsidered. *Review of Educational Research, 57*(2), 225–230.

Guskey, T.R., & Gates, S.L. (1986). Synthesis of research on the effects of mastery learning in elementary and secondary classrooms. *Educational Leadership, 43*(8), 73–80.

Halpern, D. (2001). Why wisdom? *Educational Psychologist, 36,* 253–256.

Hargreaves, A. (1994). *Changing teachers, changing times: Teachers' work and culture in the postmodern age.* New York: Teachers College Press.

Has tutoring worked? (2005, August 11). *Chicago Tribune, 2,* p. 26.

Hecker, D.E. (2001, November). Occupational employment projections to 2010. *Monthly Labor Review,* 57–84.

Herman, J.L., & Golan, S. (1991). *Effects of standardized testing on teacher and learning: Another look* (CSE Technical Report 334). Los Angeles: University of California, National Center for Research and Evaluation, Standards, and Student Testing.

Hiebert, E.H. (1994). Reading Recovery in the United States: What difference does it make to an age cohort? *Educational Researcher, 23*(9), 15–25.

Hiebert, J., Gallimore, R., & Stigler, J. (2002). A knowledge base for the teaching profession: What would it look like and how can we get one? *Educational Researcher, 31*(5), 3–15.

Hirsch, E.D. (1987). *Cultural literacy: What every American needs to know*. Boston: Houghton Mifflin.

Jacobi, M. (1991). Mentoring and undergraduate academic success: A literature review. *Review of Educational Research, 61*(4), 505–532.

Jason, L.A., Danner, K.E., Weine, A.M., Kurasaki, K.S., Johnson, J.H., Warren-Sohlberg, L., & Reyes, O. (1995). Academic follow-up data on two cohorts of high-risk transfer children. *Early Education and Development, 5*, 277–288.

Johnston, P. (1998). The consequences and the use of standardized tests. In S. Murphy (Ed.), *Fragile evidence: A critique of reading assessment* (pp. 89–101). Mahwah, NJ: Erlbaum.

Juel, C. (1996). What makes literacy tutoring effective? *Reading Research Quarterly, 31*, 268–289.

Kaiden, E. (1994). Repeat attendance at a college tutoring center: The students' perspectives. *Research and Teaching in Developmental Education, 11*, 49–62.

Kalyuga, S., Ayres, P., Chandler, P., & Sweller, J. (2003). The expertise reversal effect. *Educational Psychologist, 38*(1), 23–32.

Kantrowitz, B. (2000, Fall). 21st century babies. *Newsweek, 136*, 4–7.

Keller, F.S. (1968). Good-bye teacher! *Journal of Applied Behavioral Analysis, 1*, 79–84.

Kilpatrick, D.G. (2000). *Definitions of public policy and the law*. National Violence of Women Prevention Resource Center, Medical University of South Carolina. Available from www.musc.edu/vawprevention/policy/definition.shtml.

Klein, K. (2006, February 4). X = Karin (Johnny) > 95%. *The Los Angeles Times*, p. B15.

Kuhn, D., & Udell, W. (2001). The path to wisdom. *Educational Psychologist, 36*, 261–264.

Kulik, J.A., Kulik, C.L.C., & Cohen, P.A. (1979). A meta-analysis of outcome studies of Keller's personalized system of instruction. *American Psychologist, 34*, 307–318.

Kutner, M., Greenberg, E., & Baer, J. (2005). *A first look at the literacy of America's adults in the 21st century*. (NCES 2006470). Washington, DC: U.S. Department of Education.

Lajoie, S.P. (1993). Computer environments as cognitive tools for enhancing learning. In S. Derry & S.P. Lajoie (Eds.), *Computers as cognitive tools* (pp. 261–288). Hillsdale, NJ: Erlbaum.

Lane, C. (2002, June 27). U.S. court votes to bar pledge of allegiance use of "God" called unconstitutional. *Washington Post*, p. A1.

Lepper, M.R., & Chabay, R.W. (1985). Intrinsic motivation and instruction: Conflicting views on the role of motivational processes in computer-based education. *Educational Psychologist, 20*, 217–230.

Lepper, M.R., & Greene, D. (1975). Turning play into work: Effects of adult surveillance and extrinsic rewards on children's intrinsic motivation. *Journal of Personality and Social Psychology, 31*, 479–488.

Lepper, M.R., Greene, D., & Nisbett, R.E. (1973). Undermining children's intrinsic interest with extrinsic rewards: A test of the overjustification hypothesis. *Journal of Personality and Social Psychology, 28*, 129–137.

Lepper, M.R., & Hodell, M. (1989). Intrinsic motivation in the classroom. In C. Ames & R. Ames (Eds.), *Research on motivation in education* (Vol. 3). San Diego, CA: Academic Press.

Lepper, M.R., Keavney, M., & Drake, M. (1996). Intrinsic motivation and extrinsic rewards: A commentary on Cameron and Pierce's meta-analysis. *Review of Educational Research, 66*, 5–32.

Levin, J., & Pressley, N. (1983). *Cognitive strategy research: Educational applications.* New York: Springer-Verlag.

Levin, T. (1979). Instruction which enables students to develop higher mental processes. *Evaluation in Education: An International Review Series, 3*(3), 173–220.

Linn, R.L., Baker, E.L., & Betebenner, D.W. (2002). Accountability systems: Implications of requirements of the No Child Left Behind Act of 2001. *Educational Researcher, 31*(6), 3–16.

Lippitt, P. (1969). Children can teach other children. *The Instructor, 789*, 41, 99.

Lippitt, P., & Lippitt, R. (1970). The peer culture as a learning environment. *Childhood Education, 47*, 135–138.

Lippitt, R., & Lippitt, P. (1968). Cross-age helpers. *National Education Association Journal, 57*, 24–26.

Lizama, J. A. (2005, November 1). Don't want to transfer? Being tutored is an option. *Richmond Times-Dispatch*, p. B5.

Losen, D., Orfield, G., Wald, J., & Swanson, C.B. (2004). *Losing our future.* How minority youth are being left behind by the graduation rate crisis. Cambridge, MA: Civil Rights Project, Harvard University: Urban Institute.

Lyons, C.A., & Beaver, J. (1995). Reducing retention and learning disability placement through Reading Recovery: An educationally sound cost-effectiveness choice. In R.L. Allington & S.A. Walmsley (Eds.), *No quick fix: Redesigning literacy programs in America's elementary schools* (pp. 16–36). New York: Teachers College Press.

Madison, J., Watson, K., & Knight, B. (1994). Mentors and preceptors in the nursing profession. *Contemporary Nurse, 3*(3), 121–126.

Mantzicopoulos, P., Morrison, D., Stone, E., & Setrakian, W. (1992). Use of the SEARCH/TEACH tutoring approach with middle-class students at risk for reading failure. *Elementary School Journal, 92*, 573–586.

Manzo, K.K. (2005a, May 25). College-based high schools fill growing need. *Education Week*, p. 1, 17.

Manzo, K.K. (2005b, November 9). Against all odds. *Education Week*, pp. 32–35.

Marston, D., Deno, S.L., Kim, D., Diment, K., & Rogers, D. (1995). Comparison of reading intervention approaches for students with mild disabilities. *Exceptional Children, 62*, 20–37.

Maslow, A.H. (1954). *Motivation and personality.* New York: Viking.

Maslow, A.H. (1968). *Toward a psychology of being.* New York: Van Nostrand.

Mathan, S., & Koedinger, K.R. (2005). Benefits of tutoring error detection and self-correction skills. *Educational Psychologist, 40*, 257–265.

Mathes, P.G., & Fuchs, L.S. (1994). The efficacy of peer tutoring in reading for students with mild disabilities: A best-evidence synthesis. *School Psychology Review, 23*, 59–80.

Mayer, R.E. (1997). Multimedia learning: Are we asking the right questions? *Educational Psychologist, 32*(1), 1–20.

Mayer, R.E. (2001). *Multimedia learning*. New York: Cambridge University Press.

Mayer, R.E., & Moreno, R. (2003). Nine ways to reduce cognitive load in multimedia learning. *Educational Psychologist, 38*(1), 43–52.

Mayer, R.E., Moreno, R., Boise, M., & Vagge, S. (1999). Maximizing constructivist learning from multimedia communications by minimizing cognitive load. *Journal of Educational Psychology, 91*(4), 638–643.

McGilly, K. (1996). *Classroom lessons: Integrating cognitive theory and classroom practice*. Cambridge, MA: The MIT Press.

McNeil, L. M. (2000). *Contradictions of school reform: Educational costs of standardized testing*. New York: Routledge.

Meroney, J. (2002, June). *Lobby League Newsletter*.

Mevarach, Z.R. (1980). *The role of teaching-learning strategies and feedback-corrective procedures in developing higher cognitive achievement*. Doctoral dissertation, University of Chicago.

Miller, G.A. (1956). The magical number seven plus or minus two: Some limits on our capacity for processing information. *Psychological Review, 63*, 81–97.

Minstrell, J. (1982). Explaining the "at rest" condition of an object. *The Physics Teacher, 20*, 10–14.

Morgan, R.R., Ponticell, J.A., & Gordon, E.E. (1998). *Enhancing learning in training and adult education*. Westport, CT: Praeger.

Morris, D., Ervin, C., & Conrad, K. (1995). A case study of middle school reading disability. *The Reading Teacher, 49*, 368–377.

Morris, D., Shaw, B., & Perney, J. (1990). Helping low readers in grades 2 and 3: An after-school volunteer tutoring program. *Elementary School Journal, 91*, 187–194.

Morris, E. (1998). *Dutch: A memoir of Ronald Reagan*. New York: Random House.

Mueller, D.J. (1976). Mastery learning: Partly boon, partly boondoggle. *Teachers College Record, 78*, 41–52.

Myers, G.L., & Fisk, A.D. (1987). Training consistent task components: Applications of automatic and controlled processing theory to industrial task training. *Human Factors, 29*(3), 355–368.

Nadel, D. (2000, April). *Tutoring Industry Report*. New York: Bear Stearns.

Nader, R. (1965). *Unsafe at any speed: the designed-in danger of the American automobile*. New York: Grossman.

National Educational Research Policies and Priorities Board. (1999). *Investing in learning: A policy statement with recommendations on research in education by the National Education Research Policy and Priorities Board*. Washington, DC: U.S. Department of Education.

National Endowment for the Arts. (2004). *Reading at risk: A survey of literary reading in America*. Retrieved November 15, 2005, from www.arts.gov/ReadingAtRisk.pdf.

National Forum on Education Policy hosted by ECS in Los Angeles, July 9, 2002.

National Research Council. (2002). *Scientific research in education*. R.J. Shavelson and L. Towne (Eds.). Committee on Scientific Principles for Educational Research, Washington, DC: National Academy Press.

Newell, A., & Simon, H.A. (1972). *Human problem solving*. Englewood Cliffs, NJ: Prentice-Hall.

Norman, D.A., & Rumelhart, D.E. (1981). The LNR approach to human information processing. *Cognition, 10*(1–3), 235–240.

Ogbu, J.U. (1987). Variability in minority school performance: A problem in search of an explanation. *Anthropology and Education Quarterly, 18*, 312–334.

Orfield, G., Losen, D., Wald, J., & Swanson, C. (2004). *Losing our future: How minority youth are being left behind by the graduation rate crisis*. Retrieved November 15, 2005, from http://urbanorg/url.cfm?ID=410936.

Organization for Economic Co-operation and Development. (2004). *Learning for tomorrow's world: First results from PISA 2003*. Paris: OECD.

Paas, F., Renkl, A., & Sweller, J. (Eds.). (2003). Special issue: Cognitive load theory and instructional design: Recent developments. *Educational Psychologist, 38*(1), 1–72.

Paas, F., Tuovinen, J., Tabbers, H., & Van Gerven, P.W.M. (2003). Cognitive load measurement as a means to advance cognitive load theory. *Educational Psychologist, 38*(1), 63–72.

Palincsar, A.S., & Brown, A.L. (1984). Reciprocal teaching of comprehension-fostering and comprehensive-monitoring activities. *Cognitive and Instruction, 1*, 117–175.

Paris, S. (2001). Wisdom, snake oil, and the educational marketplace. *Educational Psychologist, 36*, 257–260.

Pellegrino, J.W., & Goldman, S.R. (2002). Be careful what you wish for—you may get it: Educational researcher in the spotlight. *Educational Researcher, 31*(8), 15–17.

Perkins, D. (2001). Wisdom in the wild. *Educational Psychologist, 36*, 265–268.

Phye, G.D. (1997). *Handbook of academic learning: Construction of knowledge*. New York: Academic.

Pinar, W. (1991). Curriculum as social psychoanalysis: On the significance of place. In J. Kincheloe & W. Pinar (Eds.), *Curriculum as social psychoanalysis* (pp. 165–186). Albany, NY: State University of New York Press.

Pintrich, P.R. (1994). Continuities and discontinuities: Future directions for research in educational psychology. *Educational Psychologist, 29*(3), 137–148.

Pintrich, P.R. (2000a). Educational psychology at the millennium: A look back and a look forward. *Educational Psychologist, 35*(4), 221–226.

Pintrich, P.R. (2000b). The role of goal orientation in self-regulated learning. In M. Boekaerts, P. Pintrich, & M. Zeidner (Eds.), *Handbook of self-regulation* (pp. 451–502). San Diego, CA: Academic.

Postman, N. (1995). *The end of education: Redefining the value of school*. New York: Random House.

Practical Parenting Partnerships. (2005). Jefferson City, MO. Available from www.pppctro.org.

Pressley, N., & Levin, J. (1983). *Cognitive strategy research: Psychological foundations*. New York: Springer-Verlag.

Puntabekar, S., & Hubscher, R. (2005). Tools for scaffolding students in a complex learning environment: What have we gained and what have we missed? *Educational Psychologist, 40*(1), 1–12.

Quintana, C., Zhang, M., & Krajcik, J. (2005). Scaffolded software environments for supporting metacognitive aspects of online inquiry. *Educational Psychologist, 40*, 235–244.

Renkl, A., & Atkinson, R.K. (2003). Structuring the transition from example study to problem solving in cognitive skill acquisition: A cognitive load perspective. *Educational Psychologist, 38*(1), 15–22.

Resnick, L.B. (1991). Shared cognition: Thinking as a social practice. In L.B. Resnick, J.M. Levine, & S.D. Teasley (Eds.), *Perspectives on socially shared cognition* (pp. 1–20). Washington, DC: American Psychological Association.

Resnick, L.T. (1977). Assuming that everyone can learn everything, will some learn less? *School Review, 85*, 445–452.

Robelen, E.W. (2002, September 25). States suffer halting start of tutoring. *Education Week*, pp. 1, 26.

Rogers, C.R. (1961). *On becoming a person*. Boston, MA: Houghton Mifflin.

Rogoff, B. (1990). *Apprenticeship in thinking: Cognitive development in social contexts*. New York: Oxford University Press.

Rose, L.C. (2004). No Child Left Behind: The mathematics of guaranteed failure. *Educational Horizons, 82*, 121–130.

Rosenshine, B., & Furst, N. (1969). *The effects of tutoring upon pupil achievement: A research review*. Washington, DC: Office of Education. (ERIC Document Reproduction Service No. ED 064 462.)

Ross, S.M., Smith, L.J., Casey, J., & Slavin, R.E. (1995). Increasing the academic success of disadvantaged children: An examination of alternative early intervention programs. *American Educational Research Journal, 32*, 773–800.

Rychlak, J.F. (1993). A suggested principle of complementarity for psychology: In theory, not method. *American Psychologist, 48*(4), 933–942.

Rychlak, J.F. (1994). *Logical learning theory: A human teleology and its empirical support*. Lincoln, NB: University of Nebraska Press.

Rychlak, J.F. (2000). A psychotherapist's lessons from the philosophy of science. *American Psychologist, 55*(10), 1126–1132.

Saulney, S. (2005, April 4). A lucrative brand of tutoring grows unchecked. *The New York Times*, p. 23.

Scardamalia, M., & Bereiter, C. (1983). Child as co-investigator: Helping children gain insight into their own mental processes. In S. Paris, G. Olson, & H. Stevenson (Eds.), *Learning and motivation in the classroom*. Hillsdale, NJ: Erlbaum.

Schank, R.C., & Cleary, C. (1995). *Engines for education*. Hillsdale, NJ: Erlbaum.

Schwartz, B. (1990). The creation and destruction of value. *American Psychologist, 45*, 7–15.

Shanahan, T. (1998). On the effectiveness and limitations of tutoring in reading. In P.D. Pearson & A Iran-Nejad. (Eds.), *Review of research in education* (Vol. 23, pp. 217–234). Washington, DC: American Educational Research Association.

Shanahan, T., & Barr, R. (1995). Reading Recovery: An independent evaluation of the effects of an early instructional intervention for at-risk learners. *Reading Research Quarterly, 30*, 958–997.

Shavelson, R., & Towne, L. (Eds.). (2002). *Scientific research in education.* Washington, DC: National Academy Press.

Shepard, L.A. (2000). The role of assessment in a learning culture. *Educational Researcher, 29*(7), 4–14.

Shuell, T.J. (1986). Cognitive conceptions of learning. *Review of Educational Research, 56*(4), 411–437.

Simmons, D.C., Fuchs, L.S., Fuchs, D., Mathes, P., & Hodge, J.P. (1995). Effects of explicit teaching and peer tutoring on the reading achievement of learning-disabled and low-performing students in regular classrooms. *Elementary School Journal, 95,* 387–408.

Sizer, T.R. (1997). *Horace's school: Redesigning the American high school.* Boston: Houghton Mifflin.

Skinner, B.F. (1973, Winter). The free and happy student. *New York University Education Quarterly,* 2–6.

Slavin, R.E. (1984). Students motivating students to excel: Cooperative incentives, cooperative tasks, and student achievement. *Elementary School Journal, 85,* 53–64.

Slavin, R.E. (1987a). Mastery learning reconsidered. *Review of Educational Research, 57*(2), 175–214.

Slavin, R.E. (1987b). Taking the mystery out of mastery: A response to Guskey, Anderson, and Burns. *American Psychologist, 57*(2), 231–235.

Slavin, R.E. (1990). *Cooperative learning: Theory, research, and practice.* Boston: Allyn & Bacon.

Smith, M.B. (1994). Selfhood at risk: Postmodern perils and the perils of postmodernism. *American Psychologist, 49,* 405–411.

Smith, M.L. (1991). Put to the test: The effects of external testing on teachers. *Educational Researcher, 20*(5), 8–11.

Spady, W.G., & Marshall, K.J. (1991). Beyond traditional outcome-based education. *Educational Leadership, 49,* 67–72.

Stallings, J. (1980). Allocated academic learning time revisited or beyond time on task. *Educational Researcher, 9,* 11–16.

Stanovich, K. (2001). The rationality of educating for wisdom. *Educational Researcher, 36,* 247–251.

Sternberg, R.J. (1998a). Abilities are forms of developing expertise. *Educational Researcher, 27*(3), 11–21.

Sternberg, R.J. (1998b). Principles of teaching for successful intelligence. *Educational Psychologist, 33*(2/3), 65–72.

Sternberg, R.J. (2001). Why schools should teach for wisdom: The balance theory of wisdom in educational settings. *Educational Psychologist, 36*(4), 227–246.

Strauss, V. (2002, December 10). Cost, tutor shortage hinder single "no child" efforts. *Washington Post,* p. A16.

Stremmel, A., & Fu, V. (1993). Teaching in the zone of proximal development: Implications for responsive teaching practice. *Child and Youth Care Forum, 22*(5), 337–349.

Strommen, L.T., & Mates, B.F. (2004). Learning to love reading: Interviews with older children and teens. *Journal of Adolescent & Adult Literary, 46*, 188–200.

Takaki, R.T. (1993). *A different minor: A history of multicultural America.* New York: Little, Brown.

Tenenbaum, G. (1982). A method of group instruction which is as effective as one-to-one tutorial instruction (Doctoral dissertation, University of Chicago, 1982). *Dissertation Abstracts International, 43*, 1822A.

Tudge, J., & Winterhoff, P. (1993). Vygotsky, Piaget, and Bandura: Perspectives on the relations between the social world and cognitive development. *Human Development, 36*, 61–81.

U.S. Department of Education. (2005, June 13). *Supplemental educational services non-regulatory guidance.* Retrieved November 1, 2005, from www.ed.gov/policy/elsec/guid/suppsvsguid.doc.

U.S. Department of Education. (2006, January 3). *No Child Left Behind Act, 21st century learning centers–after school programs.* Retrieved February 1, 2006, from www.ed.gov/about/overview/budget/budget06/06actions.pdf.

U.S. Department of Education, Office of Educational Research and Improvement, National Center for Educational Statistics. (2001). *The nation's report card: Mathematics 2000* (NCES 2001-517). Washington, DC: Education Publications Center.

U.S. Department of Education, Office of Educational Research and Improvement. National Center for Educational Statistics. (2002). *The nation's report card: Reading 2000.* Retrieved September 30, 2003, from http://nces.ed.gov/nationsreportcard/reading/results2002.

Van Merrienboer, J.J.G., Kirschner, P.A., & Kester, L. (2003). Taking the load off a learner's mind: Instructional design for complex learning. *Educational Psychologist, 38*(1), 5–14.

Vance, C., & Olson, R. (1991). Annals of nursing research. *Mentorship, 31*, 175–200.

Vellutino, F., Scanlon, D.M., Sipay, E.R., Small, S.G., Pratt, A., Chen, R., et al. (1996). Cognitive profiles of difficult-to-remediate and readily remediated poor readers: Intervention as a vehicle for distinguishing between cognitive and experiential deficits as basic cause of specific reading disability. *Journal of Educational Psychology, 88*, 601–638.

Vygotsky, L. (1962). *Thought and language.* Cambridge, MA: MIT Press.

Vygotsky, L.S. (1978). *Mind in society: The development of higher psychological processes* (M. Cole, V. John-Steiner, S. Scribner, & E. Souberman, Eds. and Trans.). Boston: Harvard University Press.

Walberg, H. (1984). Improving the productivity of America's schools. *Educational Leadership, 41*(8), 19–30.

Wang, M.C., Haertel, G.D., & Walberg, H.J. (1990). What influences learning: A content analysis of review literature. *Journal of Educational Research, 84*(1), 30–43.

Wasik, B.A., & Slavin, R.E. (1993). Preventing early reading failure with one-to-one tutoring: A review of five programs. *Reading Research Quarterly, 28*, 179–200.

Weinstein, C.E., & Marges, R.E. (1986). The teaching of learning strategies. In M.C. Wittrock (Ed.), *Handbook of research on teaching.* New York: Macmillan.

White, B., & Frederiksen, J. (2005). Cognitive models and instructional environments that foster young learners' metacognitive development. *Educational Psychologist, 40*, 211–223.

Why offer tutoring only to "eligible" children. (2005, September 11). *Education Week,* p. 41.

Wilson, E.O. (1998). *Consilience: The unity of knowledge.* New York: Knopf.

Windschitl, M. (2002). Framing constructivism in practice as the negotiation of dilemmas: An analysis of the conceptual, pedagogical, cultural, and political challenges facing teachers. *Review of Educational Research, 72*(2), 131–176.

Winne, P.H. (1985). Steps toward promoting cognitive development. *Elementary School Journal, 83,* 673–693.

Winne, P.H. (1991). Motivation and teaching. In H.C. Waxman & H.J. Walberg (Eds.), *Effective teaching: Current research.* Berkeley, CA: McCutchan.

Wraga, W.G. (1999). Extracting sun-beams out of cucumbers: The retreat from practice in reconceptualized curriculum studies. *Educational Researcher, 28*(1), 4–13.

Yankelovitch, D. (1972, April). The new naturalism. *Saturday Review,* 35.

Yankelovitch, D. (1981). *New rules: Searching for self-fulfillment in a world turned upside down.* New York: Random House.

Yoder, L. (1990). Mentoring: A concept analysis. *Nursing Administration Quarterly 15*(1), 9–19.

Zimmerman, B. (2000). Attaining self-regulation: A social cognitive perspective. In M. Boekaerts, P. Pintrich, & M. Zeidner (Eds.), *Handbook of self-regulation* (pp. 13–39). San Diego, CA: Academic.

Zimmerman, B., Bandura, A., & Martinez-Pons, M. (1992). Self-motivation for academic attainment: The role of self-efficacy beliefs and personal goal setting. *American Educational Research Journal, 29*(3), 663–676.

Zimmerman, B.J., & Tsikalas, K.E. (2005). Can computer-based learning environments (CBLEs) be used as self-regulatory tools to enhance learning? *Educational Psychologist, 40*(4), 267–271.

Index

About the Authors

Edward E. Gordon, Ph.D., is an international expert on tutoring, individualized education, and literacy issues. He is the author of *Centuries of Tutoring* (1990), *Tutor Quest* (2002), and *Peer Tutoring* (2005). Gordon is the founder and principal of the research firm Imperial Consulting Corporation in Chicago and previously taught at DePaul, Loyola, and Northwestern universities in Chicago.

Ronald R. Morgan, Ph.D., is an expert in the psychology of learning and instruction. He is a professor in the Department of Curriculum, Instruction, and Educational Psychology at Loyola University, Chicago.

Charles J. O'Malley, Ph.D., is an independent education consultant specializing in public policy-related issues and provides policy development assistance to national, state, and local organizations. He has served as executive assistant for private education to three U.S. secretaries of education (Ted Bell, Bill Bennett, and Lauro Cavazos) and recently returned to the U.S. Department of Education as a policy consultant to the deputy secretary of education.

Judith Ponticell, Ph.D., is currently associate vice president for Academic Affairs and professor of Educational Leadership at the University of South Florida, Lakeland. She has previously worked as an accreditation, program, and grant evaluator in Illinois, Texas, New Mexico, and Florida. During her career, she has also served as a consultant to schools, school districts, state departments, and businesses at local, state, and national levels.